ERRATA
(for "A Dwelling Place for God")

Please go through this book and mark the following corrections. Then as you read, the edits will be handy for you.

1. Page 23, 2nd paragraph, next-to-last line: ("blood he" should be "blood He")
2. Page 68, 3rd paragraph, 3rd line: ("Pentecos.t" should be "Pentecost.")
3. *Explanation:* The abbreviated *Scripture* references were written out in the computer, but "Mt.," the abbreviation for "Mount" was mistaken by the computer to be "Matthew." So the following places are to be changed from "Matthew" to "Mount":
   - Page 80, last paragraph, last line, to top of page 81.
   - Page 120, 3rd paragraph, 4th line.
   - Page 120, 4th paragraph, 4th line.
   - Page 137, 1st paragraph, 5th line.
   - Page 199, 4th paragraph, 4th line.
   - Page 239, 4th paragraph, 3rd line.
4. Page 75, 2nd paragraph, 3rd and 6th lines: "ram's **skies**" should be "ram's **skins**".
5. Page 168, the last line: "antetype" should be "antitype". This is from the Greek word *antitupon*, which means "the fulfillment of the type."
6. Page 81. 4th line from top. Numbers 2:7 should be **Deuteronomy** 2:7.

A DWELLING PLACE FOR GOD

All original sketches, including cover, drawn by artist Howard Morlock, transferred into graphics and edited by Duane Bagaas, editor.

A DWELLING PLACE FOR GOD

*A verse-by-verse description from
Exodus 25-30 of the Ancient Hebrew Tabernacle
with New Covenant applications.*

Revised and Enlarged Edition

by
Ruth Specter Lascelle

𝕭
Bedrock Publishing
Arlington, Washington

Copyright © 1997 by Bedrock Publishing

All rights reserved. No portion of this book may be reproduced in whole or in part in any form without the express written permission of the copyright holder.

Library of Congress Cataloging-in-Publication Data
A Dwelling Place For God /Ruth Specter Lascelle.
  The Tabernacle in the Wilderness. Study of Exodus chapters 25 through 30. OT symbols, types interpreted from the NT. Includes bibliographical references and Index. Duane Bagaas, Editor; Wuffy Evans, Associate Editor.
  1. Story of the Tabernacle in the Wilderness. 2. Portrayal of God's Dwelling with His people. 3. Messiah and God's people. 4. Interpretation of the Hebrew Scriptures. 5. Sketches, diagrams and charts illustrate text. 6. List of 200 questions and answers.

Library of Congress Catalog Card Number: 97-71131
ISBN 0-9654519-2-5

First Printing 1973; Second Printing 1979;
Third Printing 1985; Fourth Printing 1989;
Fifth Printing 1992;
Sixth Printing (first printing of revised/enlarged edition) 1997

Printed in the United States of America
by

Gorham Printing
Rochester, Washington

This Study is
lovingly dedicated to
my own dear Jewish people
to whom God's plan
of the Tabernacle
was first given.

Books by Ruth Specter Lascelle

A Dwelling Place For God
Global Harvest
God's Calendar of Prophetic Events: "Leviticus Twenty-Three"
Hanukkah and Christmas
How Shall They Hear? (With Hyman Israel Specter)
Jewish Faith and The New Covenant
Jewish Love for a Gentile: "Story of The Lascelles"
My Jewish People
New Covenant Passover Haggadah: "Remembering The Exodus of Deliverance"
On What Day Did Christ Die? "The Last Week of Christ"
Pictures of Messiah in The Holy Scriptures
That They Might be Saved: "Eight Lessons in Jewish Evangelism"
The Passover Feast
Two Loaves—One Bread: "Jew and Gentile in the Church"
We Have a Great High Priest: "A Brief Study of The Book of Hebrews"

No longer in print:
  Mission to Haiti
  Sent Forth by God
  The Bud and The Flower of Judaism

All Scriptures quoted are from the
King James Version of the Bible
unless otherwise noted. Bolding within the
Scripture portions for emphasis is mine.

ACKNOWLEDGMENTS

I want to express my appreciation to *Reverend E. W. Robinson* who first awakened my interest to study the great Bible subject on the Tabernacle. *Reverend Warren D. Combs*, who not only advanced the recording of sessions on this study (which I had the privilege to minister), but also saw to it that this same recording was put down on paper in such a form as to greatly facilitate preparation toward the completed manuscript. Howard Morlock (a former student of mine) graciously offered his artistic talent. My dear daughter *"Wuffy"* had printed the first three editions of this book and now with her brother, my son-in-the-Lord, *Duane Bagaas*, has edited this revised and enlarged edition. I also remember my departed husband *Reverend Walter (Wallie) Lascelle* for his patience, assistance, prayers and encouragement during the many hours of work on this volume.

ENDORSEMENTS

(The following endorsements were printed in the editions preceding this present volume. Two endorsers of this work have since passed away: Reverend Ernest S. Williams and Reverend Dennis Bennett.)

When I received the manuscript of "A Dwelling Place For God," with request that I review the same, my first thought was: How can I find time to do this in addition to my other duties? I then read a few pages for an idea as to its contents and became so interested that I laid aside all else until I had read every page. I have read other expositions concerning the spiritual significance of the Tabernacle and have enjoyed teaching its many lessons, but I have not seen another exposition so full and fruitful as this work which so richly portrays Christ with God's plan and purpose in redemption.

I remember the author's love and dedication to her Messiah ... but my comments here concern the book itself. It is written in simple language, yet profound. If a person wishes wealth of Christian teaching, this is a book to be read with studious care, with Bible at hand for reading the many Scripture references.

The work unfolds God, the Father as the source of all things in the plan of redemption; the Lord Jesus Christ in the many aspects of His life, ministry, and redeeming grace; and the purpose of God in Christian experience from the beginning of Christian life to the final perfection of saints.

Application of redeeming grace by the Holy Spirit of Promise reveals qualities and blessings which God would have Christian believers to enjoy. These are reviewed as the author takes a person through the book explaining verse-by-verse blessings which the verses point out. The Apostle Paul admonished his beloved Timothy to "study to shew thyself approved unto God—rightly dividing the word of truth." Those who give this writing careful study and thought will find it speaking for itself, a delightful study in all the fundamentals of Christian faith.

Ernest Swing Williams
For 20 years General Superintendent
General Council of the Assemblies of God

Ruth Specter Lascelle has been a valued friend in the Lord for some years, and we have profited by knowing her and her teachings. We are glad that through this book she will be sharing those teachings more widely with others, and we know that they will be much help and inspiration to many, both Jew and Gentile, in this crucial time when so many of God's people of old are turning to their Messiah.

Dennis and Rita Bennett
Internationally known Bible Teachers
Former Pastors of St. Luke's Episcopal Church
Seattle, Washington

PREFACE

When I undertook to author a book on the Tabernacle Type in the Bible, I knew full well that it would be impossible to cover such a study completely, for it is inexhaustible. I considered also that as I would write, many new thoughts would come which would extend the years before the finished work could be realized.

An outline for the great Tabernacle subject was begun in November of 1956, the actual writing, however, not until 1957 and thereafter, intermittently until the year 1969 when it was completed. During this writing period the manuscript continued to grow as throughout the years of research, instruction, and study, many new truths were added. In this present edition (1997) the book has been enlarged so as to include the many new truths through research and the enlightenment of the Holy Spirit.

The verse-by-verse description herein by no means exhausts the great subject of God's Dwelling Place. It is presented to the reader with the prayer that the Holy Spirit will teach new truths as it is read and studied. A list of Test Questions is offered after each section as a form of assistance with the hope that this will prompt further research. As it is studied, this Chief Type of the Bible is enlarged and many are the rich truths revealed by the Great Teacher, the Pattern-Maker who alone can explain the Pattern!

Notes of Explanation

In this book you may find different spellings for the English transliteration of Hebrew words. The reason for this is that the Hebrew transliteration into English takes on several forms of pronunciation such as: **ch**, **c** or **h** is usually from the Hebrew letter, *heth* ח, pronounced as a guttural **k**, sometimes written as **kh**. Examples: Pesah or Pesach; T'nakh or Tenach, Hannuka or Channuka; Chuppah or Huppah. Also, the letter *sheen* ש is transliterated into English as '**s**' if the dot is over the first *left* stroke, but as '**sh**' when the dot is over the first *right* stroke. When the letter *beth* ב has a dot (*dagesh*) within, it is pronounced as a '**b**' in English; however, if the *beth* does not have a *dagesh* within it then it is pronounced as a '**v**' in English!

The Jerusalem Post International for the week ending June 29, 1996 printed an article entitled *Hebrew is Not Built For Speed* by Robert Alberg in which he wrote:

> "Many Hebrew words can be read in seven different ways, with seven different meanings. MSPR can be read as *mispar, msaper, mi-sefer, mi-sapar, mi-sfar, masper, mi-saper.*"

For other pronunciations it will be safer to find a Hebrew scholar to help you if you do not know them yourself! But even Hebrew scholars do not always agree on the pronunciation, or on the spelling!

I follow the King James Version of the Scriptures. When the name "LORD" is printed with capitals within Scripture, it is not an emphasis but is the translator's code to signify that this is the Tetragrammaton (word of four letters) YHWH or JHVH which, in the Hebrew text, is יהוה ("Yahweh"). Also I use the abbreviations (OT and NT) of the Old Testament and New Testament respectively.

–Ruth Specter Lascelle, 1997
Arlington, Washington

The Ancient Hebrew Tabernacle

Table of Contents

Tabernacle Study 1
Chapter 1: EXODUS 25 7
   The Offering 7
   God's Desire for a Dwelling 13
   Pattern Helpers 15
      Test Questions 18
   The Ark of the Covenant 20
   The Mercy Seat 29
      Test Questions 36
   The Table of Shewbread 38
   The Human and the Divine Side of Christ 40
      Test Questions 46
   The Golden Lampstand 48
Chapter 2: EXODUS 26 62
   The Mishkan Covering 62
   The Ohel 69
      Test Questions 76
   The Boards of the Tabernacle 78
      Test Questions 98
   The Veil 99
      Test Questions 104
Chapter Three - EXODUS 27 105
   The Altar of Sacrifice 105
   The Grate 110
   The Altar of Sacrifice 113
   The Brazen Altar 117
      Test Questions 126
   The Court Fence 128
   The Gate, Door and Veil 132
      Test Questions 143

Chapter 4: EXODUS 28 145
  The Tabernacle Priesthood 145
  Consecration of the Priests 168
    Test Questions 175
Chapter 5: EXODUS 30 177
  The Altar of Incense 177
    Test Questions 190
  The Laver 191
    Test Questions 198
  The Anointing Oil 199
  Conclusion 209
    Test Questions 211
    Christ in the Tabernacle 213
Appendices:
  I: Notes on Typology and Bible Symbolism 216
  II: Significance of Numbers in Scripture 220
  III: God's Word and Women Preachers 222
  IV: Treasures in the Snow 231
  V: The Tabernacle as Fulfilled in John's Gospel 234
  VI: The Tabernacle in the Revelation 237
  VII: The Open Place in the North 239
  VIII: 200 Questions and Answers 241
Bibliography 273
General Index 277

ILLUSTRATIONS by Howard Morlock

The Ancient Hebrew Tabernacle	frontispiece
The Ark of the Covenant and Mercy Seat	20
The Table of Showbread	38
The Golden Lampstand	48
Cross Section of Tabernacle Building	61
The Veil	99
The Altar of Sacrifice	105
Foreshadows of Calvary's Altar	113
The High Priest of Israel	149
The Breastplate of Decision (recreated by D. Bagaas)	163
The Priest's Consecration by Blood Application	167
Levites Erecting Walls of Tabernacle	173
The Altar of Incense	178
High Priest Entering the Holiest	185
The Laver	191

DIAGRAMS, SKETCHES AND CHARTS
by the Author

Floor Plan of the Tabernacle	v
The Seven-Branched Menorah	56
A Bedouin Tent	69
The Open Frame Boards and Sockets	83
The Cross in the Tabernacle Furniture	122
Five Principle Offerings	124-125
Sixty Pillars of the Court	126
Fifty-by-Fifty Everywhere	138
Encampment Around the Tabernacle	170
Tabernacle in the Book of Revelation	238

FLOOR PLAN OF THE TABERNACLE

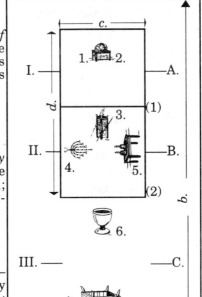

GOD

I. *The Holy of Holies*–God the Father; God's Presence; God's Throne

II. *The Holy Place*–God the Son; Heaven; Heaven's Supply.

III. *The Court*–God the Holy Spirit; Earth; Judgment for Sin.

MAN

A. *Spirit*——(God-consciousness); 5 spiritual senses; faith, hope, love, reverential fear of God, true worship.

B. *Soul*——(self-consciousness); 5 intuitive senses: reason, imagination, affections, memory, conscience.

C. *Body*——(world-consciousness); 5 natural senses: sight, hearing, taste, smell, touch.

LEGEND

Furniture / Title of Christ
1. The Mercy Seat
   Christ, the Propitiation
2. The Ark of the Covenant
   Christ, the Presence of God
3. The Altar of Incense
   Christ, the Intercessor
4. The Golden Lampstand
   Christ, the True Light
5. The Table of Shewbread
   Christ, the Bread of Life
6. The Laver
   Christ, the Word of God
7. The Altar of Sacrifice
   Christ, the Supreme Sacrifice (Symbol–The Cross)

Measurements
a. 50 cubits (75 ft.)
b. 100 cubits (150 ft.)
c. 10 cubits (15 ft.)
d. 30 cubits (45 ft.)
e. 20 cubits (30 ft.)

Entrances
(1) The Veil
(2) The Door
(3) The Gate

Height of the Tabernacle Building (Holy of Holies and The Holy Place) was 10 cubits or 15 ft.

Height of Linen Fence of the Court was 5 cubits or 7 1/2 ft.

(All measurements here are according to the Hebrew cubit which is 18 in. or 1-1/2 ft.)

TABERNACLE STUDY

Moses and his "Cabinet" accepted God's invitation to come up to the Mount of God with Him. Their reward was: *"They saw God"* (Exodus 24:10, 11)! The invitation goes out to God's people today to "come up higher" with Him in a study of the Tabernacle and theirs will be the same reward. For the Sanctuary was prepared by the hands of God Himself (Exodus 15:17), and was not only a revelation *from* Him, but also a revelation *of* Him. Here it is we meet with God face to face and learn to know Him, for in this Tabernacle story He is pictured in His fullness.

The Jewish Talmudists and Rabbinists hold that the "Tabernacle was meant to be a book of deeper wisdom, and of something more glorious than itself, and hence shadowed heavenly and eternal things." God used this method of types (similitudes) to teach His people (see Hosea 12:10).

It is true that there was a very deep meaning attached to it which God endeavored to convey to His people. It is the chief type in all the Scriptures for in it we find the most complete story of redemption. It was a "shadow" of good things to come (Hebrews 8:1, 2, 4, 5; 10:1), containing the foundation of all God's plan for a lost world. Every detail–every bit of material, color, dimension, position, and every article of furniture–had its special significance.

The Tabernacle is emphasized by God Himself for He mentions it with its offerings and service in *fifty* chapters of His Word: 13 chapters of Exodus, 18 chapters of Leviticus, 13 chapters of Numbers, two chapters of Deuteronomy, and four chapters of Hebrews, besides many other references throughout. In contrast, the account of creation is recorded in only two chapters of the Bible, showing that God considered the new creation realities, found to a greater degree in the Tabernacle, of major importance. The first Song ever recorded in Scripture which will be sung in the courts of heaven,[1] mentions it.[2] Also God's great Covenant of Peace with the Israelites included this Holy Dwelling (Leviticus 26:3-13). Another example of its

---

[1] Revelation 15:3.
[2] This Song is written in Exodus 15:1, 2, 17.

prominence is found in the Epistle to the Hebrews. This Book contains 303 verses out of which 131 refer to the Tabernacle of the Old Testament! How much better an understanding we would have of Hebrews, if first we pursue a study of the Sanctuary at Sinai for Hebrews is a commentary on the OT Tabernacle. Along with this book of Hebrews the Book of John is filled with references to the Tabernacle as representing the Messiah. Too, the Book of Revelation is built on its symbolism (see Appendices I and II).

Upon the first physical creation the Triune God stamped His signature of *Three*. In the Universe He created, there are *three* views: earth, sea, and sky; there are *three* great kingdoms: animal, vegetable, mineral; *three* parts of man: spirit, soul, body; *three* forms matter can assume: solid, liquid, aeroform (gas); *three* colors to one ray of light: blue, red, and yellow, etc.

In the Tabernacle, a picture of the New Creation, is also found the numerical signature of the Divine Being. *Three* was the number of the main parts of this Holy Structure: the Court, the Holy Place, and the Holy of Holies or The Holiest. The Holy of Holies represents God's Holy Presence, His Throne Room; The Holy Place pictures Heaven and Heaven's Provisions; The Court shows Earth and the Judgment for Sin. The innermost room tells of God, the Father; the second room, of God, the Son; the outer court speaks of God, the Holy Spirit and yet each part in itself embodies the Godhead. Collectively and individually these rooms describe the Lord Jesus Christ. They tell of the believer in Christ as well:

The Holiest represents the spirit, or the God-conscious part of man. It is the innermost shrine, the Holy of Holies of the spirit where the Law of God is deposited (Ephesians 3:16). The Holy Place symbolizes the soul, man's self-consciousness. This is the soul or mind, the Holy Place where the lamps light up the understanding, where is the bread for nourishment and also the incense of Divine fellowship.

The Court is significant of the body, or that which is world-conscious in man. It represents the external side of his being, that which is seen and recognized by all as the actual person. In 2 Corinthians 5:1,4 the word *tabernacle* is used metaphorically of the body as the tabernacle of the soul. Peter compares his life to that of a tabernacle (2 Peter 1:13,14).

The body in the Outer Court is where it is cleansed, clothed and consecrated for service. The Tabernacle is God's portrayal of a man–the Man, Christ Jesus–and the believer in Him.

God revealed to Moses, Aaron, and many of His people in that day (as well as a goodly number throughout the ages) the true meaning of the Holy Tent in the desert. We read of its significance in the books of Isaiah, Jeremiah and others, until the time when the true Tabernacle, the Lord Jesus Christ, appeared on earth, filled with the Shekinah of God. The Sanctuary of Sinai taught for nearly 1,500 years that the Temple of God, the Messiah, would personally appear in the flesh (Malachi 3:1-3). Every silver hook, brass pin, cord, and other material of this House of God prophesied of Him. Christ fulfills in every detail the pattern of the Tent in the Desert. He is the Antitype* of this sacred building in whom was fulfilled the will and desire of God to dwell with His people. *"And the **word** was made flesh and dwelt[3] among us."*

Christ Himself taught that He was to be found in the Tabernacle of the Exodus. When walking with two of His disciples on the road to Emmaus He said that it was prophesied of Him in the Law, the Books of Moses (Luke 24:27). No doubt He revealed many truths contained in the OT Sanctuary which pictured the Word who became flesh and tabernacled among them!

Notice that in the construction of the ancient Tabernacle, God was the architect and the Israelites, His redeemed people, the builders. They brought a *willing* offering. The work in the Incarnation was done by God who was the Architect, the Designer. The Sons of Israel (God's people at that time) were the Builders of this Temple, the Lord Jesus. It was prophesied that the Redeemer would be born into the human family. His ancestry is traced back to Adam. He would be a *descendant* of David of the *Tribe of Judah.* The Jewish virgin, Miriam (Mary) was submissive to the work of this Sanctuary as is indicated in her declaration to God: *"Be it unto me according to thy word"* (Luke 1:38). She brought a *willing offering*–herself.

---

[3]The Greek word here for *dwelt* is "tabernacled;" see also Hebrews 8:1, 2; 9:9.
*From the Greek word *antitupon* which means 'the reality or fulfillment of the type.'

God is the Designer of the believer (those who are "born-again"), as He was the Designer of the Dwelling at Sinai, and as He is of the body of the Lord Jesus Christ (see Hebrews 10:5). The Christians are the Builders of the Holy Sanctuary on earth even as the Old Covenant people of God were the builders of the Tent of Meeting and of Christ's flesh: *"who are Israelites; ... of whom as concerning the flesh Christ came"* (Romans 9:4, 5). Only God's people can build an habitation for God!

The camp of the Israelites surrounding the Tabernacle was arranged in a remarkable manner which surpasses nation's armies today who are the most enlightened as to order and arrangement. The Dwelling of God was in the center and surrounding it were four great camps of three tribes each. This demonstrated the fact that not only was God *with* His people but that He also was *within* them. (See Numbers 2, 3 and 4 for the order of the encampment and the diagram following section on *Camp Order and Duties* covered under chapters 28 and 29 of Exodus.)

A Short History of the Tabernacle

The sacred Tent was constructed about the thirteenth or fifteenth century BC, and continued to operate right up until the time when Solomon's Temple was dedicated (1 Kings 8:4). In addition, David had made a second tent for the Ark (see 2 Samuel 6:17, cf. 2 Samuel 17:6).

The evidence of God's presence within the Tabernacle was the pillar of cloud and fire (Exodus 13:21, 22). The evidence of God's presence within these Tabernacles of "clay" is the operation of the Gift of the Holy Spirit in our lives. At the Altar in the Court, the fire of God came down to consume the sacrifice, to atone for sin. At the Altar (Mercy Seat) over the Ark was the Shekinah fire, the abiding sign of the Divine Presence–the supernatural always manifest, witnessing to the fact He was within.

This Tent in the desert was called by various names, but the most fitting is *The Tabernacle of **Witness***, for from it 24 hours of every day the power and presence of God was manifested.

After the furniture was finished there had to be a sacrifice upon the Brazen Altar to bring the fire of God, water in the Brazen Laver for cleansing of the priests, oil in the lamps on the Golden Lampstand for the light, a coal of fire with the incense upon the Golden Altar for the fragrance of worship, and "oiled" bread with frankincense upon the Table for food. There had to be the Shekinah over the blood-sprinkled Mercy Seat and also the Pillar of fire by night, representing the presence of God. Without all this, the building constructed by the Israelites would not have been a *true* Tabernacle of *Witness*. There would have been no display of the supernatural as God intended there should be. It would have held no meaning at all.

There was an Interim Tent before the Tabernacle was set up, in which there was no Ark or priesthood. Joshua was its only minister, and it was outside the Camp of Israel called "The Tabernacle of the Congregation" (Exodus 33:7-11). (See also Exodus 24:4-8; the Tabernacle of Moses in the time of David, 2 Chronicles 5:5; and in Solomon's time, 2 Chronicles 1:3.)

The Tabernacle was as much a Tabernacle, and the Israelites were as much the people of God *before* this structure became operative. But the Tabernacle, as well as the Children of Israel, were not *witnesses* to the presence and power of God in the wilderness *until* God came down to *dwell* in their midst.

When Christ was 30 years of age, He was baptized of the Spirit at the river Jordan. By the power of the Holy Spirit overshadowing the virgin Mary He had been "conceived" in her womb. He was as much the Son of God *and* the Son of Man *before* His anointing as He was afterward, but (and I say it carefully) He was not a true Tabernacle of *witness* until the Holy Spirit descended in bodily shape as a dove upon Him. Before this Divine enablement He was not known as the Son of God, and did not reveal the Father openly. He did not perform any miracles, and did not teach or preach expressing the supernatural characteristics of God. In order to fulfill His divine mission He had to be baptized with the Holy Spirit. We read in Isaiah 61:1 concerning His anointing that He was declaring His ministry had commenced now because He had been baptized for that ministry by the Holy Spirit of God!

The followers of Christ had been made the sons of God by the regenerating power of the Holy Spirit. They were as much the disciples of Christ *before* they had been baptized with the Holy Spirit as they were afterward, but were not *true* Tabernacles of *witness, until* they had received the Promise of the Father.

Jesus taught the lesson of the Sanctuary, "as He is so are we in this world" (1 John 4:17). The body of the believer is designed to be the Abiding Place, the Temple of God (see 1 Corinthians 3:16, 17). The willing sacrifice must be upon the Brazen Altar, the water in the Laver, the oil in the Lamp, the coal of fire with the incense on the Golden Altar, the bread with the oil and frankincense upon the pure Table. The Shekinah, the Holy Spirit, desires to dwell between the cherubim over the blood-sprinkled Mercy Seat of his heart and the Pillar of cloud and fire to rest upon his life. The believer is to be a true Tabernacle of *witness* for God. He is to be God's own active testimony in this world according to His will by coming into the promise which Christ gave to all who would believe in Him: "ye shall receive the power of the Holy Ghost coming upon you: and ye shall be *witnesses* unto me" (Acts 1:8, Greek Text).

CHAPTER ONE
EXODUS 25

Verses One and Two

> *"And the LORD spake unto Moses, saying, Speak unto the children of Israel, ..."*

This portion of Scripture begins with three names involved in the Tabernacle, typifying what is to be seen in the overall structure. The Lord God is mentioned here as is Moses, and the Israelites who are the redeemed of the Lord. Everything brought in offerings, every work or service rendered, every experience, every measure, etc., concerns these "Three."

We notice that the name of the Lord is first, the Children of Israel last and Moses, in between. Moses is the mediator, the intercessor; he is likened to God's voice and is a type of the Coming One. God said to Moses:

> *"I will raise them up a Prophet from among their brethren, like unto thee, and will put my words in his mouth; and he shall speak unto them all that I shall command him. And it shall come to pass, that whosoever will not hearken unto my words which he shall speak in my name, I will require it of him"* (Deuteronomy 18:18, 19).

The Lord Jesus Christ fulfills in every detail all the prophecies concerning the Messiah of Israel, the Saviour of the world. He is the "Go-Between," the Mediator between God and Man, the Intercessor. He is the Voice of God, the Incarnate Word (John 1:1, 14).

The Offering

Though there was a mixed multitude that left the land of Egypt, God called them *all* the Children of Israel (see Exodus 12:38, cf. Nehemiah 13:3; Numbers 11:4). Those Egyptians who had intermarried with God's people, who believed in the blood over the doorpost and had obeyed this commandment of the Lord, were delivered as were the Israelites, making their Exodus with them (though later they sinned as did also the Israelites). God named all of the people together as one, as His own children. Throughout the OT we find this truth: ***The gospel is for both***

Jew and Gentile. It was in the mind and purpose of God from before the foundation of the earth that "whosoever will" may come. Not only those of Israel were to be redeemed but the Gentile was included in this wonderful salvation! God considers all people as His own children who leave their bondage of sin and come to the Messiah!

> [verse two continued] *"... that they bring **me** an offering: of every man that giveth it willingly with his heart ye shall take my offering."*

First of all, the Lord called this "***my** offering*," and the people were to bring it to **Him**. They were to give willingly that which they knew belonged to God and was rightfully His possession. They had first offered themselves (Exodus 24:7); now their gifts were requested. It was a "heave offering." The word signifies "something lifted up on high off the ground." It refers to complete separation from earthly ties and unto God. The Hebrew word is *terumah* from the root *rom*, "that which is taken off," implying that which had been reserved for special enjoyment, or that which usually belonged to the priests. A heave offering meant it was lifted up and waved before the Lord (Exodus 35:5, 21, 24; cf. Exodus 36:3, 6).

Exodus 30:13-15 calls the silver atonement money a "heave offering." It was also used to designate the right shoulder of certain sacrifices, therefore called the "heave-shoulder." The people were commanded by God to take a portion of these *choice* things, that which they could use for their earthly pleasures, and give it toward the building of the Holy Sanctuary.

God commands His redeemed today to give to Him a portion of the choice things in His own offering and to bring it willingly for His work. God is the greatest of givers and those who have been born of Him take on the characteristics of their heavenly Father. They are partakers of the Divine nature and become givers with Him. Their time, their wealth, their abilities and their influence are willingly, cheerfully given back to Him who first gave to them. Their worldly gains are hallowed to the glory and honor of God. Their hearts drive them to part with their earthly enjoyments in order to contribute to the advancement of the Heavenly Kingdom.

God did not call upon the people of Egypt left behind but upon those who had observed His command and were saved from death and bondage by the sacrifice of an innocent lamb. So God is requesting His own people today who have come out of sin's bondage, who have been redeemed by the blood of Jesus, God's Passover Lamb, to meet His conditions *following* their salvation and deliverance.

God made it possible for His people to take a prize, to take a reward for all their labor from the Egyptians upon leaving the land of their servitude. The charge against the Jewish people of robbing and cheating the Egyptians is erroneous, and without foundation, due to a wrong translation of the word *shaal* (borrowed). The primary meaning of that word is: *to ask, require as a gift* or *demand as a debt,* and **not** *to borrow.*

> *"And the children of Israel did according to the word of Moses; and they **borrowed** [shaal] of the Egyptians jewels of silver, and jewels of gold, and raiment: And the LORD gave the people favour in the sight of the Egyptians, so that they lent unto them such things as they required. And they spoiled the Egyptians"* (Exodus 12:35, 36).

However, instead of "they spoiled" the Egyptians, it should be "they impoverished," "emptied," or "stripped them."[4]

God commanded those whom He had redeemed, to bring to Him, or to return to Him some of that which He had already given to them through the Egyptians. First God gives, then he asks his people to give. He offers an abundance to His redeemed ones today and also enables them to return a small part. He demands from believers very, very little in exchange for what he has already lavished upon them.

The offering was consecrated to the Lord. "Consecrate" is "to fill the hand." It is first of all taking a handful, and then giving the handful back again. In other words, "to consecrate" means "filling of the hands of things which have already been supplied." God's people are to give "with heart." They are not to bring grudgingly nor hold back, but are to give hilariously, cheerfully, willingly. The Hebrew text is literally rendered: "on the part of every man whose heart drives him." God Himself put that willingness in their hearts in order that they might obey even this commandment. Everything that we get from God comes to us freely. Everything that we are to give back to God

---
[4]See Exodus 3:21, 22; 11:2-3; cf. Exodus 35:22–28.

is to be given generously. We are encouraged to *"Give, and it shall be given unto you; good measure, pressed down, and shaken together, and running over, ..."* (Luke 6:38).

The Israelites willingly, hilariously and cheerfully brought their gifts to the work of the Sanctuary. They had just been forgiven for their sin of idolatry (worship of the golden calf) and a remedy had been supplied for their atonement. How grateful they were for what God had done for them in redeeming, delivering, and forgiving them, so much so that they generously gave in offerings to the extent that they brought more than enough and had to be stopped (Exodus 36:3-7)! That was an experience under "law." Christians are now living under "grace" in the New Covenant. Relative to this someone stated: "The Children of Israel under law were *restrained* from giving, for they brought too much. The Church today under grace must be *constrained* to give, for they give too little. The opposite should be the case." God has done so much for us; how much more hilariously and cheerfully should we give our offerings, and of ourselves, to God for His work, than did the Israelites under the Old Covenant![5]

Often the Jewish people are condemned because they worshiped the golden calf, but are ignored, as to any of their virtues. It is true that they brought their earrings, their vessels, their utensils, their jewels of gold and melted them together for Aaron to fashion this calf (Exodus 32:4). But it wasn't long afterward God gave them the plan of their redemption in the Tabernacle and they were willing to give up the gold to the work of God! A Rabbi who lived close to the time of Jesus described the character of the Jew:

> "A peculiar people, this. Their character is hard to fathom. When Aaron asked them to give for the golden calf, they did so, and when Moses asked for the Tabernacle, they also gave!"

Verse Three

> *"And this is the offering which ye shall take of them; gold, and silver, and brass* [copper].*"*

The sum of the metal offerings and their use in the Tabernacle is written in Exodus 38:2-4. It is remarkable to discover that no

---

[5]The character of giving in this new dispensation is found in Acts 2:44-46.

iron was to be brought. Iron is a military metal. This is the House of Peace! The metals, colors, ingredients, etc., will be explained in more detail as we view them later in this study.

They could not bring just any kind of offering, but one which would be acceptable to God for His work. Of the three metals, gold, the brightest, the clearest, most beautiful, most precious and enduring metal, is mentioned first. Gold is symbolic of Divinity (see Job 22:25). *"The Almighty shall be thy **defense**."* The word "defense" is *betszer* here or *gold*. God and gold are closely associated. God emphasizes that He is first, that He begins from Himself. What we are and what we do for God, all things of beauty, of preciousness, sweetness, and brightness, like the gold, come from God and are the "best." And in turn, let us be sure that God is preeminent in our lives and that we give Him the best of ourselves.

Verse Four

"And blue, and purple, and scarlet, and fine linen, and goats' hair."

This order of colors is repeated at least 24 times in Exodus. There is an absence of green, brown or gray among the colors here. These are *earth* colors and the Tabernacle symbolizes the *heavenly* Tabernacle, the Lord Jesus Christ and those who would be born of *heaven* by believing on His Name!

Blue, which is heaven's color, is listed first. God begins from Himself, from *heaven*.

*"In the beginning God created the **heavens** ..."* (Genesis 1:1, Hebrew rendering).

Fine linen is the first of two woven fabrics. It is typical of righteousness. The Lamb's wife will be clothed in fine linen which is called "righteousness" (Revelation 19:7, 8).

The New Jerusalem adorned as the Lamb's wife will be called *Jehovah Tsidkenu* which means "The Lord, our Righteousness" (Jeremiah 33:16). Who else is righteous but the Lord God? Placing the linen at the head of these materials stresses again that: God is first. He is the Head of all things, the Beginning of Righteousness.

Verse Five

> *"And rams' skins dyed red, and badgers' skins, and shittim* [acacia] *wood,"*

The ram is the animal representing consecration in the Bible. The red dye in it tells that this consecration is unto the "shedding of blood." The Divine Will was perfectly carried out through Messiah's consecration even to death (John 10:18 w/Philemon 2:8). Before the foundation of the earth, in the very beginning, God had this plan and purpose for mankind. The Ram is the *first* skin covering: God's will is first.

The "shittim wood" is the present-day acacia which grows in the desert and receives its life and sustenance from the sand. We find this is the only substance like it in all the verses. There are *three* metals; there are *three* colors; there are *two* woven materials; there are *two* skins, and there are several different "mixtures" of oil. There are many stones too, but here the acacia wood is a substance that stands alone. There is nothing else like it or around it in all of these verses. The Lord Jesus Christ, in His humanity, is the Antitype of the acacia wood. He was born into the human family and grew in the desert wilderness of this world, receiving His human life and sustenance from its "sands." He is a Substance alone, even as the acacia wood of this verse. A Man among men is He, and though human, He is distinctly different and stands alone in the midst of all of human-kind.

Verse Six and Seven

> *"Oil for the light, spices for anointing oil, and for sweet incense, Onyx stones, and stones to be set in the ephod, and in the breastplate."*

Oil is symbolic of the Holy Spirit. It is without any other ingredient and placed first. It was to be poured into the lamps to produce light in the Sanctuary. God, the Holy Spirit, is without any mixture and, being here first, in symbol, shows again the preeminence of God in all things. The onyx stones of the Bible were precious and very brilliant. This stone shines forth as does God's wisdom and glory. It is the first stone in the order of stones and tells us again that God begins from Himself. After the onyx is mentioned then it is recorded concerning the stones which were to be put into the breastplate and on the shoulders of the High Priest's garments. The first stones tell of *heaven's* glorious

Lord, the Son of God. Then the stones tell of *earth's* glorious Lord, the Son of Man.

THE LORD IS FIRST
(as found in Exodus 25:1-7)

1. 1st Name	The Lord	His Title
2. 1st Metal	Gold	His Divinity
3. 1st Color	Blue	His Heavenly Majesty
4. 1st Woven Material	Linen	His Righteousness
5. 1st Skin	Ram	His Will
6. (Stands Alone)	Shittim Wood	His Humanity
7. 1st Ingredient	Oil	His Anointing
8. 1st Stone	Onyx	His Wisdom & Glory

God's Desire for a Dwelling

Verse Eight

"And let them make me a sanctuary; that I may dwell among them."

Sanctuary is the Hebrew word *Mikdash* or "holy place" (innermost), a consecrated place or thing. In the NT the word is *naos* meaning the central or inner shrine or holy place. Christ spoke of His body using this word *naos* in John 2:19, 22. He is the Sanctuary of God! When He talked about teaching in the temple (Matthew 26:55), the word for "temple" is *hieron*, a "sacred place," the entire precincts.

The heart cry of God is: *"that I might dwell among them."* It has been so all through the years. In the very beginning, in the Garden of Eden, God came down and walked with Adam in the cool of the day. He wanted to fellowship with this one whom He had created in His own image and likeness. God cried out then, as in this instance at Sinai, and ever does cry out: "Oh, that I might dwell in and have unbroken fellowship with my people!"

It is striking to note that the Hebrew word, *tavek*, in the above verse is translated as the English "among." It is actually a stronger expression which literally means "in the midst of," "within," "the center," "between," "in the middle," "out of," implying that God would dwell **within** them. This thought is brought out again in the following verses of Scripture:

*"And I will dwell **among** the children of Israel, and will be their God"* (Exodus 29:45). *"And I will set up my tabernacle **among** you: ... And I will walk **among** you, and will be your God, and ye shall be my people"* (Leviticus 26:11-12).⁶

Let the reader consider the foregoing with Paul's statement to the believers in the New Covenant:

*" ... for ye are the temple of the living God; **as God hath said**, I will dwell in* [Literal Greek rendering: "to be in a house"] *them; and I will be their God, and they shall be my people"* (2 Corinthians 6:16).

Here we see that the Apostle knew the true significance of Exodus 25:8 and the desire of God to dwell **within** the earthly sanctuary, the temple of "clay," which is the body of the believer!

God promised that as the glory of the *Shekinah* dwelt in the tabernacle of the wilderness *after* it was completed, so His power and glory would dwell in His people *after* they had been redeemed! *They* would be His dwelling-place, His holy temple, His sanctuary. *This is the wonderful, practical lesson of the Tabernacle in the wilderness!*

Those Israelites were the children of God, but He wanted to come down and dwell *in* them. God is everywhere, but He does not *dwell* everywhere. The apostles of Christ were believers; they had been redeemed, but their bodies were not yet the habitations of God until Christ sent the Comforter from heaven as He promised. The Holy Spirit had been *with* them but now would be *in* them, in the sense of abiding (John 14:17). In the Greek NT the word for sanctuary (*naos*) is also used for the inner temple in Jerusalem and of the believer's body (1 Corinthians 3:16, 17). This is the sanctuary God wants for His dwelling forever!

You and I who are the children of God have been delivered out of "Egypt's" bondage. *Still today* it is the desire of God that He come down and *dwell **within*** us. In this temple He wants to abide; He wants to move; He wants to walk and have His being. He wants His "home" to be in this "tent of flesh." The Tabernacle is not only a type of the Lord Jesus Christ, but it is a picture of

---

⁶Cf. Revelation 7:15 and 21:3.

the Church which is intended by God to be His dwelling place. Each one in the church is to be a habitation of God *through His indwelling Spirit* (Ephesians 2:22).

True, we already have been redeemed, but have we built a "place" for the Lord? Does He delight to live in this "house of clay?" Does He feel at home in this "tent of earth?" Does He control and permeate every atom of our being? Let us open the door of our heart, saints of God, and permit the Lord of Glory entrance to fulfill His desire! Let us build Him a sanctuary that He might ***dwell within***!

Verse Nine

> *"According to all that I show thee, after the pattern of the tabernacle* [*Mishkan*–dwelling], *and the pattern of all the instruments thereof, even so shall ye make it."*

Everything about this sacred building had to be "according to the pattern" (see also Numbers 8:4 with Acts 7:44). It was God's ideal, not organized or planned by man. Everything connected with this edifice of heavenly origin had to be made according to the purpose which God had in mind. All the vessels, instruments, garments, furniture, *everything* had to be carried out after God's own Divine order; this was Heaven's first law.

Pattern Helpers

God's House had to be a place of meticulous perfection and He gave a lot of detail in connection with the Tabernacle which showed His care in that respect. This also indicates His expectation of the same from us. On His first creation, after He had looked upon it, God declared: "It is good!" We who are born of Him should have the characteristics of our Heavenly Father, for we are partakers of His Divine Nature. When we do something for God we should be able to look upon it and say that it is good!

Now how could these former slaves carry out the instructions of God in every minute detail according to the way that God had purposed? They knew nothing of constructing a sanctuary which would meet God's requirements. True, they had learned much about building, and various mechanical arts (which would be involved in the Tabernacle) from the Egyptians, but they did not know how to apply them to the certain specifications and measurements which God gave them concerning His Holy Sanctuary in the desert. They needed wisdom from above to put to use their natural abilities (which had also been given them by God). They could have possessed much talent and intellectual knowledge obtained from Egypt (which God allowed), but this would have been useless without direction from the Master-Builder. God decided to have a Dwelling Place among us, and planned its construction piece by piece. It had to be carried out according to the Heavenly Blueprint through men who were directed by the Great Architect, their Teacher.

God did not leave them with instructions and tell them to obey them in the best way that they could. No, God commanded them that they make it *"according to the pattern that was seen by Moses on the mount."* He gave them helpers that they might be able to fulfill His plan in every detail. He equipped them for the work He gave them to do. It is true: "Whom God appoints, He anoints." "God's commandments are always accompanied by His enablements." In other words, God does not give instructions to His people today and then leave them wondering how they are to finish this work, but He "brings alongside One to help."

We discover how the Israelites were able to carry out God's directions:

> *"And the LORD spake unto Moses, saying, See, I have called by name **Bezaleel** the son of Uri, the son of Hur, of the tribe of Judah: And I have filled him with the spirit of God, in wisdom, and in understanding, and in knowledge, and in all manner of workmanship, ... And I, behold, I have given with him Aholiab, the son of Ahisamach, the tribe of Dan: and in the hearts of all that are wise hearted I have put wisdom,* **that they may make all that I have commanded thee***"* (Exodus 31:1-3, 6).

The Spirit of God was the "Helper," the Wisdom of all the Tabernacle workers, both men and women.[7] Bezaleel and Aholiab were appointed by God to make all things smooth for the Tabernacle. Bezaleel[8] represents the Holy Spirit. His name means "in the shadow (or protection) of God" (*tsel* = "shade," *El*–"God"). The word, *Betselel* is taken from *tsel* which gives

---

[7]Exodus 31:6; 35:10, 25, 26; 36:2.
[8]Today there is a *Bezalel Art School* in Jerusalem named after the Bible Bezaleel.

the idea of hovering over as the pillar of cloud was a *shade* hovering over the sacred Tent. The Holy Spirit is the Divine Umbrella. It also means "vibrate" or "to tingle" (from *tsalal*). How like the Holy Spirit, the "Holy Shade Cloud," to hover over His people, not only to protect them but to energize and enable them for service so that they "vibrate" with Divine Life!

Bezaleel was the son of *Uri*, or "light" (of the Lord), son of *Hur*, or "white," "splendid." The Holy Spirit is Light, revealing Christ. He is Holy, and He is White, Splendid. This man came from the Tribe of *Judah*, or "praise of God." The Holy Spirit prompts praise from God's people.

We learn that after the Tabernacle was built, Bezaleel was acknowledged as the Builder 74 times, *not by name* but by the personal pronoun "he," though all the Israelites were involved (see Exodus 36:8, 10 through 38:22). The Holy Spirit does not speak of Himself but praises or magnifies the Lord Jesus, and this is the reason the personal prooun "he" is used instead of the actual name "Bezaleel". Although God's people are recognized for their service to Him, yet it is the Holy Spirit who empowers and enables them to do the work. Without Him they could do nothing!

Aholiab means "who was at home in the Father's tent," or "tent of my father." He was the son of *Ahisamach*, or "brother of support." He was an assistant, a fellow-helper to Bezaleel. Aholiab seemed to have charge of the textile fabrics, both woven and embroidered (Exodus 38:23). He came from the tribe of Dan. (*Hiram*, the chief artist employed by Solomon for the *ornamental* work of the Temple, was also a descendant of Dan.) The word "Dan" is translated as "judging." Aholiab represents the gifts of the Spirit (1 Corinthians 12:4-11, 28; Ephesians 4:1-11).

The spiritual gifts judge and edify the body of Christ. God gave Aholiab *with* Bezaleel. These two chief architects were, respectively, of the tribes of Judah and Dan. Judah was the leading camp and Dan, the last camp of Israel. They stand as representatives of the complete Camp, the first and last camps. The Gifts of the Holy Spirit and the "ministry" Gifts go together (*with* Him) and God gives them "severally as He wills." The Lord has designed and distributed these "spirituals" to the church to *build* up the Church, the body of Christ. The Lord's people, through the ministry of the Heavenly Bezaleel (*with* Aholiab), are coworkers with God and Christ

All the builders were filled with the wisdom of God and worked according to the Divine plan. God has instructed His children today concerning the Sanctuary, the Temple for His habitation, and has given them a Helper, the Holy Spirit! Like Bezaleel, the Holy Spirit alone knows and searches the deep things of God. The Holy Spirit not only reveals these truths in God's Word, but enables the believer to observe God's instructions "according to the pattern."

Thank God for the infilling of the Holy Spirit and His gifts with which He endows us that we might be able to carry out *His* design for our lives. Without this enablement, time and strength is wasted, but working with it means there is going to be a maximum of fruit with a minimum of labor. As we follow the leading of God's Spirit we will "make it according to the pattern" which will please Him, as He expresses, through these Tabernacles of flesh, His own power, presence and glory.

Test Questions

1. Why is the Tabernacle the chief type in the Bible?
2. How does God emphasize the study of the Tabernacle?
3. What is the "numerical signature of the Divine Being"? Explain.
4. How many main parts were there in this Holy Tent in the Wilderness? Name them and what each one represents.
5. What does God portray in this type?
6. Why was this Sanctuary called "The Tabernacle of WITNESS"?
7. Where and how were the materials obtained for the building of the Sanctuary?
8. What was the first requirement God demanded of the Israelites in building the Tabernacle? In what manner did they meet this requirement?

9. How many metals were employed in the construction of the Tabernacle? Name them.
10. What do we learn in the order of the offering in that gold is the first metal, blue–the first color; linen–the first woven material; rams' skins–the first skin covering; oil–the first ingredient, and onyx–the first stone?
11. Memorize the breakdown of Exodus 25:1-7 according to the title, "The Lord is First."
12. What great desire did God express to Moses in the building of the Sanctuary?
13. Explain the meaning of the Hebrew word *"tavek"* in Exodus 25:8 and of what does it prophesy?
14. What is the great practical lesson of the Tabernacle?
15. How were the Children of Israel able to carry out God's instructions? Explain the meaning of the names involved, and of what do these names speak?
16. How are we able to observe God's instructions today?
17. Name the nine gifts of the Spirit in their order and give Scripture reference where found.
18. Give Scripture reference where other "gifts of the Spirit" are mentioned and tell what they are?
19. Name the five *ministry* gifts in their order, and the Scripture reference where they can be found.
20. What truth is outstanding to you in this section?

ARK OF THE COVENANT AND MERCY SEAT

The Ark of the Covenant

"A striking Hebrew tradition exists as to the ark of the covenant: That it was taken by Jeremiah and secreted in a cavern (II Maccabees 2:4-8) at the time of the Babylonian capture of the city; and that its hiding place has never been found, and never will be, until Messiah shall set up His Kingdom and restore the glory of Israel."[9]

Verse Ten

> *"And they shall make an ark of shittim* [acacia] *wood: two cubits*[10] *and a half shall be the length thereof, and a cubit and a half the breadth thereof, and a cubit and a half the height thereof."*

We see the importance of this piece of furniture in that it was listed *first* in the directions concerning the building of the Tabernacle. This Ark was to be placed in the Holy of Holies

---

[9]*Unger's Bible Dictionary*, p. 1061.
[10]*Latin,* cubitum, *"elbow," "cubit."* A measure of length based on the length of the forearm, about 18 inches. The Egyptian royal cubit (a palm or width of four fingers longer) was 20.67 inches. The Hebrew or common cubit is 18 inches.

(symbolic of Heaven or God's Throne Room), the innermost room of the sanctuary where was the Shekinah–Presence. (See placing of furniture in Exodus 26:34,35 and Exodus 40.) God works from Himself; He moves from Heaven and "comes down." He proceeds from within, outwards toward man. Man could not go to God if He had not first come to him. "The way to God is not of man's invention but of God's revelation." The Tabernacle furniture began with God's Throne. God is first; He will not be second.

This article of furniture was to be made of acacia (*shittim*) wood. It was an incorruptible wood which could not rot, swell, or shrink. It was a hard, closed-grained wood of great strength and endurance, withstanding the winds and sandstorms that would have destroyed weaker and softer wood. Here, in type, is the incorruptible humanity of the Lord Jesus who grew in the desert of this world ("a root out of dry ground" Isaiah 53:2), and received His life from it. He was strong and enduring, defeating every subtle and vicious scheme of Satan and His enemies to cause Him to sin. In all points he was tempted like we are, yet was sinless (Hebrews 4:15).

> *"For in that he himself hath suffered being tempted, he is able to succor* [help, support, champion] *them that are tempted"* (Hebrews 2:18).

He is the incorruptible Son of God who said to the Father: *"Thou wilt not suffer* [permit] *thine Holy One to see corruption"* (Psalm 16:10; Acts 13:35). He arose from the grave on the third day before death could corrupt His flesh!

God's directions to build the furniture began with the Ark. The Holy Tent was reared primarily for this Sacred Chest over which God dwelt between the cherubim. He was the very Center of the Camp of Israel. The Sanctuary of Sinai was to be built that God could dwell "within." This is the desire of God for us today: that He be first and the very Center of our lives. How He longs to be "at home" within these tabernacles of flesh and to permeate our beings with His presence!

Verse Eleven

> *"And thou shalt overlay it with pure gold, within and without shalt thou overlay it, ..."*

The Ark of Noah was pitched within and without with pitch. (Genesis 6:14). The word for "pitch" here is *kaphar*, "to cover up," from which the word *capporeth* (Mercy Seat) comes!

Gold, we have discovered already, is symbolic of Divinity. The acacia wood was to be overlaid with this pure metal. (Pure gold is distinguished from gold which is not purified, by the heat of a furnace in a capsule to remove the dross.)

> "'Overlaying' the furniture of the tabernacle must have been by gilding, both because if plates of gold, however thin, had been used, the weight of the plates would have rendered the tabernacle very difficult of transport, and because all the gold that Moses collected would not have sufficed to furnish plates for every article that was to be covered."[11]

According to some Rabbis the Ark was made in three parts and then put together as one[12]. Two were to be of gold and one in-between, of wood. This can very well represent the Trinity: the Go-Between, the Mediator who was God manifest in the flesh, as the wood; God, the Father and God, the Holy Spirit as the two layers of gold on each side of the wood.

The gold *within* the Ark "pictures" Him who would be filled with all the fullness of God (Colossians 2:9) and anointed of the Holy Spirit (Isaiah 61:1). God would dwell "within" this Tabernacle. The gold *without* is significant of Christ who is the Son of God (Proverbs 30:4; Isaiah 9:6); and the wood *between* tells of the Messiah to come who would be God manifest in the flesh, born of a woman, made under the Law (Galatians 4:4)!

The individual who believes on the Son is represented *in* the Son; therefore the Ark of the Covenant describes the Christian as well. The wood signifies our humanity, the gold *without* represents the Divine nature of which we are partakers (2 Peter 1:4; John 1:12; 1 John 3:2), and that gold *within,* the indwelling of the Holy Spirit.

> [verse eleven continued] *" ... and shalt make upon it a crown of gold round about."*

A crown indicates authority, dominion and the majesty of a king; also it implies the finishing touches to a completed task. This ornament of gold which surrounded the top of the Ark of

---

[11] Dr. Taylor, *Books of Moses*, p. 136.
[12] See *Soncino Chumash* on Exodus 25:10.

the Covenant symbolized the King with His power, dominion, and majesty who declared upon the Cross: *"It is finished!"*

The Crown was similar to a rail on the Ark which surrounded the Mercy Seat above, protecting or guarding, as it were, the Shekinah (the Holy Presence between the Cherubim) and the Blood of Atonement sprinkled there. How God does set a guard to protect His Holiness and the Blood of Atonement from desecration, and defilement at men's hands. He is the King of glory and will never permit His mercy to be removed, nor the blood he gave upon the Altar to be successfully dishonored or trampled upon by men!

> "Notice *three* crowns in the Tabernacle Furniture. They begin with the Ark of the Covenant:
>
> (1) Ark of the Covenant (Exodus 25:11). *The Crown of the Law.* The atoning blood between it, and the cherubim its executant.
>
> (2) Altar of Incense (Exodus 30:3). *The Crown of the Priesthood.* Its incense fired only by the fire from the Altar of burnt offering.
>
> (3) Table of Shewbread (Exodus 25:24). *The Crown of the Kingdom.* The 12 tribes symbolized by the 12 loaves."[13]

Verse Twelve

> *"And thou shalt cast four rings of gold for it, ... "*

"Four" is a "universal" number representing four "corners" of the earth, four elements (land, air, water and fire), four divisions of mankind (Genesis 10:5, 20, 31–lands, tongues, families, nations), four kinds of flesh (1 Corinthians 15:39–beasts, birds, fish, human), four main directions–North, South, East and West; and four seasons–summer, spring, fall and winter.

A ring symbolizes love, "forever" love, endless, infinite, immeasurable love. There is no beginning or ending to it, and it is gold, therefore it can only represent *Divine* love.

> [verse twelve continued] *"... and put them in the four corners thereof; and two rings shall be in the one side of it, and two rings in the other side of it."*

---

[13]Humphrey Milford, *The Companion Bible*, Authorized Version of 1611.

The Ark of the Covenant was surrounded by God's love. The Lord Jesus is the Ark of the Covenant, as the gold, the Son of God; as the wood, the Son of Man. He was surrounded by love, acted in love, was filled with God's love, and is the expression of God's love. He is the Universal Christ for the people in the four corners of the earth; He is the Christ of the four main directions, of the four elements, the four seasons, and of the four divisions of mankind.

> "He is the inseparable, all-enduring and unfailing love of Romans 8:35-39; the magnanimous love of Romans 5:5-8 and the impersonal, unprejudiced, all-embracing love of John 3:16 for the 'whosoever' of the world."[14]

Verses Thirteen, Fourteen, and Fifteen

"And thou shalt make staves of shittim wood, and overlay them with gold. And thou shalt put the staves into the rings by the sides of the ark, that the ark may be borne with them. The staves shall be in the rings of the ark: they shall not be taken from it."

These staves tell us of the ministry of Him who is the expression of the love of God (the rings). They were to be in the Ark, not to be removed from it, so our Lord (as the God-Man) is continually serving His own people with His Presence, not only during their pilgrimage upon earth, but forever! He promises: *"Lo, I am with thee alway, even unto the end of the age ..."* (Matthew 28:20). *"I will never leave thee, nor forsake thee"* (Hebrews 13:5). One of His Names is *Jehovah-Shammah*, "The Lord is There [Present]" (Ezekiel 48:35).

God commanded that the staves in the Ark were never to be removed. There seems to be a contradiction to this in 1 Kings 8:8 where it reads "They *drew out* the staves of the Ark." The Hebrew of "drew out" is *arak* which means "to lengthen," "make long" (extended), from the prim. root, "cause to make long." Christ will be "enlarged" to us when we see Him as He is!

After covering the Ark of the Covenant, the instructions for its transportation are to "put in the staves" (Numbers 4:6). Here, the words "put in" are to be translated *"to convey* it." The thought is *to carry* the Ark *by the* staves. The Ark itself was not to be

---

[14]Rev. Walter D. Lascelle, *Lecture Notes on the Significance of Pentecost* (unpublished).

touched by flesh. The priests (sons of Kohath) were to bear it by the staves. (Numbers 4:4-5; the Ark covered–Numbers 4:5, 20.) It was not to be carried by unclean men but by the priests of the Lord who had been chosen, called, cleansed, clothed, consecrated, and commissioned (see Exodus 28 and 29; also Chapter Seven: *The Tabernacle Priesthood).* The Lord Jesus Christ is the Antitype of the priesthood and those who are in Him are the priests of the Most High God. In love we are to bear, uphold, carry the presence of the Lord with us through this wilderness world journey to the Promised Land. We are to uphold the truth carefully and not permit the touch of flesh to contaminate or hinder the work of God! *"Be ye clean, that bear the vessels of the Lord"* (Isaiah 52:11).

Verse Sixteen

> *"And thou shalt put into the ark the testimony which I shall give thee."*

The Ark was a symbol of protection, of care, and of preservation. God's Law was placed here for safekeeping. The Antetype of the Ark of the Covenant is the Lord Jesus Christ and the Law of God is in His heart to keep it, to preserve it. He would never betray it. He would never misrepresent it. He would never forsake it. This is what God longs to do for every soul: put His Law within the innermost being where it can be preserved, where it will be kept safely. *"Thy law have I hid in my heart that I might not sin against thee"* and *"Thy law is in the midst of me"* was spoken by Messiah Jesus through David and this is the response God desires from those whom He has redeemed.

In the New Covenant God promises the Divine Enabler to help believers observe His Law. First of all, an individual must have his heart changed:

> *"A new heart also will I give you, and a new spirit will I put within you: and I will take away the stony heart out of your flesh, and I will give you an heart of flesh"* (Ezekiel 36:26).

This Covenant prophecy was given to the Israelites (see also Jeremiah 31:31-34) and was dealing with their future restoration, but, as in other prophecies pertaining to Israel which is typical of the redeemed of the Lord (both Jew and Gentile), so also it is in this case. A new heart will be given to those who come to Christ. They will be regenerated or born anew. No longer will their heart be as stone, but it will be soft and pliable in the Master's hands.

> *"And I will put my spirit **within** you, and **cause** you to walk in my statutes, and ye shall **keep** my judgments, and **do** them"* (Ezekiel 36:27).

Here we see what will transpire in the life of the believer when he is filled with the Spirit of God. This transaction takes place *after* his heart is made new. Divine enablement is promised by God to the one who has already received the work of the Holy Spirit in regeneration.

It is only when he is empowered by the Holy Spirit that the child of God can truly keep God's judgments and statutes satisfactorily. If a believer in the Lord Jesus could observe the laws and commandments of God without this ability from above, there would have been no need for this 27th verse which tells of the "God-Within" experience! And this is the significance of Pentecost: **God's enablement for the believer to do that which he could not do without Him!**

Christ told His disciples that if they loved Him they would keep His commandments. The new commandment He left with them was to love one another even as He Himself loved (John 13:34). First, Christ taught them that by keeping His commandments they would show their love to Him. Immediately after this instruction He promised another Comforter who would dwell within them (John 14:13; cf. Ezekiel 36:27). The Father was God *over* men; the Son was God *with* men; and now by the Holy Spirit, God was to be *in* men. How could the disciples love as Christ loved? He knew that it was humanly impossible to do so and therefore promised them God's enablement. The observance of all the commandments of God hangs upon this: Divine Love. Christ is the expression of that love and He desires that those who believe in Him also be representatives of God's love to the world. We cannot do it by ourselves. We need Divine ability. When we are "born again," we enter into the experience of Ezekiel 36:26 and begin to "walk with God." When we are filled with the Holy Spirit we enter into the promise found in Ezekiel 36:27 and God begins to walk in us. Then we can safely keep the Law of God in our hearts, as did Christ, and as He commanded us.

There were two other articles in the Ark of the Covenant which are not mentioned here but are recorded in the book of Hebrews:

> "... and the ark of the covenant overlaid round about with gold, wherein was the golden pot that had the manna, and Aaron's rod that budded, ..." (Hebrews 9:4).

A Brief History of the Ark

Its sojourn and abode before David's time: 1 Samuel 7:1; 2 Samuel 6:3,11; 1 Chronicles 13:13; 15:24, 25 in the border villages of Eastern Judah. It abode in a separate tent pitched for it by David in Jerusalem until the Temple of Solomon (2 Chronicles 1:4). It was probably destroyed by Nebuchadnezzar so that there was no Ark in Herod's Temple.[15]

The three objects in the Ark picture the Lord Jesus Christ. ***First,*** he was the fulfillment of the Law of God (Matthew 5:17). He was simply the Law of God in the flesh. When Moses came down from the mountain after he had broken the two tablets of the Law because of Israel's sin, he brought with him the second tablets. But he also brought something better than the Law; it was the pattern of the Tabernacle, the picture of grace, the plan of salvation in the Lord Jesus Christ.

The first time the tablets of stone were given to the Israelites they broke them. Moses then (literally) broke the tablets of stone upon the ground (Exodus 32:19), even as they (spiritually) had broken the Law in their hearts. The second time these tablets were *not* given to the people but to the *Ark* for safe-keeping. Christ, who is the Ark of God, said through David:

> "*I delight to do thy will, O my God: yea, thy law is within my heart* [in the midst of me]" (Psalm 40:8; cf. Hebrews 10:7).

Second, the Golden-Pot-That-Had-the-Manna, represents the Son of God (the gold), the Son of Man (the manna). The manna came down from heaven to feed the starving Israelites, prophesying of the Messiah who would come down out of heaven to give life to a starving world (John 6:31-35, 48-58).

---

[15] See also Exodus 16:32-34; Numbers 17:10; Deuteronomy 31:26. There was nothing in the Ark after the wilderness wanderings but the two tables of stone, 1 Kings 8:9.

From ancient Jewish writings we read:

"Most wonderful of all was the taste of this golden meal. The flavors of manna were as various as its original hues. No one needed to cook it, for the touch of it on the tongue was sufficient to appease hunger. A man had only to place a grain of manna against his palate, think of his favorite dish. and immediately his mouth was filled with the savor of it. Each was granted his desire according to his age. To children, it had the smoothness of sweet milk and strained honey; to youths, the smack of red meat ... ; to girls the comfort of curds and almond-cakes; to the weary, the vigor of green corn and wafers steeped in cordial; to the sick, the healing of barley bread and olive oil."

So Christ, the Manna from Heaven, satisfies every need of all who will partake of Him. Also, the Pot of Manna in the Ark brought to the remembrance of the Israelites the occasion when they complained against God's provision in the wilderness (Numbers 11:6). Therefore its presence in the Ark was a constant reminder of judgment.

Third, Aaron's Rod was a dead almond stick that was laid up before the Testimony, and overnight budded and blossomed. It portrays the Messiah who was dead but is alive forevermore; it tells of Him who stood at the grave of Lazarus and declared that He was the "Resurrection and the Life" (John 11:25, 26). The Budded Rod also recalled to their attention the instance when the rebellious followers of *Korah* among the Children of Israel questioned the priesthood of Aaron (Numbers 16:3; 17:10). This brought condemnation upon them.

Not only were these objects in the Ark articles of judgment against Israel (for they had broken God's Law, despised His food, and questioned His priesthood) but they prophesied of One Who would come as an expression of God's Law, His food, and His priesthood. He would bear the curse of the Law (Galatians 3:13), and would be rejected as to His Kingship and priesthood. He would be despised as the Living Word with His spiritual teachings of truth (food) (John 1:12).

The trinity of articles in the Ark speak of Him in whom dwelt all the fullness of the Godhead bodily (Colossians 2:9). The Tablets of the Law: Christ is the *Way;* the Golden Pot of Manna: He is the *Truth;* the Rod that Budded: He is the *Life* (John 14:6).

How beautifully does the Ark of the Covenant, with its contents portray Christ and believers in Him! Christ is the Ark covered "within and without" with gold, holding in His heart the Law, the manna, and the rod that budded, covered over by God's mercy, upholding the blood of atonement. He fulfills the promises of God; He is the source of Life and Resurrection power.

> "Thus it is with sons in the Son who, 'within and without' are covered with gold, upholding the blood of the New Covenant upon the mercy seat of their hearts, and who, by Divine enablement, reaffirm Christ's promises (Law: John 14:26; 16:13), reproduce His miraculous life (manna: John 14:12), and reassure of His resurrection power (The Budded Rod: Acts 4:33)!"[16]

The Mercy Seat

Verse Seventeen

"And thou shalt make a mercy-seat[17] of pure gold: ..."

"Mercy Seat," in the Hebrew rendering is *kapporeth* (sometimes spelled *Capporeth*). It literally means "covering over." In 1 Chronicles 28:11 (Hebrew text), the Holy of Holies is called *The House of the Kapporeth*. The NT gives it as *propitiation*. This "lid" was to cover the articles of judgment against the Children of Israel (and against all mankind). God's Law, which was kept inside the Ark, condemned man (see Romans 8:3, 4; Romans 3:20) as did also His Truth and Life symbolized in the manna and the rod. Man could not keep God's Law, believe His Truth, and appropriate His life. Without a covering, the Ark of the Covenant would have been a judgment throne. Referred to in Rabbinical notions of Deity, there is intimated the Ark of the Covenant and the Mercy Seat:

> "The day has 12 hours. The first three, the Holy One, Blessed be He, sits and occupies Himself in the law. The second, He sits and judges the whole world. When He perceives that the world deserves utter destruction, He ***stands*** up from the *throne of judgment*, and ***sits*** on the *throne of mercy*."[18]

---

[16]Rev. Walter D. Lascelle, *"Lecture Notes on the Tabernacle: Body of Christ"* (unpublished).

[17]Hilasterion, *"propitiary"* (spec. the lid of the Ark), "mercy seat" (Romans 3:25; 1 John 4:10).

[18]*Avodah Zarah*, fol. iii, col. 2.

This Cover was not to be made out of wood which represents humanity, but of pure gold, symbolic of Divinity. Mercy is of God not of man. Man had not fashioned it nor counseled God in it. Man had not advised God as to a propitiation for sin, a way of redemption. No, it was pure gold entirely. God alone had fashioned it; before the very foundation of the earth He had planned it. *It is Divine all the way through!*

> [verse 17 continued] *"... two cubits and a half shall be the length thereof, and a cubit and a half the breadth thereof."*

We know by this measurement, which corresponds to the measurement of the Ark of the Covenant in width and length, that the Mercy Seat completely covered the contents of the Ark. God's mercy is sufficient (because of the blood atonement) to cover over His judgment against us. Christ is our Mercy Seat, for:

> *" ... if any man sin, we have an advocate with the Father, Jesus Christ the righteous: And he is **the propitiation** [Mercy Seat] for our sins: and not for ours only, but also for the sins of the whole world"* (1 John 2:1, 2).

We must understand that Bible types or symbols themselves are *not* perfect in every detail; only that which the type or symbol represents, is perfect. Typology (the science of types) shows similarities or contrasts as well as different phases and aspects of the subject considered. The Mercy Seat is Christ and yet it is also God's Throne upon which Christ *sits*. The blood on the Mercy Seat is the requirement for atonement and yet it represents the *slain* Lamb who *stood alive* in the midst of the Throne in heaven![19]

Verse Eighteen and Nineteen

> *"And thou shalt make two cherubims of gold, of beaten work shalt thou make them, in the two ends of the mercy seat. And make one cherub on the one end, and the other cherub on the other end: even of the mercy seat shall ye make the cherubims on the two ends thereof."*

These two cherubim then were to be as one with the Mercy Seat. They typify the glorified believers who are one with Christ.

---

[19]See *Notes on Typology and Bible Symbolism* in Appendix I, p. 216.

"No cherubim appear within the Holy of Holies (in the New City) for these former symbols of redeemed humanity are now supplanted by the innumerable company of Adam's race, from whom the curse (Revelation 23:3) has been removed, and who take their places about the throne of God and of the Lamb, act as His servants there, behold His face, and have His name on their foreheads (Revelation 22:3-4)."[20]

Two is the number suggesting union and agreement; the redeemed are in union with Christ. The cherubim are the most exalted beings of the heavenly hosts, occupying the nearest position to the throne of God. What a high honor! We have been brought to the very Throne of God and given a seat with Him in the Glory! We have been made of one piece with the Mercy Seat, heirs of God and joint heirs with Christ, partakers of the Divine nature, sons of God! We rest in the finished work of Calvary and are "seated with Christ in the heavenlies!"

The cherubs were to be of "beaten work." This prophesied of the suffering of Christ who was "beaten" to become our propitiation for sin, our Mercy Seat. We are one with Him. If we suffer with Him we shall also reign with Him (2 Timothy 2:12).

Though it was called a Mercy *Seat*, no one could sit upon it. In fact, there were no articles of furniture in all the Tabernacle that God had commanded to be made where the priest could sit down. Sitting would imply his work was finished and this was an impossibility. He was continually *standing*, offering many times the same sacrifices. The priests would continue on in their ministry before the Lord, one priest after another, but they never came to the completion of their duties. There is only one Priest who sat down because His ministry (as concerning the Old Covenant) was finished:

> *"And every priest standeth daily ministering and offering oftentimes the same sacrifices, which can never take away sin: But this **man*** ["man"-not in original, Priest, more correct since this verse is about priests], *after he had offered **one** sacrifice for sins for ever, **sat down** on the right hand of God"* (Hebrews 10:11, 12).

---

[20]Milton S. Terry, *Biblical Hermeneutics*, p. 492.

It was a shock to the Hebrews to *sit* in the Temple or Tabernacle, but Jesus entered the heavenly Tabernacle and after He had completed the ritual of the great Day of Atonement He *sat down* at the right hand of God. This action meant that not only was His work of the Old Covenant finished but that He received the equal powers of God. (To be seated at the right hand of an earthly King means to receive the authority and equal powers of the King.) Once before this Christ "sat down" after He had read the prophecy concerning Himself and His work (Luke 4:20) implying that He would finish or fulfill the Old Covenant (see John 19:30; "It is *finished*" with Hebrews 1:3). All eyes were fastened upon Him when He acted in this manner for no one dared to take this authority preceding His coming. This was something new and startling to these Jews. Could it be they knew that only such a One as their Messiah would be ordained by God to do it?

Verse Twenty

> "And the cherubims shall stretch forth their wings on high, covering the mercy seat with their wings, and their faces shall look one to another; toward the mercy seat shall the faces of the cherubims be."

According to the great Jewish teacher, Rashi[21] the wings of these cherubim extended above the Mercy Seat so as to provide a space of ten hand-breadths between them and the top of the Cover. In this space dwelt the Shekinah.[22]

In present-day evaluation the gold of the Mercy Seat is estimated to have cost approximately $6,000. However, the cherubim were not to look upon one another though they were beautiful, neither upon the gold though it was precious. They were not to "look under" at the law man failed to keep, or eastward toward the people who were sinners. God commanded that their faces should be *toward the Mercy Seat*. For upon this Sacred Cover was the priceless blood of the sacrifice. The purpose for this *Kapporeth* was the blood of atonement that it held.

The word "atonement" is used 80 times in the Old Testament and only *one* time in the New Testament (which is not

---

[21]Rashi is regarded as one of the greatest Hebraists the Jews ever had.
[22]See *Soncino Chumash* on Exodus 25:20.

properly translated here) in Romans 5:11, where the word is *ketallage*, meaning *reconciliation* (satisfaction), *restoration to* [divine] *favor.* So here was a means of propitiation for Israel. Here forgiveness and pardon was offered up for them. It was by this means that a way of access to God was made on their behalf. It was the "precious blood" in which the cherubim were interested as their faces looked *toward* the Mercy Seat. You and I are not redeemed with corruptible things such as silver and gold, but we are redeemed with the precious blood of the Lamb (1 Peter 1:18, 19). We are ever to behold the blood of atonement remembering it was the work of Christ on the Cross which gives us the high privilege and honor to be *one with Him* in glory!

Verse Twenty-One

> *"And thou shalt put the mercy seat above upon the ark; and in the ark thou shalt put the testimony that I shall give thee."*

The Mercy Seat was the supreme feature (*above* upon the ark) of all the Mosaic rites. It covered over God's judgment upon His people for their sins. It was by way of the blood sacrifice. The whole Bible witnesses that without the shedding of blood there is no remission of sins (Hebrews 9:22). In the very beginning God taught this truth to our first parents. *"The LORD* [made] *coats of skins*[23]*, and clothed them"* (Genesis 3:21). Blood had been shed before such apparel could be fashioned. A "coat" suggests sufficient attire. The Septuagint[24], gives the word for "coat" as *chiton*, which was a garment reaching to the feet. In the Hebrew text the word is *kethoneth* (sometimes spelled *ketonet*) which can be translated as shirt, garment, robe, or coat but it also has another meaning: "to cover" or "to hide," indicating that the clothing is sufficient. The Hebrew word "atonement" (*kippur*) means "to cover up." The Mercy Seat, the *Kapporeth*, holding the blood of atonement, completely covered the objects in the Ark of the Covenant which were reminders of God's judgment upon the Children of Israel. (Dangerous results from uncovering or even touching the Ark

---

[23]*Or* (Hebrew text), *skin* (singular) which implies that it is "leather" or a "hide." *One* (skin) covering. There is only ONE covering made by blood sacrifice!

[24]A little over 100 years after the close of the Old Testament canon, a Greek translation of the OT Scriptures was made or commenced to be made. This was in 277 BC. It was called *Septuagint* or the *Alexandrian* version. This was the work of *70* Jewish (Rabbis) and scholars of Alexandria. The word *Septuagint* is the Latin word for *70.*

are recorded in 2 Samuel 6:6, 7.) *"Blessed is he whose ... sin is covered"* (Psalm 32:1).

The blood on the Mercy Seat testified of the Life poured out, a Life for a life prophesied as follows:

> *"For the life of the flesh is in the blood: and I have given it to you upon the altar to make an atonement for your souls: for it is the blood that maketh an atonement for the soul"* (Leviticus 17:11).

The blood on the Mercy Seat stands for the death of Christ which canceled the claims of Satan upon the sinner. No longer is the sinner under condemnation because **Christ paid the title deed**. This brings to my mind a song we used to sing in chapel when I was a student at Southern California (Bible) College. I do not know the title nor the verses of this song, only the chorus, which follows:

> "He paid the title deed with His atoning blood.
> He ever lives to make His promise true.
> Though all the hosts of hell
> March in to make a second claim,
> They all march out at the mention of His Name!
> They all march out at the mention of His Name!"

First, the Mercy Seat was to be placed on the Ark, then the Law was to be put inside. Mercy is offered first to the sinner who, if he rejects it, must suffer the judgment of the Law.

> *"He that believeth on the Son hath everlasting life: and he that believeth not the Son shall not see life; but the wrath of God abideth on him"* (John 3:36).

Verse Twenty-Two

> *"And there I will meet with thee, and I will commune with thee from above the mercy seat, from between the two cherubims which are upon the ark of the testimony, of all things which I will give thee in commandment unto the children of Israel."*

God told Moses that He would commune with him from above the Mercy Seat at His appointment. It was a privilege, an honor, a blessing to Moses that he could enter into the Holy of Holies, to the very presence of God! The High Priest could only enter once a year on the Day of Atonement but Moses could enter *at any time,* as God called him. Moses was a type of Christ. The redeemed of the Lord are represented in Him. They stand before the Father in the Beloved, and are recognized as sons in the Son. It is the privilege, the honor, the blessing that God has bestowed upon you and me who have been redeemed by the precious blood of the Lamb, to come into the Throne Room, into the Holiest Place where we can commune with God at the Mercy Seat!

> "While reason, like a Levite, waits
> Where priest and people meet,
> Faith, by a 'new and living way,'
> Hath gained the Mercy Seat."

What a wonderful appointment! At all times we have His blessing, His fellowship through the Lord Jesus Christ. No longer is it a Judgment Throne but to us it is a place of mercy (Romans 3:25). We can come boldly to the Throne of grace (Hebrews 4:15, 16; 10:19, 22) because we are washed through the sacrifice of the Lamb. And ever, always, the cherubim are looking toward the place where the blood of atonement is sprinkled. Let us continually look toward the Mercy Seat where that precious blood speaks for the remission of our sins.

> "There is a place where Jesus sheds
> The oil of gladness on our heads,
> A place than all beside more sweet,
> It is the blood-stained Mercy-Seat."

Between the two cherubs dwelt the Shekinah, the actual presence of God.[25] The cherubim represent the believers who are one with Christ. How He longs to commune in the Holy of Holies, within the inner sanctuary of every one of His children today. He desires to dwell in the *center* of their lives. This is the Promise of the Father (Luke 24:49), His coming to "dwell in," "tabernacle," in the believer. He had been *with* them, but would be *within* them by the infilling of the Holy Spirit (John 14:17). The Shekinah would *dwell* between the cherubim on the blood-sprinkled mercy seat of the believer's heart!

---

[25]See 1 Samuel 4:4; 2 Samuel 6:2; 1 Kings 22:19; 2 Kings 19:15; 1 Chronicles 13:6; Psalm 80:1; Psalm 99:1; Isaiah 37:16.

Threefold Purpose of the Mercy Seat

1. To be the place of God's Dwelling Presence.
2. To cover over the articles of judgment inside the Ark.
3. To hold the blood of atonement.

Test Questions

1. What does the Holy of Holies represent?
2. Give a definition of a cubit. What is the measure of a *Hebrew* cubit? of an *Egyptian* cubit?
3. What does the Ark of the Covenant teach us in that it was the first article of furniture to be built and placed in the Holy of Holies?
4. Of what materials was the Ark of the Covenant made and what do these symbolize?
5. Give a short History of the movements of the Ark. Was it present in Herod's Temple?
6. What does the incorruptibility of the wood teach us?
7. What does the **combination** of wood and gold represent?
8. How is the Spirit-filled believer represented in the Ark?
9. Of what does the crown on the Ark tell us?
10. Name the three crowns of the Tabernacle furniture and what they represent.
11. How many rings were to be cast for the Ark and what does this number signify?
12. What is the symbolism of the gold rings?
13. (a) What do the staves through the rings represent and of what materials were they made? (b) Explain the seeming contradiction between: "The staves of the Ark were never to be removed" and 1 Kings 8:8.

14. What were the contents of the Ark according to the record in Hebrews and what is the significance of each object?
15. (a) What is another word for "Mercy Seat" from the Hebrew text? Describe its literal meaning. (b) What is the word for *Mercy Seat* from the Greek text? Give Scripture reference where this word is found in the NT.
16. What does the absence of wood or alloy in the Mercy Seat teach us?
17. Where could the priests sit down in the Tabernacle? What does the "sitting down" imply? Compare with Hebrews 10:11, 12.
18. What was the purpose of the Mercy Seat?
19. Who is represented in the cherubim?
20. How do we see "God within" as taught by the Mercy Seat?
21. What truth is outstanding to you in this section?

THE TABLE OF SHEWBREAD

The Table of Shewbread

Verse Twenty-Three

"Thou shalt also make a table of shittim [acacia] *wood ..."*

Here we find the word "table" mentioned for the first time in Scripture. In the Hebrew text it is *shulhan* which means "to send," "to stretch forth," "extend," an object with capacity for the food upon it, "to spread out," a *meal* by implication.

The Table was closely associated with the Ark of the Covenant intimated by the word "also." The Ark which represents God's Throne and Presence, is vitally connected with the truths symbolized in the second object in the Holy Sanctuary. This is where we receive strength to overcome so that we can truly "dwell" with God in the Holy of Holies. We must sit at the Lord's Table before we can sit with Him on His throne (Revelation 3:21).

Wood is symbolic of humanity. A table made of this substance points to human activity where fellowship and service is enjoyed along with nourishment, satisfaction, and strength which is derived from the food upon it. God did not only desire a Tabernacle for his dwelling place (His relationship to His people), but He called for a table in the Holy House where He could come and feast with His children and they, in turn, could feast with Him (His people's relationship to Him). Here they would be drawn closer together in communion, one with another. God longs to satisfy His people with Himself and He wants His people to satisfy Him with their presence as well. God's desire to draw His people closer to Himself is beautifully portrayed in the *Feasts of the Lord* listed in Leviticus 23.[26] We who are born of God can bring enjoyment and pleasure to the heart of our Heavenly Father by our devotion and respect toward Him. Something better than salvation is to have fellowship with the One who saved us. We can come to His table and there we are served and nourished; we are satisfied and, in turn, we serve God and satisfy Him.

David said, concerning fellowship with God: *"Thou preparest a table before me in the presence of mine enemies"* (Psalm 23:5). He was surrounded by opposing forces, yet he could be with God in the midst of it all. Even though enemies encircled him, he could serve God and be served of Him in that wonderful sweet communion with his Lord. Thus we, who are the children of God, can enjoy the same privilege and blessing today.

We read in the book of Revelation that it is the yearning of the Lord Jesus Christ to come and feast with His own, and they, with Him. This verse has been used for the unbeliever (and it can be applied that way) but in this particular portion it is written to the churches, to the believers.

The Lord invites by His Spirit: *"Behold, I stand at the door and knock. If any man hear my voice and open the door I will come in and sup with him and he with me"* (Revelation 3:20). We can "sup" with the Master as He "sups" with us. He can be satisfied with *our* bread as we can be satisfied with *His* bread.

> [verse 23 continued] *"... two cubits shall be the length thereof, and a cubit the breadth thereof, and a cubit and a half the height thereof."*

---

[26]Leviticus 23 has been called *"God's Calendar of Redeeming Grace."*

The height of this table was to be the same as that of the Mercy Seat on the Ark of the Covenant. Fellowship with God is equal with His mercy and because of His mercy we can have this fellowship with Him. Because we have been reconciled to God we can come and sit at the Royal Table!

The Table was to be made of acacia wood. The wood is significant not only of the humanity of the believer, but first of all, the humanity of the Lord Jesus. He is the Table of the Lord God, the One who serves us, satisfies, strengthens and nourishes us. He is the Table spread by God Himself who is with us even in the midst of our enemies.

Verse Twenty-Four

"And thou shalt overlay it with pure gold, and make thereto a crown of gold round about."

Again, in this Table, we see the humanity and divinity of the Lord Jesus. He is not half God and half man, but He is whole, perfect God; whole, perfect Man. He is God, the Son of God; He is God, the Son of Man. As the gold: He came from Heaven, from Eternity. As the wood; He came from Earth into Time. Throughout Scripture Christ is presented in these two aspects: His Divine Nature, which shows that He is equal with God, and His human nature which shows that He took the form of man. Man's iniquity separated him from God; and only God could understand this position. Only man could fully sense man's temptation with regard to iniquity. In order that there be a combined understanding of these two positions Christ had to be both man and God, a Mediator, a Go-Between. The Scriptures prove Him to be exactly this. He IS the God-Man (see Acts 17:3; John 1:1; Hebrews 1:8.)

The Human and the Divine Side of Christ

He who is the Bread of Life began His ministry hungering.
He who is the Water of Life ended His ministry thirsting.
He who was weary is our True Rest.
He who paid tribute is the King of Kings.
He prayed yet hears our prayers.
He wept but dries our tears.
He was sold for thirty pieces of silver, yet redeemed
the world.

> He was led as a lamb to the slaughter, but is the
> Good Shepherd.
> He died and gave His life, and by dying destroyed
> death for all who believe.
>
> –Author unknown

The following item relative to the Ark of the Covenant is from the *Sapirstein Edition of Rashi*:

> "'And you shall make upon the Ark a golden diadem all around.' This refers to a sort of crown going all the way around it, and is a symbol for the crown of Torah (*Rashi*). That is, the figurative crown worn by the Torah scholar (see *Avos* 4:12) is symbolized by the diadem of the Ark, for the Tablets of the Covenant were kept inside the Ark. According to one opinion, the Torah scroll written by Moses was also placed inside the Ark, while according to another opinion, it was kept on a shelf that protruded from it (see *Rashi* to *Deuteronomy* 31:26). Thus the Ark represents the study of Torah." PARASHAS TERUMAH (p. 325).

A crown signifies authority, kingship, and a finished work. Our fellowship with the Father is given to us through the authority and finished work of the King!

Verse Twenty-Five

> *"And thou shalt make unto it a border of an hand breadth round about, and **thou shalt make a golden crown** to the border thereof round about."*

A handbreadth (the measure of the palm's width or four fingers) away from the outside crown was another crown of gold. Two crowns. He is the King of Kings, the outward crown; He is the King of the Jews, the inside crown. Bread, here, symbolizes humanity. The 12 loaves of bread, which the inside crown surrounded, represented the 12 tribes of redeemed Israel. (Jewish writers claim that the cakes or loaves of bread were separated from each other, to keep from molding, by thin plates of gold.) This "rail" or crown of gold kept the bread from slipping or sliding off the table. Christ is the King of those He has redeemed, His Heavenly People; He came in Person to be Ruler of Israel, King of His Earthly People. He keeps the bread from slipping, from sliding and falling to the ground. Our Lord is able to keep us from falling and to present us faultless before the presence of His glory with exceeding joy (Jude 24).

Verse Twenty-Six

" ... and put the rings in the four corners that are on the four feet thereof."

Four is significant of the Universal Christ. Rings speak of love, and gold tells of divinity. Divine Love surrounded the Table.

The four feet beneath the Table were placed upon the earth. There was no prepared flooring in the Tabernacle. Dirt, the sand of the wilderness, was the only floor (see Numbers 5:17; the dust that formed the Tabernacle floor was used in this case). In His Incarnation God came all the way down to the earth, down to where we live, to be as we are, to meet us on our own level!

As a Man, the Universal Christ walked upon the sandy floor of the world in His wilderness journey. He was the Table of the Lord, and as He was walking among men upon the earth He served and fed them; nurtured, strengthened and satisfied them. He was the Table of the Lord in the wilderness journey of the Children of Israel and He continues to be so to all His redeemed ones in their pilgrimage on the sands of this "desert" world. He serves His people and He expects His people to serve Him. In the four corners of the earth our Redeemer is the Table of God.

Verse Twenty-Seven

"Over against the border shall the rings be for places of the staves to bear the table."

The border of the table was a crown of gold: Christ is the King. The staves are significant of the Lord Jesus in His service to mankind. They were near this crown, indicating that Christ was King upon the earth, King of the Jews. It was prophesied that out of Bethlehem the *Ruler* in Israel would come. He, who is nourishment, the Staff of Life for His people, would be born in Bethlehem, the original meaning of which is "House of Bread"!

Verse Twenty-Eight

> "And thou shalt make the staves of shittim [acacia] wood, and overlay them with gold, that the table may be borne with them."

In His earthly sojourn Christ walked among men as a Man, subjecting Himself to sustenance from the desert sand of earth even as other men, yet upheld by God, empowered by the Holy Spirit as He desired that His Redeemed should be.

The priests of the Lord were to bear the Table by these staves. Christians are, with redeemed Israel, a "royal priesthood" and are to carry the Table of the Lord with them in their pilgrimage here. They are to be the messengers of "Glad Tidings." They bear the Manna to feed the spiritually hungry in this earthly journey. Note: 1 Peter 2:9, Peter was writing to *Jews* calling **them** a *chosen generation, a royal priesthood, an holy nation, a special people*. However, all believers (Jew and Gentile) inherit the promises of God and are "chosen, of the royal priesthood, a holy and special people of God"!

Verse Twenty-Nine

> "And thou shalt make the dishes thereof, and spoons thereof, and covers thereof, and bowls thereof, to cover withal: of pure gold shalt thou make them."

The word "bowls" is equated with "cups" or "goblets." Also "to cover" means "to pour with" or "to pour." This intimates the drink offering mentioned in Exodus 29:38-42. (See also Numbers 28:1-31 where wine was used as a drink offering in the Holy Place of the Tabernacle.) Following the offering which included the *wine,* Exodus 29:39-41 states, concerning *the continual burnt offering,* that this *communion* was to take place twice a day, the whole burnt offering at 9 a.m. (our time), and at 3 p.m. (our time) or "between the (two) evenings" (Exodus 12:6; Leviticus 23:5, 6; Exodus 29:38, 39; 30:7, 8).

In the Holy Place (rather, the Court is indicated here) wine (the drink offering) was *poured out to the Lord* twice daily with the lamb "whole burnt offering" (Numbers 28:3, 4 with Numbers 28:7) morning and evening. Also with the drink offering" and lamb there was to be an offering of flour mingled with beaten oil. The bread, wine and oil with the lamb were The Holy Communion. On the Sabbath, besides the "continual burnt offering" there was to be another two lambs and double the flour mingled with oil as well as another drink offering (Numbers 28:9, 10).

On the Day of Pentecost the Jews were accused of being drunk on wine. But Peter stood up and said it could not be so since it was but the *third hour* of the day (Acts 2:13-15).[27] It was the time of prayer and the morning sacrifice. They would not be desecrating this time in revelry. Also, the wine was *poured out to the Lord*, not partaken of by the worshipers (see Leviticus 10:8, 9; cf. Genesis 35:14)! "Poured it out to the Lord" was an act of worship (2 Samuel 23:16; 1 Chronicles 11:18).

These utensils or instruments that were used to help in the oiling and serving of the bread are symbols of the Holy Spirit, who is the Helper. The Bread on the Table could not be made or distributed, could not be partaken of, without the golden utensils to help. The Bread of God who came down from Heaven was "made" by the Holy Spirit, "distributed" by the Holy Spirit and can be partaken of properly, only by the Divine Helper. We too, cannot be broken bread to feed the hungry unless we are empowered by the Holy Spirit, even as was Christ, the Heavenly Manna.

Verse Thirty

> *"And thou shalt set upon the table showbread[28] before me alway."*

The Hebrew text calls this shewbread *Lehem ha-Panim* or, literally, "Bread of Faces" (a face that turns every way). The use of the term, "faces," is found in "My Presence (*panim*–faces) shall go with thee" (Exodus 33:14). Faces, then, in this connection means the Divine Presence.

Christ is God's *appointed* Wheat. There was no "unevenness or coarseness" in Him for He was sinless. He was cut down, then He was sifted through suffering, ground and bruised fine in God's mill of judgment against sin. But His life in the "fine flour" stage could not save us. He was baked in the oven of Calvary before we could partake of Him. He is the Bread of God's Presence!

---

[27]See the "charge" of the Levites, 2 Chronicles 13:10, 11.
[28]"Shewbread" is an old English word for "Showbread." The Septuagint calls the shewbread "foreplaced Loaves." The New Testament calls it "the placing of bread."

The bread was put up before the Lord, offered first to Him for six days, and then on the seventh day the priests would participate in it, would eat this bread and renew it with other freshly baked bread. Christians are New Covenant priests (1 Peter 2:9; Revelation 1:5, 6). The service of these priests is commanded as written in the New Testament: Romans 12:1.

How the bread was made, set in order on the table, and taken care of by the priests is recorded in Leviticus 24:5-10. Each cake was two-tenth deals or one gal. of flour which equals 7½ pounds (a 10th deal of flour is ½ gallon).

According to the Jewish *Mishna* the length of a loaf was 7 handbreadths, about 28 inches; the width was 4 handbreadths, about 16 inches, and the depth was equal to 7 finger's width, about 6 or 7 inches. (Problem: How could the *Table* hold 12 cakes each with the aforementioned measurement when it was only 36 inches long and 18 inches wide?–Author.)

The Jews have a custom today handed down from this Tabernacle ritual. The bread is called *challah* (*kahlah*) and after it is baked on Friday (the preparation day for Sabbath), it is covered over with a white cloth which signifies purity. On the Sabbath (Friday evening at sunset the beginning of Saturday), it is uncovered, cut, and blessed with these words in Hebrew: *"Baruch attah Adonai, Elohenu, Melech ha-olam, ha-moitzeh lehem min ha-eretz."* "Blessed art Thou, O Lord our God, King of the Universe,[29] who bringeth forth bread from the earth." The first piece of this "challah" is presented to the head of the house who is the priest and lord of his household; the remainder of it is then distributed among the family. The Bread from Heaven was revealed in Christ. He who was baked in the oven of God's wrath for sin, first offered Himself to the Lord, then became the portion of His people.

The bread was to have frankincense (meaning "to be white"), not honey, upon it. Honey is sweet but it is only a counterfeit of frankincense. The honey sweetness is not lasting; it easily ferments and turns sour. Frankincense is sweeter as it comes in contact with fire. The fire brings out its sweetness but this is not the case with honey–as soon as the *fire* touches honey, the honey is gone. The Lord Jesus Christ is the Bread with the frankincense

---

[29] Should be "Eternal King" or "King of Eternity."

(the Holy Spirit) upon Him. And we who are His redeemed ones as "one bread" (1 Corinthians 10:17) are to exercise forth, not honey or natural sweetness, but the sweetness of the Holy Spirit.

Christ not only atoned for sin, canceling the death penalty and making life possible, but He, as the Bread, the Staff of Life, sustains that life He has made possible. He is the Bread that came down out of heaven who feeds, nurtures and satisfies us. In Christ the redeemed of the Lord are likened to this bread as well. They must offer themselves first to God and then to the people. The following is by an unknown poet and should be the prayer of all God's people:

"Dear Saviour, make me
All you prayed I'd be;
Body, soul, and spirit
By Thyself made free.
Take this bread and break it
Broken bread I'd be,
And poured-out wine before Thee:
This, my humble plea."

Test Questions

1. With what do we associate the word, table?

2. Of what materials was the Table of Shewbread made and what is their significance?

3. What surrounded the Table? the Bread? Explain their symbolic meaning.

4. (a) How do we know there was no prepared flooring for the Tabernacle structure? (b) What does this teach? (c) What do the four feet of the Table on the sand represent?

5. Name the golden utensils made for the Bread and what is their symbolic meaning?

6. What was the Bread on this Table called (literal translation from the Hebrew). Explain this name from Scripture and give other names for this Bread.

7. How many loaves were there and in what order were they to be placed on the Table? Give Scripture reference.
8. Whom did the loaves of Bread represent in the time of Moses and of whom do they prophesy and represent today?
9. Who was allowed to partake of this Bread?
10. Describe the OT ritual of "The Communion." Prove from Scripture that the wine was "poured out before the Lord in the Holy Place" and give its significance.
11. How many days was the shewbread to be set in the presence of the Lord before it was replaced with fresh bread?
12. Explain the spiritual application in that these loaves were first offered to God and then to the priests.
13. Why was the Bread with frankincense called "an offering of fire" unto the Lord? What does the frankincense on the Bread teach us?
14. What truth is taught in the absence of honey and the application of frankincense on the 12 loaves of bread?
15. What truth was outstanding to you in this section?

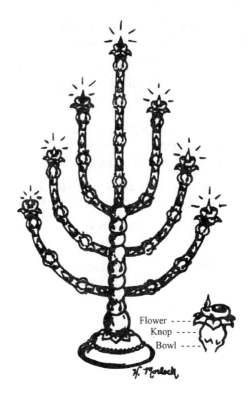

THE GOLDEN LAMPSTAND

The Golden Lampstand

Verse Thirty-One

> *"And thou shalt make a candlestick of pure gold: of beaten work shall the candlestick be made: ..."*

The Easterners called lamps on a stand, "a candlestick." The Western mind calls it a Lampstand because oil is used in a lamp for the flame. The word *"menorah"* is translated here in the English as "candlestick." However, the "candle" as we know it today was then unknown. More correctly: "Thou shalt make a *menorah* (a place of light) of pure gold."

There was no wood in this Lampstand. God instructed the Children of Israel to make it of one block of pure gold. These materials are symbolic: gold, of Divinity, wood, of humanity. God, not man, is the Author of light. God did not counsel with man in its creation. It was pure gold–all Divine throughout.

48

Christ is the Lampstand. He is the Light of the World, the Light of the Jew, of the Gentile (Luke 2:32; John 1:9, 8:12), and the Light in the New City coming down out of Heaven. In this Holy City there need not be any light of the sun, nor the moon, nor the stars because "the Lamb is the light thereof " (Revelation 21:23).

The Golden Lampstand, symbolic of spiritual light, stood in the Holy Place. Nature's light was absent and would have to be experienced on the outside of this Holy room. One must come into the Holy Place with God and walk by God's light in order to enjoy fellowship with Him. No service in the natural light is acceptable to "the Father of Lights." *"The natural man receiveth not the things of the Spirit of God, neither can he know them, for they are spiritually discerned"* (1 Corinthians 2: 14).

The Lampstand was not made into a mold nor put into sections and then connected together. It was beaten[30] into its form and shape, and that, outside of the Holy Place and then brought inside. The Lord Jesus received the hammer of God's judgment upon Him for the sins of the world *outside* of Heaven. It was *outside* of the City of Jerusalem He endured the "beatings" of the Cross. Through His sufferings He was made perfect (Hebrews 2:10) and was then received up into Heaven (the Holy Place). On earth Christ was not permitted to enter The Holy Place for He was not a Levite (cf. Hebrews 2:24). *"Ought not Christ to have suffered these things, and to enter into his glory?"* (Luke 24:26).

> [verse 31 continued] *" ... his shaft, and his branches, his bowls, his knops, and his flowers, shall be of the same."*

That is, the design, the formation of the Lampstand were all to be of this pure beaten gold. They belonged to the Lampstand, and were one with the Central Stand. Notice it is in the masculine gender. There are only two genders in Hebrew grammar: feminine and masculine. And here it is written of the Lampstand: "**his** shaft, **his** branches, **his** bowls, ..." The Lord Jesus who is the Light of the world was found "in fashion as a ***man***."

---

[30]*Mikshah* = "rounded work" (moulded by hammering), "round and hard," *i.e.,* "solid." From *kashah,* "to be heavy or stiff," "hammered out."

Verse Thirty-Two

"And six branches shall come out of the sides of it; three branches of the candlestick out of the one side, and three branches of the candlestick out of the other side:"

God was very specific concerning the form of this article of furniture even to every bud, knop, flower, and every one of the branches, but He did not give any measurement to it. God has as much purpose in omitting instructions as He does including them in His Word. There is no measure or dimensions given for this Lampstand; there is no measure to light! Light is limitless, without measure or dimension; so the Lord Jesus in His Light, Love, Truth, Grace and Mercy is matchless and limitless.

The six branches were to come out of the sides of the Lampstand (Central Shaft). It was on the *sixth* day that man was created. This number (six) signifies man and man's working day. It is an incomplete number. The six branches coming out of the sides of the Central Shaft were a very part of the Central Shaft. The Central Shaft symbolizes God; therefore, each branch is a picture of man coming out of God: born of Him, from His thigh.[31] The six branches joined together with the Central Branch made it "seven," which is the perfect number.

It is interesting to note that light has **7** colors. A prism will break up light into these **7** colors. *Seven* is the number of perfection. God emphasizes perfection in His dealings with His people: The Holy Days and Seasons was a system built on a cycle of *Sevens*: every **7**th day a Sabbath; every **7**th year a Sabbatic year; every **7**th Sabbatic year was followed by a Jubilee year; every **7**th month was especially holy, having three feasts; there were **7** weeks between Passover and Pentecost; the Passover Feast lasted **7** days; the Feast of Tabernacles lasted **7** days; at Passover 14 lambs (twice **7**) were offered daily; at Tabernacles 14 lambs (twice **7**) were offered daily and 70 (10x**7**) bullocks; at Pentecost **7** lambs were offered. We are complete in Christ. The six branches represent the Church of the Living God.

The Lord hung upon the Cross and from His *side* there flowed a stream of blood which gives life to those who come to Him and are a part of Him. We, the Church, come out of the

---
[31]"Shaft"–*yarek* from an unused root meaning "to be soft," "thigh," by euphemism the generative parts, the seat of life.

side of the Central Branch and from the *Thigh* of the Central Shaft!

Now this Lampstand was in the Holy Place, and it could only stand there because the branches were joined to the Central Branch and Shaft, making it *seven* in number. Without the Central Branch and Shaft there would be six, an incomplete number, and they would fall. The Lord Jesus Christ said:

> *"I am the vine, ye are the branches: He that abideth in me, and I in him, the same bringeth forth much fruit: for without me* [severed from me] *ye can do nothing"* (John 15:5).

Severed from the Central Figure we cannot stand in the Holy Place, but we are joined to Him made possible by His wonderful sacrifice and His resurrection from the dead.

Verse Thirty-Three

> *"Three bowls made like unto almonds, with a knop and a flower in one branch; and three bowls made like almonds in the other branch, with a knop and a flower: so in the six branches that come out of the candlestick* [lampstand].*"*

We find that the design of the almond was in each of the branches which proceeded from the Central Stem. "Like unto almonds" is like the bloom of the almond tree. The Septuagint gives it as "lilies." Some describe the candlestick with the design of the pomegranate. (The almond bloom is similar to that of the peach bloom.) The "bowls" are the cups or calyxes which proceed from the stem of the tree and hold the almond blossom. The knop or "knob" is described as a "capital" in the Hebrew text, intimating a crown or disk. This "capital" or circling crown of the calyx is composed of the sepals (individual 'leaves" of the calyx) of the flower. From this "knop" comes the petals and stamens of the almond bloom. Thus we see in the order: "a bowl (the calyx), a knop (the sepals), and a flower (the bloom)"– the beginning, the finishing, and resulting of the wondrous redemption in Christ who is the Light of the World!

The design of the almond is the central feature in the formation of the branches. The almond tree is the first to bud and bring forth its fruit after the dead of winter. Seed must first die before it can bloom. In His earthly life Christ Himself said He remained alone, but when He died He would bring forth *much fruit* (John 12:23, 24). It is only by His death we can be joined to Him. It is by His resurrection that we can live in Him and bear fruit for the Master.

The branches reach up to heaven. Abundant and resurrection life comes from heaven. The word for almond implies *expectation*.[32] It is a prophetic word. The Lord Jesus is expecting to come again and His Church is expecting His coming as well.

Notice that the *flower* of the almond tree is mentioned last in the formation of the branches. The almond blossom has 5 petals (the flower), 5 sepals (the knop) to each calyx (the bowl), and a multiple of 5 stamens. Every part of the flower bloom shows this number *five* which represents the grace of God. God's grace crowned each branch and the Central Shaft!

The three bowls each had a knop and a flower *with* them according to this verse of Scripture. "Three bowls...*with* ..." (cf. verse 34). Three times three (there were 3 sets of 3 in each of the branches) equal nine. There are nine gifts of the Spirit and nine manifestations of the fruit of the Spirit (1 Corinthians 12:8-10, 28; Galatians 5:22, 23). It is only because the Lord Jesus Christ rose from the dead that His Church now receives the nine "spirituals." It was only after He ascended on high that He gave gifts to the Church (Ephesians 4:1 1). The fruit of the spirit was intensified in the believers' lives *after* Christ returned to the Father, for when He "went away" He sent the Divine Enabler to His waiting disciples that He might "dwell within."

Verse Thirty-Four

> "*And in the candlestick* [lampstand, central shaft] *shall be four bowls made like unto almonds, with their knops and their flowers.*"

The branches, as also the Central Shaft, were called "the Lampstand." This Central Branch that came out of the center stand was different from the other six branches. It is described as having had *four* bowls with *four* knops and *four* flowers, whereas in the others there were *three* sets of *three*. This Branch of the Center, being four sets of three, would have elevated it to be higher than the other six branches and lamps. Christ is the Highest Light. We are the "lower lights." Christ is called "The

---

[32]Almond, *shaqad*–"to be alert," i.e., "sleepless" hence "expecting," "to be on the look out," "wakeful," "watchful."

Righteous Branch," (Jeremiah 23:5), "The Branch of Righteousness," (Jeremiah 33:15), and "The Branch of the Lord" (Isaiah 4:2; Zechariah 3:8; 6:12). He is the Central Branch that comes out of the Central Shaft (God, the Father). He is ***The Branch***; His people are the branches. The fourfold picture of Messiah as *The Branch* is connected with the four Gospels in which the Holy Spirit presents Christ to us: Jeremiah 23:5,6 with Matthew, as the King; Zechariah 3:8, to Mark as the Servant; Zechariah 6:12, to Luke as the Man; and Isaiah 4:2, to John as the Son of God. He is like those He has redeemed, yet distinct from them. The Central Shaft is called "The Lampstand" and the whole, that is, the six branches and Central Branch together, is also called "The Lampstand."

Christ gives His Name to His people. The branches are called by the same name; the disciples of Christ are called Christians (Acts 11:26), "Christ-Ones," and called by the title, "Sons of God" (John 1:11, 12; 1 John 3:1, 2).They are all of the same pure gold; members of Christ are partakers of the Divine nature. As He was in the world so are His followers to be. Take away the Shaft, where are the branches? They have gone too. Cut out the Shaft, they fall to the ground. There is no standing, no usefulness, no light, nothing **without Christ**!

Here the number "four" represents the Universal Christ who offers Himself for "whosoever will." He comes out of the Central Shaft and is the Branch of our Righteousness. He is the Root (Central Shaft: Divinity) as well as the offspring (Central Branch: Humanity) of Jesse (see Isaiah 11:1, 10 with Revelation 22:16). Four sets of three formations equal "12," the number which represents Divine Government. "... the government shall be upon his shoulder" (Isaiah 9:6). Christ is the *Governor* of His redeemed people.

Verse Thirty-Five

> *"And there shall be a knop under two branches of the same, and a knop under two branches of the same, and a knop under two branches of the same, according to the six branches that proceed out of the candlestick* [lampstand]*."*

The almond plant buds in January and is the "firstfruits" from the dead. The bowl, knop and flower speak of the almond tree's nature, the first to "rise" after the death of winter, which very well represents Christ, who is the "Firstfruits," the Resurrection and the Life (1 Corinthians 15:20).

The branches rested upon knops or capitals shaped like sepals of the almond bloom. They were held up in their places by these knops and lifted up toward the Central Branch. Believers in Christ are the branches; they have the formation of the almond present in their lives for they are held up by the *resurrected* Christ. They rest in the *finished* work (capitals) of Calvary, (Christ's resurrection testifying to that fact), and will be resurrected (lifted) with Him in glory! *Two* branches on either side were held up by these knops. "Two" signifies union, balance, and agreement. The Church of the living God is in union one with another, members of each other, balanced in agreement on the foundation of the resurrected Christ!

Verse Thirty-Six

> *"Their knops and their branches shall be of the same: all it shall be one beaten work of pure gold."*

Out in the courtyard God's people are pictured as resting upon a foundation, but here we read "one beaten work of pure gold." Here they are viewed, not as *resting* upon a Saviour, but *rather* as *members* of a Saviour !

All of the branches were the same. They were beaten into their formations even as was the Central Shaft and Branch. The branches came out of the Central Shaft and Branch even as they came out of one another. That is, they were a part of one another, and were all considered as the Lampstand. Our Lord Jesus became as one of us that we might be able to become as He is. He took our place that we might be able to take His place. He is the Son of God who makes us sons of God. We are one with Him. He is one with us. He is a very vital part of us; and we are a very vital part of Him. We are all "made" of this same pure gold of beaten work. The Lord Jesus Christ suffered "without the gate" as an outcast and we, who are in Christ Jesus, partake of the same.

The branches of the Lampstand were all alike. Each branch was not only a part of the Shaft but also part of the branches on either side. We are members one of another. The same gold that joined the branch on the left side of the shaft also united the branch on the right side of it. God's children are all members of

Christ and also joint members of each other (1 Corinthians 12:21, 25).

Verse Thirty-Seven

> *"And thou shalt make the seven lamps thereof: and they shall light the lamps thereof, that they may give light over against it."*

On top of each of these branches were lamps into which oil was poured (Exodus 27:20).

> "Each lamp was supplied with cotton and about two wineglasses of the purest olive oil, which was sufficient to keep it burning during a long night."[33]

The wick in the oil was lighted by a coal of fire from off the Altar of Sacrifice out in the Court. These lamps were to shine forth, to light up the Holy Place and were the only light in this room. Responsible for the light was the Sacrifice Altar; responsible for the "lesser lights" to shine upon the earth is the Supreme Sacrifice of Calvary! As we partake of Him in the Holy Place, we, the "lesser lights," shine forth in this world with the wonderful story of redemption.

The oil that was put in the lamps was a symbol of the Holy Spirit. Each of the seven lamps with the oil contained in them was significant, first of all, of Him who is the Highest Light (John 1:9; 8:12; 9:5); then of the Christians who are "lights" (Matthew 5:14; Ephesians 5:8) empowered by the Holy Spirit to "shine" (Matthew 5:16; Acts 1:8).

---

[33]*Smith's Bible Dictionary.*

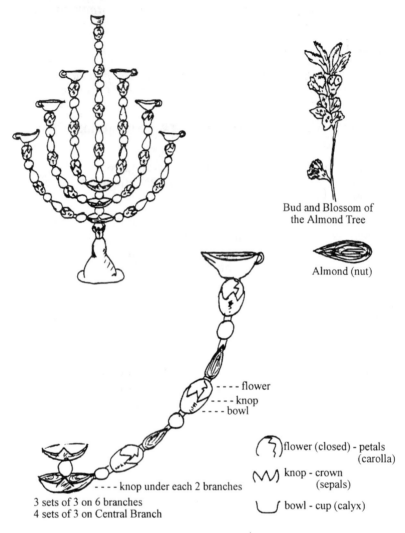

Bud and Blossom of the Almond Tree

Almond (nut)

- - - - flower
- - - - knop
- - - - bowl

- - - - knop under each 2 branches
3 sets of 3 on 6 branches
4 sets of 3 on Central Branch

flower (closed) - petals (carolla)

knop - crown (sepals)

bowl - cup (calyx)

THE GOLDEN LAMPSTAND
(Exodus 25:31-40)

Some Bible commentators state that the entire lamp was made of hollow tubes which received a continual flow of oil from beneath, but this could not be the case since the lamp was of "beaten work," implying that it was *solid* (from *"mikshah,"* "round and hard," also, the lamps were "renewed" with oil by the High Priest at specified times as commanded by God).

The lamps were filled from *above*. Christ arose, ascended on high and poured out the oil from *above* upon His waiting disciples (Ephesians 4:8-11). "There came a sound from *heaven* ... and they were all *filled* with (oil) the Holy Spirit" (Acts 2:4).

The Lampstand was as much a Lampstand and as beautiful a Lampstand *before* the oil was poured into the lamps as *afterward*; but it did not function, show forth any light, reveal the beautiful colors and design of the Veil and the curtains, the gold of the furniture, the silver sockets. It did not operate in the Tabernacle at all, until *after* the oil had been poured into the lamps. So it is with you and me who are in Christ Jesus. We are as much the sons of God before we have been filled with the Holy Spirit as we are afterward; but we do not function as effectively, do not shine brightly as lights; we are not "active" as God desires until after the oil is poured into our "lamps"! In order to function properly as a lamp, as a light in this world of darkness, we must be filled with the oil from above![34] Some Rabbis say that the *central lamp* was to be kept continually burning from which the other six lamps on the lampstand were lighted, both morning and evening.

The lamps on the branches were to show forth their light "over against the Lampstand." They were to manifest the beauty of the Central Branch and Shaft. The Lord Jesus is the Golden Lampstand in the midst of His Church. The Light He has given His people is to shine against Him who is the Central Figure to reflect His beauty and loveliness.

The "candlestick" of the Tabernacle[35] was different from those of today and not exactly like the one depicted in the bas-relief of the Arch of Titus in Rome. We do not see the details of the Tabernacle lampstand on the best photographs of that sculptured lamp.

When Solomon's Temple was pillaged, the lampstands were also destroyed. Several centuries later when Herod built his temple he had no way of knowing just exactly how the *Mosaic Menorah* looked and so it could not be duplicated. And also the original "candlestick" was lost long before the temple built by Solomon was started. No mention was made of the ten

---

[34] See Leviticus 24:2–"olive oil to *cause* the lamps to burn continually."
[35] See Zechariah 4:1-14. The "Candlestick" of Zechariah's vision was not the Lampstand of the Tabernacle.

candlesticks required for the Temple being similar to the lampstand of the wilderness tabernacle.

For more than 550 years after the time of Nebuchadnezzar or until Herod's Temple there is no record of any Holy Lampstand. Also, Ezra and Nehemiah did not mention the candlestick, which tells us they knew nothing of the location of any consecrated lamp dating back to the days of Solomon, much less to one made hundreds of years before Solomon's time. By this foregoing information we can conclude that the only *dependable* source for the formation and construction of the Tabernacle candlestick was given in the books of Moses.

The lamps on the branches, of necessity, would have to have been at different levels in order to throw their light upon the shaft, or "against the lampstand" (Numbers 8:2, w/Exodus 25:37) as God commanded it should be. Placing the lamps on a level line would not have conveyed this thought and would have failed in structural and teleological problems (problems in design). Situating them on the same level would have made the branches unequal in length. We are all equal in the sight of God.

The formation of the knops, the bowls, and the flowers were all the *same* size. The work of the Holy Spirit is the same to all His people and each believer is a candidate for His fullness. He is not received in measure (a little to one, more to another), but as the believer submits to Him, He manifests His power and presence to a greater degree.

There are different levels and proximities. Two of these branches were nearer to the Central Branch and Shaft. Next was an intermediary or middle position, and last, one that was farthest from the Central Stem. You will discover that there are always these three classes of Christians: those who are closer to the Lord, who continually draw nearer to Him than do the others; those who remain in the middle position; and those who walk at a distance. *All* these are Christians with the same "formation of the almond" in the branch; they all have the lamps; all are shining, and all are in the Lampstand. But there are different positions of nearness to the Lord.

Verse Thirty-Eight

> *"And the tongs thereof, and the snuffdishes thereof, shall be of pure gold."* (Tongs–Numbers 8:2 w/Exodus 25:38).

It was very important that the wicks of these lamps be trimmed every day (Christ trims the lamps in Revelation, chapters 2 and 3). The officiating priest had to keep it clean and pure with the snuffers. His daily task (Exodus 27:21) was to enter the Tabernacle with these golden tweezers and with them he would lift the partly burned wicks, and break off the black carbon so the light could shine more evenly and brightly. This carbon was placed in a golden pan and taken away.

These golden instruments were to help in the trimming of the lamps and in the carrying away of the char from the wicks that were trimmed. They were helpers, and being of pure gold (representing Divinity), were significant of the Holy Spirit who is the Divine Helper. The Holy Spirit trims our lamps in order that we might shine brighter. He is "called alongside to help" so that we can shine for the Master. We are drawn closer to God by this cleansing (trimming). Those things of the flesh (carnality) are taken away, that the Spirit can manifest the Light of the world through our lives. Then we are true witnesses of Him (Acts 1:8).

Verses Thirty-Nine and Forty

> *"Of a talent[36] of pure gold shall he make it, with all these vessels. And look that thou make them after their pattern, which was showed thee in the mount."*

In the actual construction of the Tabernacle though many workers were used, yet the Scriptures acknowledges *one* ("... shall *he* make it"). Bezaleel is the one (Exodus 36:1, 2; 37:1-17; 38:22), and He represents the Holy Spirit.

Over and over again God emphasized to the Children of Israel that they were to make it after the pattern that was shown on the mount. Every detail had to be exact with meticulous care. Moses was called up to Mount Sinai and saw the pattern of the Tabernacle or the Heavenly Blueprint, even as John saw it on the Isle of Patmos. The Israelites, we are told, knew the *acts* of

---

[36] A talent of gold was worth $29,085.00, *Dake's Annotated Bible*, p. 106. (Of course this estimate was before inflation!)

the Lord, but Moses (and John) knew the *ways* of the Lord. (Psalm 103:7). Moses, even as John on Patmos, was called up and saw the heavens open revealing the Holy Furniture: The Golden Altar (Revelation 6:9; 8:3-5; 9:13); a Sea of Glass (laver)–(Revelation 4:6); Seven candlesticks (Revelation 1:12); Hidden Manna (Revelation 2:17); and the Ark of the Testament (Revelation 11:19; see also Appendix VI, Diagram and *The Tabernacle in the Book of Revelation*, pp. 237-238).

The Holy Tabernacle was made according to the pattern of things in the Heavenlies. All the sacred furniture which Moses saw and which John saw, we also see through the eye of the Spirit. "Bezaleel" reveals to us our wonderful Christ in all these things and we are to carefully follow "the pattern" in our lives; show forth Christ in every area of our being as we are empowered by the Holy Spirit to do so.

Test Questions

1. Explain the meaning of the Hebrew word for "candlestick"–"menorah."
2. What does the absence of wood or alloy in the Lampstand tell us?
3. What does the beaten gold represent?
4. Give a reason why no measurements were given for the Lampstand. What does this tell us?
5. What does the Hebrew word for "almond" imply?
6. Give the symbolic meaning of the design of the almond in the branches of the Lampstand. Describe the Lampstand design and ornamentation.
7. Whom does the Central Shaft represent; the Central Branch; the Design of the Almond bloom in each branch?
8. Explain the Gifts of the Spirit as we see them in the formation of the branches of the Lampstand.
9. What do the seven branches hold on top of each one?
10. What does the oil symbolize?

11. When, how, and by whom was the Lampstand "dressed" and lighted? Explain with Scripture.

12. What Names of Christ do we see in the Central Branch and give Scripture references.

13. Give the Name of the person who made the "candlestick" and who does he represent?

14. What do the snuff dishes, tongs, etc., represent?

15. What truth was outstanding to you in this section?

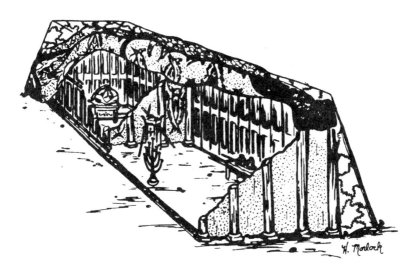

CROSS SECTION OF THE TABERNACLE BUILDING

CHAPTER TWO
EXODUS 26

The Mishkan Covering

Verse One

> *"Moreover thou shalt make the tabernacle with ten curtains of fine twined linen, and blue, and purple, and scarlet: with cherubims of cunning work shalt thou make them."*

The Hebrew word for "tabernacle" in this verse is *mishkan*. It is taken from another Hebrew word *"shakan"* meaning "to dwell," connecting itself with the Jewish word, *Shekinah*. The building proper was called "The Tabernacle" as also the court fence with the building. But this first "cover" in particular was named "The Tabernacle," the "Mishkan," the place in which God dwells.

Bezaleel made all the coverings. He was the Cunning Workman (Exodus 38:22; 36:8-19). God gave instructions concerning this curtain before any specifications for the other coverings of the building. God's dwelling is first; in the beginning, God. God begins from Himself.

We think of starting a building with the foundation, and this was the procedure for the Tabernacle structure; however, God began His *instructions* for its building with the ceiling and the roof. From the top, God comes down. From Heaven, God comes to earth. This order is also significant in the fact that each covering represents the Lord Jesus Christ. The boards symbolize the Church. Jesus Christ is first, and next, those who are in Him.

The Tabernacle (*Mishkan*) was to be of fine twined linen. Fine denotes spotlessness, innocence and faultlessness as seen in Christ (1 Peter 1:19; 2:22; 2 Corinthians 5:21; Matthew 27:3, 4). He is the Righteousness of God. What is righteousness? Simply defined, it is right standing or relationship with God. His name is *"Jehovah Tsidkenu,"* "The Lord, our Righteousness" (Jeremiah 23:6). One day this same name will be given to the city of Jerusalem and the people of Judah (Jeremiah 33:16; Isaiah 1:26) implying that believers who are a part of God's city and nation are also called by the righteousness which is the character of Jehovah (cf. 2 Corinthians 5:21 and Revelation 19:8)!

Christ was righteous, loved righteousness (Hebrews 1:9), and did right in all things. He was referred to by Jeremiah as a "righteous branch" (Jeremiah 23:5; Luke 23:47; 1 John 2:1; Isaiah 53:11). The centurion said of Him: *"Certainly this was a **righteous** man."* The Spirit of God through John spoke of Him as "Jesus Christ, the Righteous" and Isaiah referred to Him as God's "Righteous Servant."

Twined linen refers to the work of bleaching the linen in ancient Egypt. The piece of wet linen first was marked and then wrapped in a strong sack. One end was fastened to a post, and a staff was inserted in a loop in the other. Two men then bleached and rinsed the linen, and united their strength, taking hold of the staff and turning it, thereby wringing the linen to force the water out of it. Thus it was called "fine twined," or "twisted," or "wrung linen." The Egyptians were the only ones to ever manufacture this "fine linen" (*shesh*). It was of such fine, delicate work that even today it cannot be reproduced or manufactured.

This was the ceiling and completed the building. Without this covering that Holy Structure would have been open and unfinished. It is thus when we step into the Lord Jesus Christ: He is made to us, righteousness (1 Corinthians 1:30). He completes us, for we are covered over by Him and called the very "righteousness of God in Him" (2 Corinthians 5:21).

The colors of this curtain are significant.

"Colors play a very important part in explaining the Tabernacle significance because color is truly the basis of form. Color is based by our sight and this is carried out in the meaning of the word. The basis for determining the shape and perspective of an object is our sight or vision. Seeing the outline of an object from a different aspect or point of view can sometimes cause an object to have several different meanings. But, a definite color or colors give a constant image no matter from what point of view it is looked at."

Blue represents Heaven. *Blue* is a serene color closely linked with *gold* which represents Divinity (see Exodus 28:6 and 15; 39:2, 5, 8). *Gold* taches inserted in *blue* loops connected the Tabernacle curtains. Laces of *blue* passed through rings of gold fastened on the breastplate of the *ephod*; Laces of *blue* bound the *golden* plate *mitre* of the High Priest; the gold vessels of the Sanctuary (with the exception of the Ark of the Covenant) were covered with *blue* cloth in traveling. Christ came from heaven. Blue is the first color; God is first. Scarlet (red) is mentioned last. It is the color significant of earth. "Adam" is literally translated as "red earth." The Lord Jesus Christ is the *Last Adam* (or "the Second Man"). He not only came from Heaven (blue), but He came from earth (red).

Purple is the blending, the "in-between" color. There is a "clash" when red and blue are placed side by side, but purple blends the two harmoniously. Purple is the royal color, being a combination of the blue and red, and is the emblem of heavenly and earthly glory. The Lord Jesus Christ is as the purple, for He is a "combination of the blue and the red." He is the God-man (blue-red). He is the Royal One (purple), the King of the Jews (red), the King of Kings (blue).

The Redeemed are pictured also in these colors for they are *one* with their Redeemer. (The royal apparel of *Mordecai* lists these colors; see Esther 8:15.) Humanity and Divinity were blended in the Lord Jesus for He was the "earthly child of a heavenly Father and the heavenly child of an earthly mother." Not in the same sense of origin as Christ but with the same "combination of colors" are the "twice-born" ones: born of earth (red) and born of heaven (blue)!

The Lord said, "with cherubim of *cunning work* shalt thou make them." ("Cunning-work"–*chashav*, "to interpenetrate," "to weave.") The "cunning work" was a weaving which penetrated both sides. This represented workmanship of a more skillful and costly kind than needlework, and was used, not only in the working in of the figures of the cherubim upon the inner covering of the roof of the tabernacle, but also the veil before the Holy of Holies, and upon the ephod and the breastplate of the High Priest. The Mishkan curtain with its "cunning work" displayed figures on both sides, while the needle-work (*raqam*–"to variegate color," "to embroider") was without figures of the cherubim and exhibited the pattern (clearly) only on one side.

The Skillful Weaver is the Holy Spirit. The glory of God is hidden to all who stand outside Jesus Christ. The elaborate curtains were to hide the sacred furniture and services of the sanctuary from those on the outside. Only such as entered the Tabernacle saw the glory, the beauty exhibited by the colors and design of the inner curtains, the beautiful gold-covered boards and furniture, etc. God is only known in Christ. Here on the inside the Skillful Weaver is predominate in the person, life and ministry of the Lord Jesus Christ. We see the Holy Spirit in His incarnation (Luke 1:30-31, 34-35. Matthew 1:18-20), His baptism in Jordan (Matthew 3:16; Luke 4:1), His temptation by Satan (Luke 4:1, 2), His anointed ministry (Luke 4:18), the performance of His miracles (Acts 10:38), His death (Hebrews 9:14), His resurrection (1 Peter 3:18), and His post-resurrection directions to the apostles (Acts 1:1, 2). The cunning "weave" of the colors, perfectly blended together with the design of the cherubim, all tell us of the perfect work of the Holy Spirit.

The "curious work" of God in the First Curtain also speaks of the ministry of the Holy Spirit in the believer. We are His workmanship (Ephesians 2:10; 4:24; Colossians 3:10). We are identified with Christ in the "cunning work." By the Holy Spirit we are born of Him, caught up in the curtain, intertwined with Christ, woven in Him, partakers of the Divine nature! The *Mishkan* curtain covered the boards of the building. The Holy Spirit covers, envelops, submerges the Church, baptizes the believer with Himself. ***This is the great desire and promise of the Father.***

The Cherubim, according to Ezekiel's vision, had four faces: that of an ox, a lion, an eagle, and a man (Ezekiel 1:10; 10:21). A Jewish proverb states: "Four are the highest in the world: the lion among wild beasts, the ox among tame cattle, the eagle among birds, man among all (creatures); but God is supreme over all."

The four faces tell us of the four-fold ministry of the Universal Christ:

The ***OX*** (symbolic in Mark's gospel, the Servant, the earthly scarlet) is the patient, enduring servant of man. The Lord Jesus came as a servant; He is the Saviour. He serves mankind with His wonderful salvation. He came, not to be ministered to, but to minister and give His life, a ransom for many (Matthew 20:28).

The *LION* (symbolic in Matthew's gospel, the King, the royal purple) is the king of the beasts. He has power and dominion on the earth. Our Lord is called "The Lion of the Tribe of Judah." He has dominion and power and exercised this power while on earth as *King* of the Jews. He came to destroy the works of the devil (1 John 3:8). He is the Great Physician.

The *EAGLE* (symbolic in John, the Son of God, the heavenly blue) is the King of the birds, soaring high into the heavens. Christ is the King of Kings. He is the mighty Baptizer with the Holy Ghost (Matthew 3:11) causing His people to rise on eagle wings into the Heavens with Him.

The *MAN* (symbolic in Luke's gospel, the Son of Man, the righteous linen) Daniel saw Jesus coming in the clouds of glory. He calls Him the Son of *Man* (intimating that He had been born into the human family). When Christ came the first time He was rejected of men but in His return He will be the Man over men. He will be Ruler over mankind. All the governments of the world shall be upon His shoulder (Isaiah 9:6). They shall be turned over to our Christ and He will reign forever and ever!

Those four faces of the cherubim strikingly portray (as in the ox): Jesus, the Saviour; (as in the lion): Jesus, the Great Physician; (as in the eagle): Jesus, the mighty Baptizer with the Holy Ghost, and (as in the man): Jesus, our Soon-Coming King!

In these 4 faces is also found the fourfold character of God's messengers: Their service is to be by the *sacrifice* of the Ox, the *strength* of the Lion, the *sight* and *swiftness* of the Eagle, and the *sympathy* of the Man.

According to Jewish commentators, the encampment of Israel around the Tabernacle was marked by banners or standards picturing the four faces of the cherubim. Every Camp had its own standard (see Numbers 2:2-3, 10, 17-18, 25, 31, 34.)

The banner of the first corps (comprising 3 tribes) bore the outline of a *lion*, that of the second (another 3 tribes) the picture of a *man*, that of the third (another 3 tribes) the image of an *ox*, and that of the fourth (another 3 tribes) the emblem of an *eagle*, thus representing the same idea as the cherubs of the Holiest, the Veil, and the Tabernacle Covering. The Lord Jesus Christ is the fulfillment of all these emblems and designs. He is the

Standard or Banner heading all His redeemed. His name is *Jehovah-Nissi*, "the Lord, my Banner" (Exodus 17:15).

Verse Two

"The length of one curtain shall be eight and twenty cubits, and the breadth of one curtain four cubits: and every one of the curtains shall have one measure."

Each curtain was to be of *one* measure. There was no inconsistency, but *unity*. Nothing was out of proportion. Christ is the perfect measure to complete those who come to Him. He is the same Christ for everyone and He offers the same measure of salvation for all. With His same righteousness each one is covered completely who receives Him.

Verses Three and Four

"The five curtains shall be coupled together one to another; and other five curtains shall be coupled one to another. And thou shalt make loops of blue upon the edge of the one curtain from the selvedge in the coupling; and likewise shalt thou make in the uttermost edge of another curtain, in the coupling of the second."

There were ten curtains of two sets of five coupled[37] together with blue loops and gold taches. The blue was in imitation of the skies, and emblematic of heavenly origin or destiny. Christ is the Heavenly One on earth (John 3:2; 17:5, 8). As a symbol of consecration, the Israelites wore blue ribbons in the fringes (*tzitzit*) of the four quarters or wings of their garments (see Numbers 15:38-40; Deuteronomy 22:12; Matthew 23:5). This being the heavenly color indicated that the wearer was a servant of the Most High in his observance of the commandment concerning the fringes. The woman who suffered an infirmity for 12 years "grasped" this tassel[38] on the garment of Jesus and was made well (Luke 8:44). In a similar manner healing was given to the vast multitude as recorded in Mark 6:56.

These loops were to be in the selvedge of each coupling of five curtains. The selvedge of any material is very strong and finished, making it impossible for that material to ravel or wear out. It is the fine intertwining of the same material, making it

---

[37] Hebrew–*chabar* "to join," "to have fellowship with."
[38] Luke 8:44, "hem" (*kraspedon*)–"tassel," "fringe," "hem," "border."

complete. God's grace is strong like the selvedge and will never "ravel." His grace and righteousness is all complete and fulfilled in Christ Jesus.

Verse Five

> *"Fifty loops shalt thou make in the one curtain, and fifty loops shalt thou make in the edge of the curtain that is in the coupling of the second; that the loops may take hold one of another."*

These five and five curtains were to be joined together by fifty loops of blue on each set. Blue is the color for heaven and fifty tells of Pentecos.t[39] Fifty is also the number for *Jubilee* when the slaves were set free (see Leviticus 25.) Christ came from heaven, joined man and God together by His grace, "finished" (fulfilled) the Old Covenant and established the New. By this work of God's grace He set the slaves free and poured out the Gift of the Holy Spirit upon His Church.

Verse Six

> *"And thou shalt make fifty taches[40] of gold, and couple the curtains together with the taches: and it shall be one tabernacle."*

The curtains were coupled together and made *one* by clasps of "gold." This was the First Covering which completed the Building. God covers His Church by His grace, making the Building, *One*. Believers who looked forward to the coming of their Messiah and believers since His first coming are to be enveloped by Him, completely covered over and united in Him. It is God's desire that the "blue loops" take hold of one another and that the "gold taches" make it ***One*** Tabernacle!

---

[39]*Pentecost* (Greek)–"fiftieth" (Hebrew) = *Shavuot*, "weeks," "week of weeks" (a period of 7 weeks), Leviticus 23:15-22.
[40]"Taches"–"a rounded pin" (like staples), "a hook," "clasp."

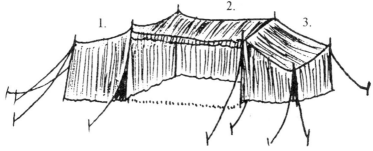

1. The Women's Quarters. 2. The Public Room.
3. The Men's Quarters.

A BEDOUIN TENT

The Ohel

Verse Seven

> *"And thou shalt make curtains of goats' hair to be a covering upon the tabernacle: eleven curtains shalt thou make."*

The women who were wise-hearted spun goats' hair (Exodus 35:26; "hair" is not in the original; the Hebrew word for "goat" is used elliptically for "goats' hair"). Today the Bedouin lives in a tent made of black goats' hair which has been woven into a canvas. He calls it his "house of hair." In the Song of Solomon, mention is made by the "bride" that she is as "black ... as the tents of *Kedar*"[41] and "as comely...as the curtains of Solomon" (Song of Solomon 1:5, 6). She refers to the darkness of sin symbolized in the black-haired goat in contrast to the white tent of Solomon, a symbol of righteousness. In the Bible, the goat signifies sin as does the *black* or dark "color," therefore, no contradiction is found here. This interpretation is in harmony with the general teaching of the first two curtains covering the Tabernacle building (and the rest of the coverings), for the *white* linen of the *Mishkan* (the first curtain, the inside covering) tells of Christ's righteousness (first, He is righteous), the *black* of the *Ohel* (the tent, the second curtain) tells of Christ who was made the sin-offering; then the rams' skins (dyed red, typical of Christ, the Substitute) which covers the blackness of sin, etc.

---

[41]"Kedar" signifies "swarthy" or "suntanned," "a dark color." (Kedar was one of the sons of *Ishmael*, the *Bedouin* or Arab of today.)

At four of the "set times" or Feasts of Jehovah (Unleavened Bread, Firstfruits, Pentecost, Day of Atonement), there was a goat slain on behalf of the people's sins. Since the foul odor of this animal signified the stench of sin in the nostrils of God, the priests were commanded to purify themselves from defilement by washing with water after handling it (Numbers 31:20; Leviticus 16:26-28). The Lord Jesus is the fulfillment of the goats' hair curtain, for He was "made" sin, a stench to God, upon that Roman Cross. Isaiah prophesied of this:

> *"When thou* [God] *shalt make his* [the Messiah] *soul an offering for sin"* (Isaiah 53:10) or, as it is in the literal rendering: *"... his soul shall make an offering for sin."* He came in the likeness of sinful flesh, yet without sin, and died upon the Altar (as did the goat) on behalf of the people. He is the **sin offering** to God for us.

The Lord said that there should be 11 curtains (panels) for this Covering *(Ohel).* This is an uneven number but there is a reason for six and five to be joined together. Christ came as man (6) to be the sin-offering because of God's grace (5) to man in his weakness.

Verses Eight and Nine

> *"The length of one curtain* [panel] *shall be thirty cubits, and the breadth of one curtain* [panel] *four cubits: and the eleven curtains* [panels] *shall be all of one measure. And thou shalt couple five curtains by themselves, and six curtains* [panel] *by themselves, and shalt* **double the sixth** *curtain* [panel] *in the forefront of the tabernacle."*

This second curtain was two cubits longer than the first curtain *(Mishkan),* covering the Tabernacle curtain completely. It was called the *Ohel* or the "Tent," it is *man's* dwelling place. The Tent of the *Bedouin* in the near East was, and is, flat-topped made of black goats' hair.[42] The tent is divided into *three* sections, (1) the women's quarters, (2) the public room, and (3) the men's quarters.

> "Ancient tents seem to have been very much like those in use in the deserts of today. A favorite material for the weaving of tent cloth was goat hair or camel hair, and the favorite color was *black* (Song of Solomon 1:5) or dark brown, in order to

---

[42]See George Mackie, *Bible Manners and Customs,* p. 89 and L. Sale Harrison, *Palestine, God's Monument of Prophecy,* p. 143.

keep out the glare and reflection of the desert sun. The usual tent of desert dwellers was very large, with at least two central poles called 'pillars' (Exodus 26:32)."[43]

The sixth panel of the "Tent" was to be doubled over in the forefront of the building and this made it possible for the Israelites to see it on the outside. Always before them, always as the priests would come toward the door of the Tabernacle, they would see the goats' hair curtain facing them. The Israelites who were camping around the court fence could also see this curtain (as well as the outer skin covering), always reminding them that they were sinners, that they needed a sacrifice for their sins and that there was One who would come to be the sin-offering for them. It was the *sixth* panel of the Ohel curtain doubled over in front. It is a man, *the* Man, their Messiah, who would become an offering for their sins!

Verses Ten and Eleven

"And thou shalt make fifty loops on the edge of the one curtain that is outmost in the coupling, and fifty loops in the edge of the curtain which coupleth the second. And thou shalt make fifty taches of brass, and put the taches into the loops, and couple the tent together, that it may be one."

Fifty was the number for the year of Jubilee when the slaves were set free. Slaves to Satan, bound by the fetters of sin, are set free when Christ becomes their sin-offering.

There were six panels and five panels joined together, blended into one, by taches of *copper*, a symbol of Divine judgment for sin (see Section on *The Copper Altar*). Man (6) and God's grace (5) are joined together; slaves are set free ("fifty" is for Jubilee) because Divine judgment for sin (copper) was laid upon Christ, the Sin-Offering!

There were no directions for a "selvedge," neither was there any mention of a "color" for the 50 loops as in the First Curtain. This is *man's* dwelling place upon earth, his tent of sinful flesh, as it were, and Heaven's color is absent here as well as the never-raveling "selvedge." Christ came down to man's level, made Himself of "no reputation" (unknown loops), emptied Himself of the "blue" by death at Calvary where He "raveled out" sin forever (no selvedge)!

---

[43]Arthur W. Klinck, *Home Life in Bible Times*, pp. 61, 62.

Verse Twelve

> "And the remnant that remaineth of the curtains of the tent, the half curtain that remaineth, shall hang over the backside of the tabernacle."

Two and one-half sections of the five curtains would cover the Holy of Holies and the remaining two and one-half sections would fall over the back or west side of the building. This would make the complete curtain the same length all the way around the three sides of the Holy Structure. The building (boards) represents the Church and the Ohel curtain typifies Christ as the Sacrifice. The sin offering on behalf of the Church is the same measure to all. Each one in the Holy Building is served with equal salvation through Him Who is the Sacrifice of Calvary. All receive the same measure.

Verse Thirteen

> "And a cubit on the one side, and a cubit on the other side of that which remaineth in the length of the curtains of the tent, it shall hang over the sides of the tabernacle on this side and on that side, to cover it."

How very carefully God instructed Israel in the making of the Tabernacle! Each measure of the Ohel was planned to cover the Sacred Building completely, as well as the Mishkan curtain. The Sin Offering, the Lord Jesus Christ, takes care of the sin question completely in the lives of those who believe in Him.

Verse Fourteen

> "And thou shalt make a covering for the tent of rams' skins dyed red, ..."

This rams' skins dyed red was to cover the "Ohel" (the tent), the black goats' hair canvas. The blood of Christ (red) blots out the blackness of sin (the goat). The ram is the animal representing substitution and provision in the Bible. *Jehovah Jireh* (*Yahweh-Yireh* = "The Lord-Will-See-and-Provide") is God's Name, first used in the instance when there was a substitution of the ram for Isaac (Genesis 22:13, 14). Isaac lived because a ram died in his place.

The ram was also the animal used for the consecration of the priesthood. When Aaron and his sons were set apart for their office, a ram was slain for them and its blood applied (Leviticus 8:22-24). So then we find in this skin a symbol indicating the Lord Jesus and His consecration to the work of the ministry. He humbled Himself and became obedient to the Father, even to death on the cross. He said: *"I delight to do thy will, O God;"* *"Not my will, but thine be done"* was His consecration (Luke 22:39-46; Isaiah 50:5-7). He was a Substitute for many, for the "whosoever will" to come and receive of His life. He is the Ram of consecration, provision, and substitution.

The skin of the ram was beautiful but it could not be seen on the outside or the inside of the building. It was hidden by the other coverings; neither were dimensions given for this skin. Only the Father saw the complete consecration and obedience of Christ to the Divine will. We cannot fathom the depths of love in the consecration and death of Christ; neither can we limit the blood (Hebrews 10:4-9; Psalm 40:6-9).

Christ was the Lamb; meek, lowly, *submissive* to the Father's will; but He was also a Ram: vigorous, strong, and *determined* to do the Father's will (John 4:34; 6:38; 8:29; Luke 9:51; John 18:11, cf. John 18:5-6). Those who believe on Him are sheep of His pasture and should be as the Ram in their consecration to follow Christ (Romans 12:1; 8:35, 36; 1 Corinthians 6:19-20; Acts 20:24; 1 Corinthians 9:26-27; Philemon 3:8; Hebrews 12:1). The cry of their hearts also should be: "Thy will, not mine be done;" "I delight to do thy will, O God."

(verse 14 continued) *" ... and a covering above of badgers' skins."*

We find no description or measurements, only that it is the *"covering above."* It represents the humiliation of Christ which cannot be measured. We do not know the height from which He came; therefore we cannot know the depth to which He stooped. He emptied Himself (Philemon 2:5-10). He who was in the *highest* heaven came down to the *lowest* earth, came *down* to where we are so that we could go up to where He is!

According to some translators the outside skin covering was that of either dolphin, porpoise, seal, antelope, or goat, and some give it as "rough leather." Most translations render it as "badger skins" but this animal was not a native of the East and it (as well as the antelope) was an unclean animal for sacrifice, so could not be used in the "holy habitation." The Septuagint Bible gives it: "an upper covering of skins dyed blue." The Jewish version in English by Dr. Benisch leaves the word untranslated, calling it *tachash* skins. The conclusion of the whole matter is that this is an "unknown" skin. How like our Lord Jesus who was **unknown** to men! He made Himself of no reputation (Matthew 13:55-57; Philemon 2:5-8). The world cannot see Him as He is in His glory until there is an entrance inside, for the glory is within, even as with the Christian; beauty is within. The believer in Christ is "black as the tents of *Kedar*" in the eyes of the world, but is comely, graceful, handsome as "the curtains of Solomon" in the eyes of God (Psalm 45:13; Song of Solomon 1:5; 1 Peter 3:3, 4).

The outside skin was all that the Israelites could see of the Tabernacle from a distance and when they approached the sacred building they saw on the Door in front, the goats' hair curtain. This covering above of dolphin skins was not very beautiful or attractive to them. They could not see the gold, silver, nor the articles of furniture inside the building. The beautiful curtains, the colors, the cherubim surrounding on every side, were hidden. All they could look upon was the unattractive skin on the outside. In the words of Isaiah here is a picture of the Saviour:

> *"... he hath no form nor comeliness; and when we shall see him, there is no beauty that we should desire him. He is despised and rejected of men; a man of sorrows, and acquainted with grief: and we hid as it were our faces from him; ..."* (Isaiah 53:2, 3).

Our Lord Jesus came to the Jewish people. They were expecting their King to come in pomp and glory with a royal crown upon His head, a royal robe about His shoulders, sitting upon a white horse, setting up His kingdom immediately when He came but He came as other men. He fulfilled the prophecy of Him as the unattractive outward skin of the Tabernacle! That is all that the Jewish people (as a nation) noticed about Him. Therefore, as they saw Him in this light, they rejected Him (John 1:11, 12). They are, even as many today (both Jew and Gentile) people whose eyes are blind to Jesus in His beauty. They have not come inside the building. All they see is the unknown outside covering of the Tabernacle.

The outer skin was a protection for the Sanctuary (cf. Isaiah 4:5, 6; Psalm 27:5; 61:3, 4). It covered the building completely and protected its contents, the underskin and curtains, and the priests who ministered there, from all the surrounding elements. Our Lord Jesus Christ is this covering which indicates Him in His service, not only to His people, but to God. Through Isaiah God calls Him "My Servant" (Isaiah 52:13-15). The NT emphasizes this title which is applied to Jesus: "God hath glorified his servant Jesus" (Acts 3:13, Revised Version). He came to serve the interests of God on earth. *"Jesus ... being in the form of God ... emptied himself, taking the form of a servant"* (Philemon 2:5-7). He protects us from all the wind storms of life, from all the sand of trouble seeping up about us, from all the strong winds of false doctrine blowing all around us.

We, who believe on Christ, are not content to stand on the outside and behold the outward covering only, but we go on beyond it to that rams' skies dyed red, and there we see the substitution and consecration of our Lord to the ministry of salvation for all those who come to Him. We are not content to stop there at the rams' skies dyed red, but we penetrate beyond that to the "goats' hair curtain, to see the reason for it all, our Lord Jesus dying upon the cruel gibbet of Golgotha being made as sin in order that we, believing upon Him, might be made as righteousness in Him. And we penetrate the outer goats' hair curtain through to the fine twined linen curtain, to behold Him in His beauty, His loveliness, His majesty, glory and power. When we have penetrated beyond the curtains, we see the colors, the cherubim all around us; we enter the Holy Place and into the Holy of Holies where we behold the *Shekinah* between the cherubim.

Test Questions

1. Of what was the ceiling and roof of the Tabernacle building made?
2. What is a reason for God giving directions for the ceiling and roof before the framework and foundation of the building?
3. Give the *Hebrew* name for the First Covering listed in Exodus 26? What is the English translation?
4. What do we learn in that this First Covering completed the Boards?
5. Of what material was the First Covering made? What is the spiritual application?
6. Name the colors of this First Covering and what does each color symbolize?
7. (a) Explain "cunning work" and its significance. (b) What is the difference between "cunning work" and "needlework"?
8. What were the four faces of the cherubim of Ezekiel's vision? Give the symbolic meaning of each one.
9. How many panels comprised the First Curtain (Mishkan) and what does this number represent?
10. What joined the two sets of five panels to make it "one Tabernacle"?
11. What was the Second Covering of Exodus 26 called (Hebrew and English)?
12. (a) Of what material was the Second Covering made?; (b) How was it made, and by whom (other than Bezaleel)? Give Scripture reference.
13. What does the material of the Second Covering tell us?
14. How many curtain panels were in the Second Covering?
15. What joined the two sets of curtain panels of this Second Covering?
16. What was to be done with the "extra" curtain of the Second Covering? Why?

17. What does the copper taches of the Tent symbolize?
18. What do the 50 loops of the First Covering, and the Second Covering represent?
19. What is the "color" of the Tent? Explain.
20. What is the material and color of the Covering over the Tent?
21. What does the ram symbolize?
22. Give the Antitype of the rams' skins.
23. What is the measurement of the rams' skin covering? Explain.
24. Why is the skin of the outer covering of the Tabernacle not known? What does this teach us?
25. What is the outer skin according to some translators?
26. What titles of Christ could be found in the outside skin covering?
27. What did the outer covering do for the Tabernacle and the priests? What does this represent?
28. What coverings could the Israelites see of the Tabernacle?
29. What coverings could the priests see?
30. What truth was outstanding to you in this section?

The Boards of the Tabernacle

Verse Fifteen

"And thou shalt make boards for the tabernacle of shittim [acacia] *wood standing up."*

Whenever, in the Word of God concerning the Tabernacle, there is mention of only one article or material, it is primarily representative of Christ and then the individual believer. But the Church is "pictured" in Christ when it is written of more than one, as in the boards of the building (or in the pillars of the fence). Many boards, one building. There are many members but one body of Christ.

These boards were to be "standing up." This Hebrew word *omdiim* is the plural of *ahmahd* which means "to continue firm," "abide," "endure" "withstand." So it is with the Church of the Living God which stands erect in the desert of this world. She is not "at ease" or "reclining" but firmly standing, enduring in honor and attention to her great Leader to do His bidding–constantly ready, willing and obedient to observe His commandments. *"Wherefore take unto you the whole armour of God, that ye may be able to withstand in the evil day, and having done all, to stand"* (Ephesians 6:13).

The boards were to be made from wood of the *shittah* tree (probably the shittah tree was the burning bush of Moses Exodus 3:2, called *seneh*) which grew in dry places where no other tree could live. It was secured from the Egyptians before Israel left Egypt (see Exodus 35:24, cf. Exodus 25:1-5; 3:21-22; 11:2-3; 12:35-36).

The name (*shittim*) is derived from another Hebrew word, *shotet* meaning "to pierce, to scourge" because of its scourging thorns, the sharpness of its spines. This plant is hard and solid, and is incorruptible. It has been suggested that it was from the *shittah* tree that the crown of thorns was made for Christ. He who created the tree was nailed to it and He who cursed the ground because of man's sin that it bring forth thorns and thistles, received that curse upon Himself on Calvary!

The Boards, being made of this *shittah* tree, were taken from their former position and transferred to another place in the wilderness. The thorns were removed and the boards made smooth for the Holy Dwelling. We, who are the children of God, were removed from the position we held in the world, smoothed of the thorns, and fitly framed together to form an habitation of God (Ephesians 2:19-22). Those in the Lord Jesus are made of the "incorruptible acacia wood." For it is prophesied that this corruption shall put on incorruption (1 Corinthians 15:51-53), and we shall be transformed; we shall be changed in a moment, in a twinkling of an eye. We shall never die!

The acacia wood is a picture of humanity, or, in this particular case, the Church of the Living God who is dressed up in the Lord Jesus, both Jew and Gentile in the body of Christ. This mystery of the Church was revealed to Paul but was hidden to those of more ancient times. In God's sight there is no Jewish-Christian church or Gentile-Christian church, but **The** Church, the Body of Christ (Ephesians 3:3-7).

In preparing these trees to be fitly framed together, all their beautiful crest was taken off. All their good deeds, their beauty to the world, was counted for nothing. They used to draw their life and sustenance from the earth but the world can no longer nourish a child of God. Christ says of them: "They are not of the world even as I am not of the world" (John 17:16). They are then ripped into boards, that is, all their inner parts examined.

This wood will not rot, neither will worms eat it. Christ's flesh saw no corruption (Psalm 16:10). The acacia tree flourishes in dry beds of extinct water courses and where no other tree can find moisture. It lives in spite of its circumstances. More than 700 years before He was born, Isaiah said of Jesus that He would be as a root out of dry ground (Isaiah 53:2). There was no natural condition that contributed to the well being of Jesus. From His birth in a stable until His last words on the Cross He was despised and rejected of men, a man of sorrows and acquainted with grief. Through all His earthly pilgrimage He lived in a body of His humiliation in spite of circumstances. Circumstances were against Him and it is said of His Church:

> *" ... as he is so, are we in this world"* (1 John 4:17). *"But rejoice, inasmuch as ye are partakers of Christ's sufferings; that, when his glory shall be revealed, ye may be glad also with exceeding joy"* (1 Peter 4: 13). *" ... joint-heirs with Christ; if so be that we suffer with him, that we may be also*

glorified together" (Romans 8:17) *"If we suffer, we shall also reign with him: ..."* (2 Timothy 2:12).

The Tabernacle pictures Christ and *those connected with Him*. These trees figure Christ in that they are incorruptible. They represent the saints in that they were cut off from the earth to form a habitation for God. They figure humanity in that they were the only timber wood in the desert. God is not building His church from birds, beasts, fish and reptiles. He is building His Church from human beings, who, when they are born again, are partakers of the Divine nature and will have incorruptible bodies like Jesus (Philemon 3:20, 21). *"Being born again, not of corruptible seed, but of incorruptible, by the word of God, which liveth and abideth for ever"* (1 Peter 1:23).

This tree furnishes the gum arabic of commerce, which exudes from it spontaneously in hot weather but is also obtained more systematically by *making incisions in the bark.* Arabs collect it for sale. It is also used for food in times of scarcity and it will quench thirst too. How beautiful a picture of Christ's life which was independent of circumstances, and in overcoming death, yielded spontaneously! He is given to us as the precious Sustenance for our souls because of "incisions" into His frame nailing Him to the "tree."

Verse Sixteen

"Ten cubits shall be the length of a board, and a cubit and a half shall be the breadth of one board."

Ten is the number of "completeness" in Bible numerics. Nothing can be added to it. The "board" represents the individual in the Church-that one who is complete only in Christ Jesus.

It was necessary that this building be one which could easily be taken down because in the long wilderness journey (**40 years**) it was taken down and set up a great many times (see Deuteronomy 2:14). These 38 years mentioned in this verse are those years between the first encampment at *Kadesh* when Israel rebelled (Numbers, chapters 13-14) and the actual crossing of the brook *Zered* along the north border of *Moab*. The **40 years** of Numbers 2:7 take in these 38 years, besides the whole period of the Exodus to Kadesh, which includes the stay at Matthew

---

[44]See Finis J. Dake, *Dake's Annotated Reference Bible*, p. 205.

Sinai of about 11 months. Altogether the time from the Exodus to Kadesh was nearly two years.[44] (So the 38 years of Deuteronomy 2:14 and the two years from Egypt to Kadesh equal the **40 years** mentioned in Numbers 2:7.)

There were four wagons each drawn by a pair of oxen to transport the boards, bases and pillars (Numbers 7:8 w/4:29-33). This would not have been adequate for the boards if they each weighed a ton, according to Josephus[45] and others. Also, it would have been impossible to secure beams of such measurements from the acacia tree of Egypt. The species of the shittah tree or *acacia nilotica* which grows in the southern part of the peninsula of Sinai and Egypt is a small tree from 15-25 ft. high and grows only 2 ft. in diameter. The acacia never gets to be a great tree, often being gnarled and twisted. It is difficult to find a piece more than 2-3 feet long that is straight. Since this was the case there must have been many pieces of wood put together to form the frame of each board. Just so is every member of the body of Christ composed of many parts. There is a diversity of ministries, yet, by the same Spirit (1 Corinthians 12:4).

Notice that no dimensions were given for the *thickness*. Therefore it is suggested that these were not solid boards but frames. A frame has, strictly speaking, no measure for thickness. The "boards" *qeresh*–"a slab" or "plank" were light and strong which held up the curtains, and gave the necessary firmness to the walls. It was open so as to allow the rich embroidery of the inner curtains to be visible on the inside of the building.[46] The beautiful curtains with their cherubim figures were specifically called (*Mishkan*) "The Tabernacle," suggesting that this was to be seen in the building proper, and not hidden from view, as would have been the case if the boards had been solid.

> "The 'Boards' constituting the framework of the tabernacle were, not solid planks, but really open 'frames,' through which the finely wrought covering could be seen from within."[47]

Physically, we are a framework, a skeleton of bones covered over by two skins even as the literal Tabernacle in the desert

---

[45]Flavius Josephus, *Jewish Antiquities*, 1.c, 116ff.
[46]A.R.S. Kennedy, HDB, IV, p. 659 f., and cf. Driver in *Cambridge Bible*.
[47]James Orr, General Editor, *The International Standard Bible Encyclopaedia*, Boards of the Tabernacle.

was a framework or "skeleton" of boards covered by two skins. The inner skin *dermis* carries the blood vessels, veins and arteries. The outward skin *epidermis* protects; it is the nonsensitive layer of skin. The Church is a "framework" for the habitation of God, covered by His righteousness though walking in the likeness of sinful flesh. Just so, the Wilderness Tent "housed" the presence of God in the Holy of Holies covered by the finetwined linen and the goats' hair curtains. The Tabernacle portrays, both in the physical and spiritual sense, Christ and the believer in Him.

> *"Now therefore ye are no more strangers and foreigners, but fellowcitizens with the saints, and of the household of God; And are built upon the foundation of the apostles and prophets, Jesus Christ himself being the chief corner stone; In whom all the building fitly framed together groweth unto an holy temple in the Lord: In whom ye also are builded together for an habitation of God through the Spirit"* (Ephesians 2:19-22).

Verse Seventeen

> *"Two tenons shall there be in one board, set in order one against another: thus shalt thou make for all the boards of the tabernacle."*

The Rabbis explain that the "arms," or "hands" (tenons *yadoth* "hands") were to be joined together as the rounds or rungs of a ladder (see *Soncino Chumash* on Exodus 26:17). Again, it seems evident that the *qeresh* (boards) had to be a *frame* of wood "such as the builders in all countries have employed in the construction of light walls."

Exodus 26:15, 16 could be translated: "And thou shalt make the frames for the dwelling of acacia wood, standing up, two uprights for each frame, joined to each other by cross rails, ten cubits the height and a cubit and a half the breadth of a single frame."

Verses Eighteen and Nineteen

> *"And thou shalt make the boards for the tabernacle, twenty boards on the south side southward. And thou shalt make forty sockets of silver under the twenty boards; two sockets under one board for his two tenons, and two sockets under another board for his two tenons."*

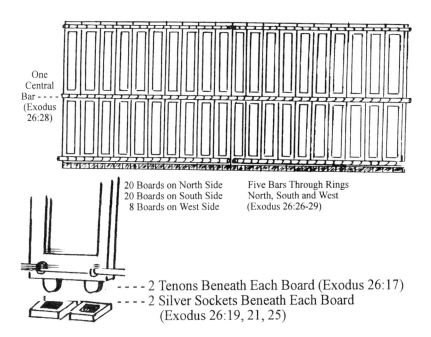

One Central Bar (Exodus 26:28)

20 Boards on North Side
20 Boards on South Side
8 Boards on West Side

Five Bars Through Rings
North, South and West
(Exodus 26:26-29)

- - - - 2 Tenons Beneath Each Board (Exodus 26:17)
- - - - 2 Silver Sockets Beneath Each Board
(Exodus 26:19, 21, 25)

**OPEN FRAMES (Boards) OF THE TABERNACLE BUILDING AND THE FIVE BARS
(Exodus 26:15-29)**

The *silver foundation* beneath the boards was acquired by the atonement money (the ransom price) which Israel brought for the work of the Sanctuary (see Exodus 30:11-16; 38:25-28).[48] This was a memorial of the redemption ("to redeem" means "to regain possession of by paying a price") that was provided for them when they were slaves in Egypt. The silver foundation beneath the boards was a reminder to the Israelites that they were ransomed by the blood of a lamb. The Church of Christ today, which is the antitype of these boards, is standing upon a *silver foundation* in the desert of this world; she is purchased with the blood of God's Lamb.

It has been estimated that the base of each of the 48 boards was valued at a little less than $4,000. How expensive was this foundation of silver, but how precious and of inestimable value is the redemption of our Lord Jesus Christ (1 Peter 1:18-19). The

---

[48]Note: The *silver* of Daniel's image was *not* made from the half a shekel atonement money, therefore does not have the same symbolism.

100 sockets (Exodus 38:27) of silver for the Sacred Building symbolize the 100 percent foundation of redemption through the blood of the Divine Lamb (Colossians 1:14) upon which His Church stands today. It is interesting to note that the earth was created as standing upon *sockets*. (See Job 38:4, 6 where the word "foundation" is the Hebrew word for "sockets.")

"Bought with a price, not of silver and gold,
Bought with a price of value untold.
'Tis the blood of Jesus shed on Calvary
Purchased my redemption and set me free."

Because they were standing upon the *silver sockets*, the boards could not sink down into the earth, neither could they lose equality with each other. This close relationship prevented a tilting to right or left, to divide or separate. "United we stand, divided we fall." We need each other.

Though these boards were in the wilderness, they were not a part of it because of the silver foundation beneath them. You and I, who are in the Church, are standing upon the silver sockets; we have been redeemed by the blood of Christ, the Lamb of God who takes away the sin of the world. We are in the "wilderness," this desert world, but are kept from sinking down into the "sands" of sin because we have a silver foundation beneath us!

There were many boards yet they stood so fitly framed together that they appeared as one complete building. Many members are there of Christ, but *one **body***. Not one of these boards was any more nor any less than the other, for they were of the same height, material, and position. There was no rubbing or chafing because they were well-balanced on an equal foundation. There is no place in the Church for one to look down upon or despise another (1 Corinthians 12:12-27).

Verses Twenty and Twenty-One

"And for the second side of the tabernacle on the north side there shall be twenty boards: And their forty sockets of silver; two sockets under one board, and two sockets under another board."

The south side was equal with the north side in the number of boards, making the length of the Tabernacle building 30 cubits, each of the 20 boards being one-and-a-half cubits wide. Each board was balanced by the two tenons in the two sockets. The number "two" represents union, agreement and balance. If the board had only one tenon it would have toppled over in the desert. The word "tenons," in the Hebrew text, is *yadoth* "hands," and being at the bottom of the boards, they acted as feet–a balance to the board, a union and agreement with the board and with that which it grasps. The two tenons hold redemption (the *silver* sockets); "the hand is occupied with nothing else. The hands that are occupied with redemption have not time to quarrel; they have no scope for quarreling; they are simply holding redemption and all the anti-typical boards of the spiritual Sanctuary stand up, resting on redemption and holding redemption. We not only rest on redemption, but we grasp that on which we stand."

Verses Twenty-Two and Twenty-Three

> "And for the sides of the tabernacle westward thou shalt make six boards. And two boards shalt thou make for the corners of the tabernacle in the two sides."

God began to make a distinction between the two boards at the corners and the rest of the boards. They were to be made out of the same acacia wood with two tenons beneath them and standing on the same silver foundation, but were to be more prominent than the others by their location in the building. Next to the foundation, the corner is the most important part of a house. It is at the corner that special care must be taken to bind the walls together. Christ is as one of us and yet He is distinct from us. He became as one of us so that we might become as He is. Although He is with us He is distinctly apart from the Church in this, that He holds and strengthens the building, keeping it in its place. He is spoken of as "a precious cornerstone," "a Chief Cornerstone" and "a sure foundation" (Isaiah 28:16; 1 Peter 2:6-8; Psalm 118:22).

Verse Twenty-Four

> "And they shall be coupled[49] together beneath, and they shall be coupled together above the head of it unto one ring: thus shall it be for them both; they shall be for the two corners."

---

[49] "*Coupled*" (tam) from primary root "to be made complete," "doubled," "twinned," "complete," "whole."

> "The word for 'corners' is used by Ezekiel to denote projections popularly known as 'horns' of his altar of shewbread (41:22). It is used by later writers to indicate the projecting bastions (2 Chronicles 26:9; Nehemiah 3:24) which guarded the walls of Jerusalem. We conclude from this information that the word in the passage before us must denote something of the nature of a projecting buttress at the two western corners of the wooden framework. These corner frames shall be made 'double' *i.e.* consist of two ordinary frames braced together for the sake of strength; further, that each is intended to form a buttress sloping upwards and terminating short of the top of the framework, at the first or 'topmost' ring, that is, underneath the top bar of the west side."[50]

> *"And they were twain* [twinned] *below; but they were whole together toward its head in the one ring"* (Exodus 36:29, *The Numerical Bible* translation).

The evident thought is that what might naturally be two, and thus divided, is "fitly joined together" (Ephesians 4:16) to be *one*. They are doubled or twinned beneath and come up to the head as whole. The corner frames terminated as one and with its head in the "topmost" ring. A ring is the symbol of love; of God's eternal love, because it is gold and because it has no beginning or ending. All the boards of the Holy Dwelling received these "rings." Divine Love held the Building together. The Head of the Church said that the world would know that we are His disciples if we manifested love one to another (John 13:35).

Verse Twenty-Five

> *"And they shall be eight boards, and their sockets of silver, sixteen sockets; two sockets under one board, and two sockets under another board."*

For the west side of the building there would be eight boards. Eight is the number representing resurrection, a new beginning, eternal life. The habitation of the Almighty God is everlasting. It is composed of the Church which has been given new life and walks in the power of Christ's resurrection! All things are made *new* to us who are in the Building of God for:

---

[50] James Hastings, editor, *A Dictionary of the Bible.*

"We are born *anew* (John 3:3, 7), receive a *new* life (Romans 6:4) and a *new* heart and spirit (Ezekiel 36:26), become members of a *new* creation (2 Corinthians 5:17), put on the *new* Man (Ephesians 4:24), receive a *new* Name (Revelation 2:17), and will sing a *new* Song (Revelation 5:8-9) in the New Heavens and the New Earth (Revelation 21:1). Christ makes all things *new* (Revelation 21:5)." (Preceding quote by unknown author.)

Two sockets of *silver* were under each board to balance them as were all the boards of the building. All the Church is balanced upon solid *redemption ground.*

Silver Sockets
by C.H. Spurgeon

The Lord commanded that every male over twenty years of age should pay half a shekel as redemption money, confessing that he deserved to die, owning that he was in debt to God, and bringing the sum demanded as a type of a great redemption which would by-and-by be paid for the souls of the sons of men.

The truth was thus taught that God's people are a redeemed people: they are elsewhere called 'the redeemed of the Lord.' If men reject the redemption which He ordains, then are they not His people, for of all His chosen it may be said: *'The Lord hath redeemed Jacob, and ransomed him from the hand of him that was stronger than he.'* Whenever we attempt to number up the people of God it is absolutely needful that we count only those who at least profess to have brought the *redemption price* in their hands, and so to have taken part in the atonement of Christ Jesus. David, when he numbered the people, did not gather from them the redemption money, and hence a plague broke out amongst them. He had failed in obedience to the Lord's ordinance, and counted his subjects, not as redeemed people, but merely as so many heads.

The redeemed have personally accepted the ransom which the Lord has provided and personally brought their redemption money in their hands by taking Christ to be theirs and presenting Him by an act of faith to the great Father.

Observe that this redemption, without which no man might rightly be numbered among the Children of Israel lest a plague should break out among them, must be *personal* and *individual.* There was not a lump sum to be paid for the nation, or 12 amounts for the twelve tribes, but *each man* must bring *his own* half-shekel for *himself*.

In the Exodus 38:25 we find that this mass of *silver* which was paid by 600,000 and 3,550 men were redeemed, each one paying his half-shekel, came to a great weight of *silver*. It must have weighed something over *four tons*, and this was dedicated to the use of the tabernacle: the special application of the precious metal was to make sockets into which the boards which made the walls of the Tabernacle should be placed. The mass of silver made up one hundred talents, and these upheld the fifty [48] boards of the holy place. They were in a wilderness, constantly moving, and continually shifting the Tabernacle. Now, they might have dug out a foundation in the sand, or on coming to a piece of rock where they could dig, they might have cut out foundations with great toil; but the Lord appointed that they should carry the foundation of the Tabernacle with them.

A talent of silver, weighing, I suppose, close upon one hundred pounds, was either formed into the shape of a wedge, so as to be driven into the soil, or else made into a solid square plate to lie upon it. In the wedge or plate were made mortises into which the tenons of the boards could be readily fitted. These plates of silver fitted the one into the other, tenon and mortise-wise, and thus they made a compact parallelogram, strengthened at the corners with double plates, and formed one foundation, moveable when taken to pieces, yet very secure as a whole. *This foundation was made of the* **redemption money.**

See the instructive emblem! The foundation of the worship of Israel was redemption. The dwelling-place of the Lord their God was founded on atonement. All the boards of incorruptible wood and precious gold stood upon the redemption price, and the curtains of fine linen, and the Veil of matchless workmanship, and the whole structure rested on nothing else but the solid mass of silver which had been paid as redemption money of the people. There was only one exception, and that was the Door where was the entrance to the Holy Place. There the pillars were set upon sockets of brass, perhaps because, as there was much going in and out of the priests, it was not meet that they should tread upon the token of redemption. The blood of the paschal lamb, when Israel came out of Egypt, was sprinkled on the lintel and the two side posts, but out of reverence to that blood it was not to be sprinkled on the threshold. Everything was done to show that atonement is to be the precious foundation of all holy things, and that man of whom it shall ever be said, *"He hath trodden under foot the Son of God, and hath counted the blood of the covenant, wherewith he was sanctified, an unholy thing."*

The foundation of the Tabernacle was very valuable, so our Lord Jesus as our Redeemer is *exceedingly precious* to us. His redemption is made with His precious blood. The redemption money was of pure and precious metal, a metal that does not lose weight in the fire. *"The redemption of the soul is precious."* What a redemption price hath Christ given for us; yea, what a redemption price *HE is*! Well did Peter say, *"Unto you that believe he is precious;"* silver and gold are not to be mentioned in comparison with Him.

The Tabernacle was a type of *The Church of God* as the place of divine indwelling. What and where is the Church of God? The true Church is founded upon *redemption*. Every board of shittim wood was tenoned and mortised into the sockets of silver made of the redemption money, and every man that is in the Church of God is united to Christ, rests upon Christ, and cannot be separated from Him.

Christ is a *sure foundation for the Church*, for the Tabernacle was never blown down. It had no foundation but the talents of silver; and yet it braved every desert storm. The wilderness is a place of rough winds - it is called a howling wilderness; but the sockets of silver hold the boards upright, and the holy tents defied the rage of the elements. To be united to Christ by faith is to be built on a sure foundation. His church will never be overthrown let the devil send what hurricanes he may.

And it was an *invariable foundation*, for the Tabernacle always had the same basis wherever it was placed. One day it was pitched on the sand, another on a good piece of arable ground, a third time on a grass plot, and tomorrow on a bare rock; but it always had the *same foundation*. The bearers of the holy furniture never left the silver sockets behind. Those four tons of silver were carried in their wagons, and put out first as the one and only foundation of the holy place."

–end of article

Directions were given for the boards on the south, north and west sides, but no boards at the east end. We know by this, that the Building faced east where the sun rose, where the Gate into the Court and the Tribe of Judah was located. The Church of the Living God is to ever face the Son who rises with healing in His wings. Continually She is to look toward the "East" where is "The Lion of the Tribe of *Judah*." Always within her heart there is to be the praise *(Judah* means *praise*) of God for His Way (Gate) into salvation's Court!

Verses Twenty-Six and Twenty-Seven

> *"And thou shalt make bars of shittim wood; five for the boards of the one side of the tabernacle, And five bars for the boards of the other side of the tabernacle, and five bars for the boards of the side of the tabernacle, for the two sides westward."*

The boards of the Tabernacle were set in sockets of silver which kept them from sinking into the sand. But to hold them from tipping, from tossing back and forth should a wind come against them, five bars were supplied. God in His grace to the Church, has made provision to keep it steady, though strong winds blow against it.

> *"Wherefore he saith, When he ascended up on high, he led captivity captive, and gave gifts unto men"* (Ephesians 4:8).

It was after He ascended up to Heaven that He sent the Divine Enabler. God's grace was manifested to the Church in her weakness through these five "bars" which were fulfilled in the five ministry gifts:

> *"And he gave some, apostles; and some, prophets; and some, evangelists; and some, pastors and teachers"* (Ephesians 4:11).

As the bars on the boards kept them from being separated, so the five ministry gifts are given ...

> *"For the perfecting of the saints, for the work of the ministry, for the edifying of the body of Christ: Till we all come in the unity of the faith, and of the knowledge of the Son of God, unto a perfect man, unto the measure of the stature of the fulness of Christ: That we henceforth be no more children,* **tossed to and fro, and carried about with every wind of doctrine,** *by the sleight of men, and cunning craftiness, whereby they lie in wait to deceive; But speaking the truth in*

love [the rings which hold the bars], *may grow up into him in all things, which is the head, even Christ* [the Corner Boards]: *From whom the whole body fitly joined together* [by the bars] *and compacted by that which every joint supplieth, according to the effectual working in the measure of every part, maketh increase of the body unto the edifying of itself in* ***love*** [the rings]" (Ephesians 4:12-16).

The five bars were put through, or "shot through" the rings on the boards like a bolt. (See Exodus 40:18, "put in the bars," vs. 34–"places for the bars." Bars–*beriah*, "a bolt," from *barah*, "to pass," or "shoot;" cf. Exodus 36:33, 34. ***All*** the bars were shot through the boards or rather, the rings of the boards.)

The bars were of no use without the rings to hold them. The gifts of the Spirit have been given to believers by God, but there is a more excellent way; it is the operation of these gifts in *Divine love* (see 1 Corinthians 13).

The boards received the bars through the rings; they did not refuse them. Each board with its rings, received each of the five bars. What would have happened to the board which did not have the bar through its ring? It would have toppled and the rest of the boards would have done the same. The Church is to receive these "graces" of the Lord in Divine love. Each individual in the body of Christ must receive God's ministry gifts in the love of God and not despise or refuse any one of them (see 1 Corinthians 12:25-31), for then the whole body would suffer. The assembly would topple to the ground; it would collapse!

Verse Twenty-Eight

"And the middle bar in the midst of the boards shall reach from end to end."

"In the midst" simply means halfway from the top to the bottom of the timbers. The middle bar, being singled out as reaching from end to end, indicates that the other four bars did *not* do so but extended halfway so that it took two of them to reach entirely across. This explanation is taken from Jewish writings and Rabbinical descriptions according to the making of Hebrew words and phrases. This would have caused each side to present the appearance of having only *three* bars, two at the top, each extending halfway, and on the same line; one in the middle extending all the way, and two at the bottom similar to those at the top. These bars were *all* held in their places by rings of gold. Thus was the appearance of the bars: three on the north side, three on the south side, and three on the west side equaling *nine,* the number of Holy Spirit gifts and the manifestations of the fruit of the Spirit (Galatians 5:22) which is given to the Church.

Love has been described, not only as *heading* all the nine parts of this Holy Fruit, but expressing itself in all these manifestations as well, for "***Joy*** is love rejoicing; ***Peace*** is love resting; ***Longsuffering*** is love's patience; ***Gentleness*** is love's touch; ***Goodness*** is love's character; ***Faith*** is love's trust; ***Meekness*** is love's humility, ***Temperance***, or self-control, is love's strength."

And Williams translation of 1 Corinthians 13:4-8 puts it this way:

> "Love is so patient and so kind; Love never boils with jealousy; It never boasts, Is never puffed with pride; It does not act with rudeness, Or insist upon its rights; It never gets provoked; It never harbors evil thoughts; Is never glad when wrong is done; But always glad when truth prevails; It bears up under anything; It exercises faith in everything; It keeps up hope in everything; It gives us power to endure in anything; Love never fails."

Each bar was made of acacia wood overlaid with gold, men (wood) made sons of God (gold). The two bars that were on the bottom-most parts of the board represent the first two ministry gifts, the apostles and the prophets. They are, in a secondary sense, the foundation of the Church, and Jesus Christ, the Chief Corner Stone (Ephesians 2:20). Then the middle bar that went through the midst of the boards, that one which reached from end to end, is the evangelist who was mentioned next in the order of gifts. It is his ministry to "reach from end to end," to draw others into the Church. Each one in the Church is exhorted to do the work of the evangelist as well (Acts 1:8; 2 Timothy 4:5). The two bars on the topmost parts of the boards are typical of the pastors and teachers who *elevate* the Church into a higher plane with God. The work of the ministry is to be in *all* the members of the body. *All* the boards have this bar. The five ministry gifts center in the work of *evangelism* to bring others into the body of Christ.

According to the Greek translation of Ephesians 4:11, *pastors and teachers* are considered as one gift since there is not the word, "some," preceding each of them as is the case with the other three gifts. They are individual gifts, but so closely associated (the pastor should also be a teacher) that they are combined into one ministry. This too, shows a beautiful spiritual truth: the five ministry gifts represented in the four upper and lower bars on the boards, the one Central Bar (which reaches from end to end and incorporating the whole) representing the Lord Jesus Christ who is the Central Figure uniting all the ministry gifts in *one Body*.

Verse Twenty-Nine

> *"And thou shalt overlay the boards with gold, and make their rings of gold for places for the bars: and thou shalt overlay the bars with gold."*

The boards for the Tabernacle were made of wood from the *shittah* tree. All the grains, knots and stains were then covered by gold. We are *"hid with Christ in God"* (Colossians 3:3). *"Thou art all fair, my love; there is no spot in thee"* (Song of Solomon 4:7). Notice that it was after the silver foundation was described, that the gold was to be applied to the wood. The silver of redemption in which the Church stands makes it possible for her to partake of and be covered with the gold of Divinity.

The grain of the *shittim* (acacia) wood is such that if it is smoothed and polished it can be made very beautiful. This typifies reformation of the natural man and the outwardly good and beneficial results that can be obtained thereby. But as you will observe, God made no provision whatsoever for developing the grain to improve the natural appearance of those boards, but simply had them overlaid with gold. Believers are to be clothed in God's own perfect, immaculate, enduring righteousness and holiness.

> *"Therefore by the deeds of the law there shall no flesh be justified in his* [God's] *sight: for by the law is the knowledge of sin. But now the righteousness of God without the law is manifested, being witnessed by the law and the prophets; Even the righteousness of God which is by faith of Jesus Christ unto all and **upon all them that believe:** ..."* (Romans 3:20-22).

The boards were all overlaid with gold and the bars were also overlaid with the same metal which speaks of divinity. The building of golden boards represented to the Israelites the glory, dignity and wealth of Jehovah. The tree was chopped down, made into boards, covered with gold, and then put into a new position in the desert. So it is with any individual who comes to the Lord Jesus and is converted. We, in the Church, have been "chopped down" from our place in the world and have been "overlaid with gold" for we have been given the power to become the sons of God. We are as the acacia wood, but we are beautified or glorified with the gold upon us, for we have become partakers of the Divine nature (2 Peter 1:4; John 1:12). Christians, when taken in a fault, often use the expression: "I am only human." Strictly speaking, this is unscriptural, for Christians are *not **only** human*; we, who are born-again, also have been given the *Divine* nature! We are transferred into a new position in the "desert," standing on the silver foundation, grasping the silver sockets beneath us that we might not sink down into the sands of sin. We are strengthened, kept from tossing to and fro with every wind of doctrine in the Church.

> "There are strong things in the world," says the *Talmud*, "Rock is strong but iron cleaves it; fire melts iron; water extinguishes fire; the clouds bear aloft the water; the wind drives away the clouds; man withstands the wind; fear unmans man; wine dispels fear; sleep overcomes wine; and death sweeps away sleep. But strongest of all is *love* (loving kindness), for it defies and survives death."

Take away the bars—the wind would scatter the boards. Take away the ministry gifts—the Church is swayed with every wind of doctrine; the whole structure would collapse.

Verse Thirty

> *"And thou shalt rear up the tabernacle according to the fashion thereof which was showed thee in the mount."*

There were 48 boards for the Tabernacle which is a remarkable number that God used in connection with the priesthood! The only times the number *forty-eight* appears in the Bible is in two passages referring to the cities given to the *Levites* (Numbers 35:7 and Joshua 21:41). *Forty-eight* Boards were in the structure consecrated for the use of the Levites!

The first day of the first month of the second year was the date appointed for the setting up of the Tabernacle (Exodus 19:1; 40:17; Numbers 9:1-5). Israel left Egypt on the 15th day of the first month of the first year (Numbers 33:3). It took about 50 days to march to Sinai from Egypt, and there were two periods of 40 days each when Moses was in the mount with some days' interval between, besides other periods, so it is estimated that the actual work on the Tabernacle occupied approximately six or seven months. Again God emphasized the careful observance of His instructions. The Levites were filled with the wisdom of God that they could do so. Believer priests today are endued with power from above in order to carry out every detail "according to the pattern."

The Rearing of the Tabernacle

(The following article is by an unknown author.)

"We know that though every bar may be shaped, and every board overlaid, and every piece of scarlet and purple and linen cut exactly to pattern, as long as they are only *individual* boards and bars laying on the building site, the glory cloud of God cannot fill them. Not until they have lost their *individualism* and submitted themselves to the Masterbuilder that He might set each one board, bar, and curtain in its place and build them all into *one* Tabernacle, *one* Dwelling Place of God, *one* Body of Christ. Only *then* shall the glory cloud of God's nature fill it and the world see the glory of God in a manifestation of the nature of Christ in His Body (John 17:23). The world is never going to know that Jesus was truly sent by the Father to redeem the world till they see divided Christianity become *one* Body of Christ with the glory cloud of God's nature filling it.

"As beautiful and well-shaped as one golden bar ministry might be, no matter how well it might glitter and reflect the light of the Sun (Jesus), it can never manifest the full glory of God. One golden board may be beautifully overlaid with the anointing of God, but alone it can never contain the full glory of God. Only when we have all died to our individualism and our desire for individual ministry and individual recognition and individual relationship with Jesus, and individual life in God, and let God build us into one body, one tabernacle of God shall the glory cloud of God's nature so fill us that the world shall see a manifestation of Christ in His Body, that shall make them know that God sent Him into the world.

"We, like Israel, might swell with pride as we gaze on beautifully shaped golden bars, that is, ministries that are greatly anointed, and gifted, and can expound the Word, prophesy beautifully, and pray down great miracles. We may look out at our various works and see the gold of God's anointing glittering everywhere, as the overlaid boards worship in the Spirit. But the Tabernacle reared up presented a different sight than the individual materials laying on the building site. In order for there to be something for the glory cloud to fill, the boards had to be holding the bars up and the bars had to be holding the boards together. Board had to be joined to board. Board had to be joined to bar and bar had to be joined to board. Only then could there be a tabernacle that could contain God's glory.

"Even so, it must be with us. The Body must be holding up the ministry, and the ministry must be holding the members of the Body together. Member must be joined to member, and member to ministry, and ministry to member before there can be a dwelling place that can contain the glory of God's nature."

Bible-Science Newsletter
May, 1980

"The Bible Is Scientific ... In 1964 space scientists discovered *four corners* on a round earth and the 1969 pictures taken by astronauts show an earth *hanging on nothing* as we read in Job 26:7. Science is confirming what Scripture teaches. In Job 38:4 we read of *foundations* of the earth and the Hebrew word used is Eden which refers to *sockets* used in construction of the tabernacle. Since the Alaskan earthquake on Good Friday of 1964, seismographic studies have revealed *literal foundation sockets,* or mantlerock under each of the seven continents. Science has just recently learned that what Job wrote 4000 years ago is scientifically accurate."

The Boards of the Tabernacle, symbolizing the Church of the Living God, is described in the following article by another unknown author. This paper was given to my students who attended the class in "Tabernacle Study" which I taught at Seattle Bible College:

ALL–NECESSARY MEMBERS

The Carpenter's tools had a conference. Brother Hammer was in the chair. The meeting had informed him that he must leave because he was too noisy. But he said, 'If I am to leave this Carpenter's shop, Brother Gimlet must go too; he is so insignificant that he makes very little impression.'

"Little Brother Gimlet arose and said, 'All right, but Brother Screw must go also; you have to turn him around and around, again and again, to get him anywhere.'

"Brother Screw then said, 'If you wish, I will go, but Brother Plane must leave also; all his work is on the surface, there is no depth to it.'

"To this, Brother Plane replied, 'Well, Brother Rule will have to withdraw if I do, for he is always measuring other folks as though he were the only one who is right.'

"Brother Rule then complained against Brother Sandpaper and said, 'I just don't care, he is rougher than he ought to be and is always rubbing people the wrong way.'

"In the midst of the discussion, the Carpenter of Nazareth walked in. He had come to perform His day's work. He put on His apron, and went to the bench to make a pulpit. He employed the *screw*, the *gimlet*, the *sandpaper*, the *saw*, the *hammer*, the *plane*, and all the other tools. After the day's work was over and the pulpit was finished, Brother Saw arose and said, 'Brethren, I perceive that all of us are very necessary members of this family; we are laborers together; let us no longer complain as *individualists* but instead act as necessary parts of the whole'."

Test Questions

1. Of what were the Boards of the Tabernacle made? Explain the Hebrew word *omdiim* in connection with these boards. Compare with NT passages. What is the symbolism of the Boards as a unit?
2. Give reasons why the Building is considered to have been composed of open frames and not solid boards.
3. From what other word does "shittim" come which describes the appearance of the wood? Give significance.
4. What was part of the Boards, made of the same materials, which grasped and stood in the silver sockets? What is its significance?
5. (a) After leaving Egypt, how was the silver secured for the foundation of the Boards? Give two Scripture references and spiritual applications. (b) What were the measurements of each Board? (c) How many were there on each side? (d) How many boards altogether?
6. Explain the meaning of the Corner Boards as concerning their antitype.
7. Give at least 3 similarities of the Boards (as a whole) with what they represent (the Church).
8. Explain the word "bar," and the phrases: "in the midst" and "shot through the boards."
9. (a) How many bars were to "shoot through the boards" or to be "put in" the boards? (b) Explain their arrangement.
10. Of what materials was each bar made?
11. What do the bars represent and what is their main function?
12. Of what material were "the places for the bars"?
13. Of what are the rings a symbol?
14. What is the "more excellent way" for the operation of the gifts of the Spirit? Memorize Scripture reference relative to this.
15. What truth was outstanding to you in this section?

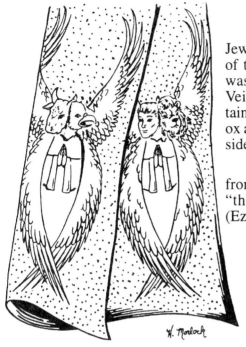

According to some Jewish scholars, the face of the man and the lion was on one side of the Veil and Mishkan Curtains, and the face of the ox and eagle on the other side.

This interpretation is from Ezekiel's vision of "the living creatures" (Ezekiel 1:5-11).

The Veil

Verse Thirty-One

"And thou shalt make a veil of blue, and purple, and scarlet, and fine twined linen of cunning work: with cherubims shall it be made:"

The veil was on the inside of the Tabernacle building in the innermost room from which God began with His instructions concerning the three entrances of the entire structure. It separated the Holy of Holies, a picture of God's very presence, from the Holy Place which represents Heaven on earth. First, God is concerned with the Veil, beginning from Himself, from the inside, before He comes to the outside court. He presents Himself to man from Heaven, then He comes to earth.

Blue "tells" of Christ's origin–the Heavenly One; He is the Son of God as described in the book of John. Purple "tells" of

Christ's Kingship-the Royal One; He is the King of Israel as pictured in Matthew. Scarlet "tells" of Christ's sacrifice–the Life-Giving One; He is the Servant as found in the book of Mark. Fine twined linen "tells" of Christ's sinless life–the Holy One; He is the Son of Man as portrayed in Luke.

"Cunning-work" indicates there was a weaving in and through the material so that the design and colors appeared on both sides of the Veil. How beautifully does this portray the Holy Spirit with His skillful weaving in the life of Jesus whose humanity and divinity were intertwined. The beauty of the Veil could be seen on both sides of the linen curtain so that when the priest came in through the Door of the Holy Place he beheld the beautiful colors and the cherubim designed into it. One side of the Veil was toward man, the other side toward God. Not only is *God* always beholding Him in His glory, but *man*, too, can see the beauty and loveliness of the Lord Jesus as portrayed by the Holy Spirit [the cunning work]. Christ has promised:

> "He that hath my commandments, and keepeth them, he it is that loveth me: and he that loveth me shall be loved of my Father, and I will love him,**will manifest myself to him**. ... If a man love me, he will keep my words: and my Father will love him, and we will come unto him, and **make our abode with him**" (John 14:21, 23).

Verse Thirty-Two

> "And thou shalt hang it upon four pillars of shittim wood overlaid with gold: their hooks shall be of gold, upon the four sockets of silver."

The "hanging" of the curtain reminds us of the death of Christ who "hung" upon the Cross. "Four" refers to those in the classification of "whosoever." It was "whosoever" who "hung" Him there. The hooks of gold represent Divinity. It was in the counsels of God before the foundation of the earth that there should be the crucifixion of the Son of God (Acts 4:27-28; Acts 2:23). God ordained it and used human instruments to carry out His plan.

The believer ("whosoever") who is an overcomer is described also as a "pillar" in the House of God (Revelation 3:12). He has accepted God's promised salvation; He stands on redemption ground: sockets of *silver*!

Verse Thirty-Three

"And thou shalt hang up the veil under the taches, that thou mayest bring in thither within the veil the ark of the testimony: and the veil shall divide unto you between the holy place and the most holy."

"Taches"–50 gold clasps in the Ceiling *Mishkan* curtain (Exodus 26:6) and 50 copper clasps in the *Ohel* curtain above it (Exodus 26:11).

The Veil separated the Holy of Holies (Hebrew text is "Holiness of Holinesses") from the Holy Place, *"The Holy Ghost this signifying, that the way into the holiest of all was not yet made manifest, while as the first tabernacle was yet standing"* (Hebrews 9:8). "Veil," in the original text, is *paroketh* meaning "to separate." This Veil stood there as if to bar man from the presence of God. However, this "barrier" was not made of steel or stone, but of a lightweight material which was easily lifted and drawn aside. And though, by this Veil God was shut out from man, yet He has provided an entrance for us to the Holiest through our perfect High Priest. When Christ was crucified, the Veil of the Temple (a copy of the Wilderness Tabernacle Veil) was rent (Matthew 27:45-52). Now we enter *boldly* to the Throne of grace (Hebrews 4:16) by a new and living way (Hebrews 10:20).

The cherubim of the Veil represented the Lord Jesus and those who are in Him. They were torn when the Veil was torn. Those who are redeemed are identified with Christ in His sufferings and death as well as His resurrection and glorification.

When our Lord yielded up His spirit, *"the veil in the temple was rent in twain from the top to the bottom"* (Matthew 27:51). It was from the ceiling first, from heaven, from the hand of God, that the Veil was torn. It was to the bottom, the earth, that the work was done on behalf of mankind. God came down.

The Veil hid the "beauties" of God and barred the way into the Holiest. It was Christ's flesh which kept man from seeing or entering the Holiest Room; in life He was alone, but through His *death* (the *Veil* was torn in two), man could now see His glory (John 12:23, 24); man could enter in to His Holy Presence! Christ "hung" upon the tree of death to make it possible for us to have access to the Tree of Life (Revelation 2:7; 22:2, 14)!

The Veil not only represents Christ's flesh, but also the self-life of the believer. When Christ died, the Veil Entrance to the Innermost Room parted as though to reveal the Presence of God in the Holy of Holies. The Veil, *our flesh*, separates us from God. When self dies, His power and presence is revealed. The more we die, the more He lives. The more we empty of our self, the more Christ fills us with Himself. Let the self-life die and enter into the Holiest Place with God!

Verse Thirty-Four

"And thou shalt put the mercy seat upon the ark of the testimony in the most holy place."

This instruction concerning the Mercy Seat was given after instructions for the making of the Veil–the Veil to hide the awful presence of God and His Holiness. The Mercy Seat was to cover all the articles of the Ark which were reminders of judgment for sin. Only through the Veil can we come to the Mercy Seat; only through the death of Christ can we find forgiveness for breaking God's law. Only through the perfect life of Christ which was laid down for the sins of the world can we expect to come boldly to the Throne Room and have fellowship with God (Hebrews 4:16).

Verse Thirty-Five

"And thou shalt set the table without the veil, and the candlestick over against the table on the side of the tabernacle toward the south: and thou shalt put the table on the north side."

The Table and the Lampstand were before the Veil in the Holy Place. The Lampstand displayed the beauties of the Table. Here was Light and Food in the service of the King. While walking with Him we have fellowship (we partake of His Bread) and the Light of His Presence.

The north side was the place of judgment (Numbers 2:25: "Dan" means "judging;" see section on *The Altar of Sacrifice*). The sacrifices were judged and killed at the *north* of the Altar in the Court. At the table we examine ourselves and make things right before we come to communion with our Lord (1 Corinthians 11:28). We cannot partake of the table of God and the table of devils at the same time (1 Corinthians 10:16-21).

Verse Thirty-Six

> *"And thou shalt make an hanging for the door[51] of the tent, of blue, and purple, and scarlet, and fine twined linen, wrought with needlework."*

Blue represents the Heavenly One on earth; purple, the royal One among men; scarlet, the Suffering One, the Lamb of God for the world; and fine-twined linen, the Holy One of Israel.

This curtain was to be made of *needlework* which signified embroidery on one side of the material, according to the Hebrew rendering of the word. This was to be on the inside of the entrance to the Holy Place where there was fellowship, satisfaction, and service with God. Christ is this Door and He is not seen from the outside in this relationship. One must enter in to behold the "beautiful colors and the design of needlework" in the Curtain!

Verse Thirty-Seven

> *"And thou shalt make for the hanging five pillars of shittim wood, and overlay them with gold, and their hooks shall be of gold: and thou shalt cast five sockets of brass* [copper] *for them."*

The Door was to hang on *five* pillars. *Five* names were given to the Child born (wood), the Son given (gold) (Isaiah 9:6). There were *five* Covenants with two parties involved: Man, wood; God, gold. These *five* Covenants are:

1. The Adamic (Genesis 3),
2. The Noahic (Genesis 9:8-17),
3. The Abrahamic (Genesis 12 to 25),
4. The Mosaic (Exodus 19-32),
5. The New Covenant (Hebrews 9:15-26).

The gold and the wood of these columns represent the dual nature of the Person of Christ. He was equally human and divine at the same time. They also tell of the believer, "pillars in the temple of God" who are as the wood covered over by gold–men who are made *sons* of God.

The copper sockets of the Court ended at the Door into the Holy Place. The priests would pass this copper for the last time

---

[51] "Door," *pethach*–"opening," "entrance."

when they entered the Door to Heaven's Holiness. Being set in this copper (symbol of God's judgment for sin), these "pillars," for the last time will be judged. The saints of God will openly be made manifest and judged for their works at the Judgment Seat of Christ (Romans 14:10; 1 Corinthians 3:13-15; 2 Corinthians 5:10). Then they will enter God's Holy Place "without sin unto salvation," never more to pass the "copper," but now free to enjoy His light, glory, and Holiness forevermore!

Test Questions

1. Describe the material and colors of the Veil and where the Veil was located? Give spiritual applications.
2. What was the pattern and kind of sewing designed in the Veil? Give symbolic meaning.
3. Upon how many pillars did the Veil hang?
4. Upon what did the pillars of the Veil stand? Give symbolism of this foundation.
5. What did the Veil represent? Give a NT verse.
6. What was immediately over the Veil? Explain significance.
7. What did the Veil do for the priests?
8. What is the Veil in relation to the Christian walk?
9. (a) What is the typical meaning of the rending of the Veil, and what does this act do for the believer? (b) Where were the colors obtained?.
10. Explain the significance of the position of the Mercy Seat and the Table of Shewbread after the description of the Veil is given.
11. Describe the material and colors of the Door. Give symbolism.
12. What kind of sewing was in the Door and where was the Door located? What are the typical applications?
13. Upon how many pillars did the Door hang?
14. Upon what did the pillars of the Door stand? Give meaning of this foundation.
15. What truth was outstanding to you in this section?

CHAPTER THREE
EXODUS 27

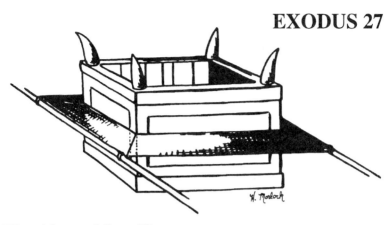

The Altar of Sacrifice

Verse One

> *"And thou shalt make an altar of shittim* [acacia] *wood, five cubits long, and five cubits broad; the altar shall be foursquare: and the height thereof shall be three cubits."*

"Altar"–*mizbeach* from *zebach* meaning "to slaughter" an animal (as a sacrifice). The first mention of the "altar" in the Bible is in connection with Noah's disembarkation from the Ark after the flood (Genesis 8:20). Bezaleel made the altar of the Tabernacle (Genesis 38:22; see also the reference to him in 2 Chronicles 1:5).

The acacia wood is representative of the humanity and humiliation of Christ. He grew, like the acacia tree, in the desert of this world. He gave up His life on the Sacrificial Altar in the wilderness.

This "slaughter place" was to be five cubits square–*five* all the way around. It is interesting to note, that relative to the "slaughter place," that there were not only *five* wounds but *five kinds* of wounds given to Christ when God's grace to man was manifested on Golgotha's Altar: *Two* wounds in His hands (work), *two* wounds in His feet (walk), and *one* wound in His side (life). He suffered every type of flesh wound known to medical science:

105

1) Bruising–Isaiah 52:14; 53:5, 10; Matthew 26:67.
2) Laceration–Psalm 129:1-3; Matthew 27:26.
3) Penetration–Zechariah 12:10; Matthew 27:29, 30.
4) Perforation–Psalm 22:16; Matthew 27:35.
5) Incision and Bursting–Zechariah 12:10; John 19:33, 34.

> "Five bleeding wounds He bears"
> Received on Calvary,
> They pour effectual prayers,
> They strongly plead for me.
> "Forgive him, O forgive" they cry,
> "Nor let that ransomed sinner die!
> Nor let that ransomed sinner die!"

This "raised place" was built and placed so that each of its four sides faced three tribes of Israel (see Section: *The Priesthood and Encampment*). It was "foursquare" for "whosoever" in the Camp surrounding it. The Cross of Christ (of which this Altar is symbolic) is for every tribe, tongue, nation, and all peoples of all ages. It pictures God's love and mercy extended to the "whosoever" of the world (John 3:16).

The height of the Altar was to be three cubits (see 2 Chronicles 6:13; we find the same measurements of the Copper Altar for the platform upon which Solomon prayed).

Verse Two

> *"And thou shalt make the horns of it upon the four corners thereof: his horns shall be of the same: and thou shalt overlay it with brass* [copper].*"*

In the English Bible the word is "brass." The Hebrew word is *nechosheth* or "copper." God is dealing with pure metals and "brass" is an alloy, a mixture of zinc and copper. (What copper was used for in the Tabernacle is recorded in Exodus 38:29-31.) "The Egyptians and Israelites knew how to make copper harder than steel."[52]

Horns are the power and strength of an animal used for fighting and conquering. The four horns of copper and wood signify that the power and strength to conquer sin and judge sin is manifested by God to the four corners of the earth by the

---

[52]Deputy W.P. Partridge, *The Tabernacle and Other Object Lessons*, p.15.

death of Christ. They announced, as it were, to all the surrounding tribes of Israel that they were to come to God this way, for the horns were pointing upward and outward (God-ward and man-ward) "whosoever will" could come to God only by way of this Altar.

Four sides of the Altar–it was for *all* (2 Corinthians 5:15). It was a propitiation for the *world* (1 John 2:2). It was a ransom for *all* (1 Timothy 2:6). It was where Christ tasted death for *every* man (Hebrews 2:9). *Everyone* must kneel there: Jew and Gentile, rich and poor, black, white, red, yellow and brown, high and low, king and pauper, educated and illiterate; all must bow before God at the Altar of Sacrifice, the Cross of Christ. The blood of bulls and goats before the cross could not take away sins, but *faith* in the thing for which they were offered as types *did take away sins* (Ephesians 1:7; Hebrews 9:11-15, 21, 22, 26; 10:10-18; 1 John 1:7-9; Revelation 1:5).

"... bind the sacrifice with cords, even unto the horns of the altar" (Psalm 118:27).

The horns of the Altar of Burnt Offering "held" the sacrificial victim. The horns were also a place of refuge in time of trouble (see 1 Kings 2:28 and 1 Kings 1:50-53; cf. Luke 1:68,69). Salvation is associated in Scripture with the *horns of the Altar.* Christ is called "Horn of our Salvation." Our Lord Jesus was "bound" to the horns of His Copper Altar with the cords of love (John 13:1), of obedience (Philemon 2:8; John 10:18), of Godly zeal (Psalm 69:9; John 2:17), and of the joy set before Him (Hebrews 12:2).

Copper was to overlay the wood of the "offering place". This metal is significant of God's judgment for sin as shown in the instance when Moses was leading the Children of Israel through the wilderness and they complained against him. They were tired of wandering in the desert and wanted to return to Egypt. Because of their murmurings, God sent serpents to poison them. As their bodies became weaker and were beginning to swell they cried to Moses for a remedy from the venom of the serpent's bite (Numbers 21:5-9; Deuteronomy 8:15).

Moses called upon God who gave him instructions to make a *"fiery"* serpent, place it upon a pole, and command the Israelites to look upon it. When they would look upon it, they would be healed, delivered from the poison that had come because of their sin. They did not complain any longer, nor did they question God's method of healing, but they obeyed the words of the Lord through Moses, and everyone who looked, lived.

The word "fiery" (serpent) is from *seraph* meaning "burning," poisonous or symbolic creature from their *copper* color (see destruction of Moses' copper serpent in 2 Kings 18:4). This serpent was called *Nehushtan* meaning "piece of copper" from *nachash* or "nechash" (serpent, copper). The pole must have had a crosspiece at the top, because a metal serpent could not be hung upon a bare pole. It is said by Josephus that the banner *poles* of the Israelites had such a crosspiece. (The Hebrew word for "standard," "flag" or "banner" is the same word for "pole".) Also, in roasting the whole paschal lamb, there was the necessity for a crosspiece because this "roasting over the fire" could only be accomplished by suspending it upon a longitudinal pole with a transverse bar to spread open the body. The *cross* of Christ is the fulfillment of this "pole" in the wilderness. It is called *stauros* in the NT Greek text, "a stake" or "post" ("a pole" *as set upright*), or "cross" from "stag"–"to stand."

The pole, upon which the copper form hung, prophesies of Golgotha's "slaughter place" (John 3:14). The serpent is a symbol of sin pointing to the Lord Jesus who was the Sin-Offering. God's judgment for sin, represented in the copper, was received by Christ–that judgment which should have been ours (1 Peter 2:24)–but God made Him to be sin for us (Isaiah 50:5, 6; John 3:14-16; Galatians 3: l3). He bore our sins in His own body (copper overlaid the wood) on the "tree" (2 Corinthians 5:21). All who "look upon Him" will live, will be delivered and healed from sin's venom.

Remember, it was 20 years later that *Korah* rebelled against the leadership of Moses and Aaron in the wilderness (Numbers 16:36-40). The judgment of God came in the form of fire which destroyed him and his followers (250 men) when they offered incense in copper censers. These censers were then beaten flat and made into an additional covering for the Altar in the Court of the Tabernacle. Their sin of rebellion, so to speak, was judged, and died there at the Altar of Sacrifice. Though Korah was destroyed, "his sons died not" (Numbers 26:11). Korah was a

Levite, a *Kohathite*, and his family was not to be extinguished. We find that some of the Psalms are addressed to Korah's sons. Oh, the mercy of God! Though their ***father*** had sinned, they were reminded that they could find pardon for their *own* sin at the Cross of Christ, of which the Copper Altar was a symbol!

Verse Three

> *"And thou shalt make his pans to receive his ashes, and his shovels, and his basins, and his fleshhooks, and his firepans: all the vessels thereof thou shalt make of brass* [copper].*"*

There were five different kinds of copper instruments for the copper Altar. This "portrays" God's grace in measuring out sin's penalty. It is remarkable to also note that there were *five* great offerings associated with these *five* copper instruments (see Chart of *Five Principle Offerings*):

1. The ***Burnt*** Offering (Leviticus 1:1-17; 6:9-13; 9:24)–Christ, our Passover (Ephesians 5:2).
2. The *Meal* Offering (Leviticus 2:1-16; 6:14-18)–Christ, the Corn of Wheat (John 12:24).
3. The *Sin* Offering (Leviticus 4:1-35; 6:24-30)–Christ, our Sin Offering (2 Corinthians 5:21).
4. The *Trespass* Offering (Leviticus 5:1-19; 6:7; 7:1-10)– Christ, our Trespass Offering (Colossians 2:13-14).
5. The ***Peace*** Offering (Leviticus 3:1-17; 7:11-21)–Christ, our Peace Offering (Ephesians 2:14).

The heave offering (vertical) and wave offering (horizontal) of Exodus 29:27 passing each other form a Cross! (Heave offering–elevated and lowered; Wave-offering–swung back and forth.)

The pans, in which the hot coals were carried were also called "censers," and held the ashes. These ashes were taken to a clean place outside the camp (Leviticus 6:11), typical of our Lord's body after His crucifixion and death. Even as they were carried to a clean place, just so His body was laid in a new tomb in which no body had been laid, as it is written (Matthew 27:59, 60). The ashes revealed that the sacrifice had been consumed, that it was completed and accepted. The basins were for the carrying of the blood into the Holy of Holies. The blood had been shed; a life had been given; a life had been laid down. These pans, shovels, basins, and fleshhooks speak of the work of the Holy Spirit in the sacrifice. God's judgment for sin was carried out with the "assistance" of the Divine Executive, the Holy Spirit (Hebrews 9:14; Christ offered Himself "through *the Eternal Spirit*"). He "helped" in the consuming of the sacrifice so that it would be accepted by the Father.

The Grate

Verses Four and Five

> *"And thou shalt make for it a grate of network of brass* [copper]; *and upon the net shalt thou make four brazen rings in the four corners thereof. And thou shalt put it* **under the compass** *of the altar beneath, that the net may be even to the midst of the altar."*

The network of copper in the Grate provided a way of access to the Altar of Sacrifice. It was also a reinforcement which kept the boards from expanding when earth was poured inside. God protects and reinforces the means by which His judgment is delivered.

He provides an access for the sinner's acceptance of this sacrifice as well. The four rings represent God's love, even in judgment for sin, expressed to the four corners of the earth in the Universal Sacrifice–the Sin-Offering for "whosoever."

"And thou shalt put it **under** *the* **compass**"–"Compass"–*karkob*, "environment," "a rim," "top margin" of the altar *from beneath* (literal rendering). This *karkob* refers to an *external* copper network, *i.e.*, the rim compassing the Altar. The Grate (sieve, plaited) was to be put under the rim to act as a bank or ledge upon which the priest stood when he ministered anything concerning the sacrifices of the Altar. It would have been impossible for the priests to lift the bullock 4½ feet so as to drop it into the Altar if there had been a grate in the center of it as pictured by so many artists! Also, the ashes had to be removed to a clean place outside the camp and it would have been difficult to do this if the ashes had fallen through a grate in the center!

Since there were no directions for any support of this grate, and since God commanded that there be no steps to His altar, it seems reasonable that the "box" was set down into the earth and that the earth was just a short distance below the grate (see illustration, *The Court Altar*). We recall that the Cross Altar was set down into a hole in the ground, and the Supreme Sacrifice upon it was lifted up from the earth according to prophecy!

The grate, extended halfway up the three cubits of the Altar, making it one and a half cubits in height. This was equal with the height of the Mercy Seat and the Table of Showbread in the Tabernacle Building. God offers His mercy and His fellowship, but equal with His love and mercy is His judgment for sin as exemplified in the copper grate. God's heart of love is accompanied by His justice! The mercy and fellowship of God inside the Holiest was given to the sinner because he had already met with God's judgment for sin which was meted out at the altar in the court!

Verses Six and Seven

> *"And thou shalt make staves for the altar, staves of shittim wood, and overlay them with brass. And the staves shall be put into the rings, and the staves shall be upon the two sides of the altar, to bear it."*

The grate that surrounded the altar was to have the rings in it for the staves (see verse 4), and the priests carried the altar by the staves as they walked through the wilderness. The four rings for the staves signify love (everlasting love since a ring has no beginning or end). Because of His great love for all mankind Christ bore the judgment of God when He voluntarily laid down His life as a Sacrifice. The rings and staves also represent the daily Cross which accompanies the believer everywhere. In love we are to carry the message of the Crucified One and remember His invitation, *"... If any man will come after me, let him deny himself, and take up **his cross** daily, and follow me"* (Luke 9:23). The Christian's cross is compared to the Cross of Christ in this, that it is *voluntary self-sacrifice for the needs of others.* The believer can say along with Paul: "I am crucified with Christ and now Christ lives in me," in other words: "I am identified with Christ in His Cross. The nails that were pounded into His hands were pounded into mine and now my work is His work. The nails that were driven into His feet were driven into mine and now my walk is His walk. The crown of thorns upon His head was pressed upon mine and now my thoughts are His thoughts. The spear that was thrust into His side was thrust into mine and now my life is laid down, my heart broken over the sins of others; I have entered into the fellowship of His sufferings. I have taken up my cross and I am following Him."

Verse Eight

*"**Hollow with boards** shalt thou make it: as it was showed thee in the mount, so shall they make it."*

There was no top or bottom to the Altar that was to be built; it was to have a cavity to hold earth or stones, the only kind of Altar God would accept:

*"An **altar of earth** thou shalt make unto me, and shalt sacrifice thereon thy burnt offerings, and thy peace offerings, thy sheep, and thine oxen: in all places where I record my name I will come unto thee, and I will bless thee. And if thou wilt make me an altar of stone, thou shalt not build it of hewn stone: for if thou lift up thy tool upon it, thou hast polluted it. Neither shalt thou go up by steps unto mine altar, that thy nakedness be not discovered thereon"* (Exodus 20:24-26).

Emphasis was placed on *plainness* so that the Altar itself would not become the object of veneration or worship. God's instructions to His people Israel excluded metal and hewn stone in the offering place because this would have involved man's ability. (Being *hollow*, the altar man built could not have anything man-made in its center!) God wants an altar that He Himself has planned and fashioned.

"God decreed that His Altar had to be built of stones which had not been touched by hammer or chisel, so that there might not be any trace of human skill or labor upon it ... chiselers, using the tools of human wisdom and sagacity, delight in trimming, changing and arranging the doctrines of the Cross into an artificial system of logic and works, into a code of ethics or standard of morals ... What sacrilege, what blasphemy it is to lift up human tools upon the Altar of God! ... God's plan of salvation is finished. It is already a complete work; the price has been paid by the shed blood of the Lamb of God upon Calvary's tree ... Consider again the command of God, given to Moses, a command which thunders down the corridors of time through the centuries as a warning and an indictment to those who would defile the Altar; "If thou lift up thy tool upon it, thou hast polluted it!"[53]

---

[53]Paul Myers ("First-Mate Bob") *Log of the Good Ship Grace*, No. 16, Vol. XIX. ("First-Mate Bob" was one of my teachers at Southern California College.)

Foreshadows of Calvary's Altar

The Altar of Sacrifice

No steps were to lead up to this structure, for by this means man would expose his self-righteousness, work out his own goodness in the offering of the sacrifice. God demanded of man an altar of *earth* (or unhewn stones). It was upon the *earth* that the Cross was erected, and where the Lord Jesus, the Supreme Sacrifice, died.[54]

The priest's body had to be covered when he ministered there (Exodus 28:3). No place was given to the flesh! God does not want *man's* righteousness, but that righteousness which is of the *Lord Jesus Christ,* working in each and everyone who believes. Man cannot provide his own salvation. It has already been accomplished by God; all one need do now is rest in the finished work of Calvary.

---

[54] At the time Christ was crucified, history tells us that there were about 30,000 Jews who had already been crucified!

The altar was to be ***hollow*** *with boards*. There is no "top or bottom" to God's love for the world which was manifested in His great sacrifice. The heights of it cannot be reached, neither can the depths of it be explored! From the physical standpoint the finite mind can comprehend it, only in a very limited capacity. Even the Holy Spirit, through the human writers of the gospel story, did not dwell upon the *physical* sufferings of Christ. He did not wish to encourage any morbid contemplation on the "body" pain of the Cross. Christ's sufferings were far deeper!

When the Lord was crucified, the powers of Hell, Earth, and Heaven were arrayed against Him. Not only did He experience bodily torture, but an anguish within which cannot be fathomed by the human heart or brain. This prophecy is recorded by Isaiah: *"And he* [Jesus] *made his grave with the wicked, and with the rich in his death* [Hebrew rendering is ***deaths***] ..." (Isaiah 53:9). His physical life on earth terminated, but three hours before this, His soul had "died." In order to understand this more clearly, we refer to God's warning in the Garden of Eden. God said to Adam that in the day he would partake of the forbidden *"fruit,"* "dying [spiritually] *thou shalt die* [physically]" (Genesis 2:17, Hebrew text). We understand from the events which followed their transgression that Adam and Eve did not "die" the very day they disobeyed their Maker, therefore this was not the physical, but the spiritual death which God implied. The moment they ate of the forbidden fruit they "died," or were cut off from God, and *dying* thus, they eventually *died* physically. The curse of the Law was upon them, and through them, upon all mankind (Romans 5:12, 18). But Christ has redeemed us from this curse since He was made a curse for us on Calvary (Galatians 3:13).

Christ ("the Last Adam") taking the place of the sinner, had to fulfill the *two **deaths*** of Genesis 2:17. He died "inwardly" (spiritually) and He died "outwardly" (physically). The physical suffering, horribly painful as it was, did not begin to compare with a deeper agony. He poured out His *soul* unto death as an offering for sin (Isaiah 53:10,12). The pain of His bones, loins, throat, etc. recorded in the Psalms can also reverently be transferred to the inward mental feelings and untold agonies of spirit which our blessed Lord endured as He hung upon Calvary's "tree."

It is remarkable to note in Scripture that most every time Christ spoke to God He called Him by the name "Father" except when He was dying as man's substitute. Then He cried: "*My God, my God*, why hast thou forsaken me?" He put Himself in the place of the sinner when He cried, not to the *Father* this time but to His *God*! Forsaken, abandoned, separated from all holiness, purity and goodness; how awful it must have been for the Holy One of Israel! He who had never sinned became as the sinner ("made sin") and received the sinner's penalty. He tasted of spiritual death (separation from God). This was the reason for the three-hour period of darkness on Nisan 14, from 12 noon to three o'clock. The Light of the World was extinguished as God withdrew Himself from the presence of sin. Our Christ was separated from God that we might never have to be separated from Him. He was made sin that we might become righteous. He died that we might live. Halleluia!

The Altar was to be "hollow" and yet this same "hollow" was to be made "with boards." The acacia wood, not covered by copper as was the outside, was to surround the recess, the place into which earth or unhewn stones was poured. The acacia tree grew in the earth and now because of "death" (that is, "chopped down") was covered by the earth. He who created the earth, grew in it, and sinking deep into *the heart of the earth* through death (Matthew 12:40), was covered over by it.

Into the hollow of the Altar the Israelites poured the sand, the earth, or unhewn stones upon which they could then place the wood and the sacrifice which the priests would offer to God. The fire was kindled miraculously (Leviticus 9:24), and never went out while the Tabernacle was stationary (Leviticus 6:9). They would use the flesh-hooks, the firepans and the shovels to help in this offering. When they would move to another location at the direction of the Lord through the pillar of cloud and fire, the earth and ashes of the Altar were left behind. This showed that their sins had been dealt with, left behind them, and remembered against them no more!

The Lord commanded that there was to be a whole burnt offering given to Him in the morning and another of the same kind given in the afternoon between the two evenings (at even) (Exodus 29:38-42). The Lord Jesus fulfilled this to the very letter, for He was both the whole burnt offering in the morning (at 9 a.m. He was nailed to the Altar of Calvary), and He was the whole burnt offering of the evening (at 3 p.m. He died).

The *north side* was the place of judgment where the sacrifices were killed by the Altar and their blood was sprinkled (Leviticus 4:7, cf. Leviticus 1:11). The Tribe of Dan was located on the *north* outside the Fence of the Tabernacle Court (Numbers 2:25). *Dan* means "judge" or "judging." The prophecy concerning him was that he would "judge his people as one of the tribes of Israel" (Genesis 49:16). God is Judge who sits in the *north* (Heaven is *north* from the earth). Samson was a judge in Israel: *"The Spirit of the Lord came upon him* [Samson] *and moved him at times in the camp of **Dan**"* (Judges 13:25), *i.e.*, the Spirit of the Lord came upon him and he *judged* Israel. Zion on the *north* (Psalm 48:2)–Jerusalem is implied (see Matthew 5:35). In Psalm 75:6-7 East, West, and South[55] are mentioned but when it comes to the *northern* direction, these words are used: "God is *Judge*" (see Appendix VII: *The Open Place in the North*).

This is remarkably fulfilled in Christ on Golgotha! Those who passed by Him on a highway that ran to the *north* out of Jerusalem and who railed on Him (Matthew 27:39-40) would not have spoken to Him in this way had the Cross been between Him and the road hiding Him from their view. With this arrangement Christ poured out His blood on the *north side* of the Cross, His Copper Altar! The Cross is typified in the heave offering and the wave offering (see Exodus 29:27). Observe that the heave offering is elevated and lowered in a vertical line and the wave offering swung back and forth in a horizontal line. The two lines passing over each other make the form of the ***cross***!

The beautiful Wilderness Tabernacle with its golden walls, its golden furniture and its magnificent blue, purple, scarlet, and white fine twined linen, was covered with blood (Hebrews 9:19-22)! There was blood upon the horns of the Altar of Incense (Exodus 30:10), the Altar of Sacrifice (Leviticus 4:7; 16:19), upon all the vessels of the Sanctuary (Hebrews 9:21) and the furniture in the Tabernacle (Leviticus 16:14-15). There was blood upon the High Priest and upon the priests who ministered there, the sons of Aaron (Exodus 29:20). The balance of the blood was poured on the ground by the Copper Altar (Leviticus

---

[55]South also means "desert" indicating earth as being south and heaven as being north.

4:7), foretelling that the earth would share in the final redemption (Romans 8:19-23). Christ's blood was poured on the ground when His life was laid down.

The "blood" is everywhere in the Word of God. It is the lifeline, the power of the gospel. This substance is the conveyor or vehicle of life. Giving up or surrender of life, the blood, is the underlying principle of atonement. We read about it from the first of the Word of God to the very last page of the Book of Revelation: The blood makes an atonement for the soul!

The Brazen Altar

(The following article, which I wrote, appeared in *The Pentecostal Evangel*, Springfield, Missouri, Gospel Publishing House, March 25, 1966.)

The first object seen by the worshiper upon entering the court of the ancient Tabernacle in the wilderness was an unpretentious and ghastly looking altar made of shittim wood (acacia), covered with brass (copper) and sprinkled with blood. It was made according to the directions God gave to Moses on Mount Sinai and placed at the door of the Tabernacle, where the sacrifices were repeated every morning and evening.

Upon each of the four corners of this foursquare vessel was a projection, called a horn, pointing upward and outward, to which the sacrifices were bound. This Altar was the largest and tallest article of furniture in all the Tabernacle structure. But it was only three cubits high (4½ feet) and rested on the ground, so that it was easily accessible to all.

The Hebrew word for altar is *mizbeah*, meaning "slaughter place." And truly it was a symbol of suffering, bloodshed and death. The only approach to a holy God in His Tabernacle was by way of this object of wood and copper.

The Altar would have been of no avail without the offerings which were presented to God upon it. No Israelite could approach it without the sacrifices and the blood. *"Without shedding of blood is no remission."* The best, cleanest and finest of the Israelites' bullocks, sheep, goats, and fowl were brought according to the Law of the Lord. These were brought to the horns, slain and burned upon the Altar. What do we see in all this? What is the meaning which God was trying to convey to the children of Israel? What significance does it have for us today? Here we see God's goodness and severity, His love and wrath, His righteousness and peace. It is here that the heart of man and the heart of God are revealed, and atonement for sin is made. At this Altar the innocent bore the judgment of the guilty, and God was reconciled with the sinner who killed and shed the blood of the sacrifice. This "slaughter place" pictures the Cross of Calvary, a vessel on earth which is the only way of entrance into God's presence. It depicts the Cross which is easily accessible to the world but towers over all the wrecks of time. It was the Cross upon which the Prince of Glory died, where He was bound with the cords of love for lost humanity. This brazen Altar foreshadows the Cross, universal in its mercy as well as its judgment-the horns pointing God-ward and man-ward, inviting "whosoever will" to come!

The sacrifices brought to that Altar–the innocent doves and pigeons with their heads wrung off, their feathers plucked from their bodies, their blood wrung at the side of the Altar; the bullocks cut to pieces and burned; the lambs and goats sacrificed–all of these tell of the Lord Jesus Christ. He is the innocent Dove of the heavens who came to earth, whose head was crowned with thorns whose beard was plucked from His cheeks. He is the Ox (bullock) of God who was cut to pieces (bruised) by the whip of the Roman soldiers, whose blood was shed, who was burned with the fire of God's judgment upon Him for the sins of the entire world. He is the Lamb of God, whose heart melted within Him like wax, who opened not His mouth in His own defense, who was led to the slaughter, and whose visage was marred more than any other man's.

Day by day, year by year, the offerings were continually being made upon the Altar of the Wilderness Tabernacle. These sacrifices continued in Solomon's Temple until the Great Sacrifice upon the "brazen altar" of Calvary. From the Cross on Golgotha we hear the words from the lips of our Lord Jesus Christ" *"It is finished!"* The types, the offerings of the Old Covenant were now done away, fulfilled in the Messiah of Israel and the Saviour of the world.

Some years ago a Jewish rabbi said in a radio address:

"Speaking as a Jew, I ask you to believe me when I say that I know what the Cross has meant to believers through the centuries. I know that the simple and the learned, the grieving and the rejoicing, the toiling and the driven, behold in the Cross of Christ the symbol of a love that is sacrificial, the sign of a hope that is redeeming, the token of an inner peace, which the world could neither give nor take away. But I want you to know also that to a Jew the Cross of Christ represents no such sacrificial love, no such redeeming hope, no such inner token of peace. To the Jew, the Cross is a symbol of persecution, opposition, discrimination, of pyre and gibbet. It is by the sign of the Cross that hundreds of Jewish communities were annihilated, thousands of Jews slaughtered, millions of Jews robbed of happiness, by those who failed to grasp the significance for Christians of that drama of which the Lenten season is the monitor and Easter Day the culmination"!

In the days of the early apostolic Church (composed of Jewish believers), there was a Jew named Saul who persecuted and put to death many who had embraced the Cross of Christ. He hated that "ugly tree" and thought of it with contempt. He looked upon it as a symbol of shame, defeat, and a curse; for it was written in the Law: *"Cursed is everyone that hangeth on a tree"* (Galatians 3:13). But something happened to Saul when the Lord appeared to him on the road to Damascus. His heart, as well as his mind, was changed. Paul's eyes were opened to behold the true significance of the Wilderness Tabernacle's Brazen Altar. His mind was illuminated to understand the meaning of the Cross. He declared not long afterwards: *"God forbid that I should glory, save in the **cross** of our Lord Jesus Christ."*

What the Jewish people do not know is that in their own OT are all the prophecies of the Cross they *hate*. We see it in the Book of Genesis immediately after sin comes into the Garden of Eden. God made coats of skin for Adam and his mate. An innocent victim was slain and its blood shed, to provide a covering for those who had disobeyed God's Law.

We see the Cross in the first promise of a Redeemer: *"I will put enmity between thee and the woman, and between thy seed and her seed; it shall bruise thy head, and thou shalt bruise his heel."* The seed of the woman, Christ, was indeed bruised by the serpent when He was lifted to the cross. But our Lord also dealt a death blow to sin, crushing the head of the serpent.

The Cross is pictured in the law of Moses and the history of the Jews. When Israel sinned in their wilderness journey to the promised land, God allowed fiery serpents to poison them. The remedy for their healing was a brazen serpent on a pole, upon which they looked in obedience to the command of God. The serpent, the brass, and the pole were symbols of sin, judgment, and the Cross. *"As Moses lifted up the serpent in the wilderness, even so must the Son of man be lifted up."*

We see the Cross pictured in the Tabernacle, too. The colors and materials of the curtains and coverings show forth the sacrificial death of the Messiah. In the pattern given to Moses on Matthew Sinai there was a peculiar arrangement of the furniture. It formed a Cross! When God led the Children of Israel to move the sanctuary to another place, there were specific directions as to how they were to march. It was in a *cross* formation!

The story of Abraham and Isaac reveals a coming Saviour. For Abraham declared in faith, "God will provide himself a lamb!" After Isaac had carried wood upon his back up the mountainside, he lay down upon it, on an altar on Matthew Moriah. In the lamb for Israel's Passover, and in the sprinkling of the blood on the upper doorposts and sideposts, we see Christ crucified. At the greatest council ever held on earth (Luke 9:28-31), the conversation concerned this most important subject. Moses, Elijah, and the Christ on the Mount of Transfiguration talked about Christ's death "which He should accomplish at Jerusalem."

This was that in which all Heaven was interested. This is the central theme of the Bible. It begins in Genesis and continues through Revelation. In that Book we read John's account of a scene in glory: He sees a Lamb as it had been *slain*! Yes, it is only at the Cross, through the finished work of the crucified (and risen) Christ, that both Jew and Gentile can be saved.

Let us see the deep significance and spiritual application of the Brazen Altar. Let us view the scene at Golgotha afresh. Oh, let our hearts be warmed by the message of the Cross until our hearts are filled with praise to God and our all is yielded to Him as a living sacrifice.

Love so amazing, so divine,
Demands my soul, my life, my all.

—End of Article

THE CROSS IN THE TABERNACLE

Heave offering and wave offering in Exodus 29:27. Heave offering elevated and lowered in a vertical line. Wave offering swung back and forth in a horizontal line. The two lines passing over each other make the form of the cross!

According to Josephus, the lambs were roasted for Passover on a cross-shaped pole.

Christ was to be lifted up as a serpent on a *pole*. The word for "pole" is used for *sign, standard, mark, flag, banner* or *cross* (OT *nace*–pole).

According to Josephus, the *standards* or *banners* of the Israelites hung on a cross-shaped stand.

The last letter of the Hebrew Alphabet is *Tav* meaning *sign* or *mark*, and its ancient pictograph form was a cross. Of course we know this is combined with the first letter of the Hebrew alphabet as one of the names of our Lord Jesus.

The Greek word for cross is *stauros* ($\sigma\tau\alpha\acute{\nu}\rho o\varsigma$), to *set* upright a pole, a stake or a cross, especially as an instrument of capital punishment, is taken from the word -stao ($\sigma\tau\acute{\alpha}\omega$)–"to stand."

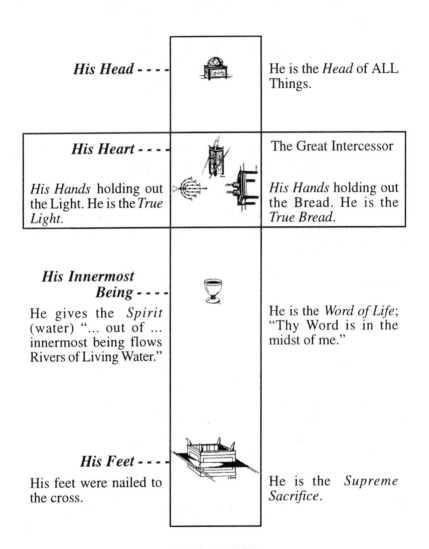

His Head - - - -		He is the *Head* of ALL Things.
His Heart - - - - *His Hands* holding out the Light. He is the *True Light*.		The Great Intercessor *His Hands* holding out the Bread. He is the *True Bread*.
His Innermost Being - - - - He gives the *Spirit* (water) "... out of ... innermost being flows Rivers of Living Water."		He is the *Word of Life*; "Thy Word is in the midst of me."
His Feet - - - - His feet were nailed to the cross.		He is the *Supreme Sacrifice*.

**THE CROSS
IN THE TABERNACLE FURNITURE**

THE CROSS

Blest they who seek,
While in their youth,
With spirit meek,
The way of truth,
To them the sacred Scriptures now display Christ as the only true and living way. His precious blood on Calvary was given To make them heirs of endless bliss in heaven; And e'en on earth the child of God can trace The glorious blessings of his Saviour's grace.
For them He bore
His Father's frown;
For them He wore
The thorny crown;
Nailed to the cross,
Endured its pain,
That His life's loss
Might be their gain.
Then haste to choose
That better part,
Nor dare refuse
The Lord thy heart,
Lest He declare,
"I know you not."
And deep despair
Should be your lot.
Now look to Jesus, who on Calvary died,
And trust in Him alone who there was crucified.

–Author Unknown

The Five Principle Offerings of the Tabernacle Services
(first half)

	The Offering	References	What the Offering could include	God's Part on Court Altar	Priest's Portion
Sweet Savour - Voluntary	**Burnt Offering**	Leviticus 1:1-17 Leviticus 6:8-13 Ephesians 5:1, 2 Hebrews 10:7 Romans 12:1, 2	Bullocks, goats, sheep, rams, lambs, turtle-doves, young pigeons, male only.	All burned.	Skin.
	Meal Offering	Leviticus 2:1-16 Leviticus 6:14-23 Hebrews 7:26 Hebrews 13:15	Fine flour, frank-incense, oil, salt, green ears of grain.	A handful, all frank-incense, part of oil, all priest offering.	All remainder.
	Peace Offering	Leviticus 3:1-17 Leviticus 7:11-34 Romans 5:1 Colossians 1:20	Male and female of herd and flock, bullocks, lambs, goats.	All the fat.	Heave-shoulder and wave-breast.
				The remainder was the offerer's.	
Non-Sweet Savour - Mandatory	**Sin-Offering**	Leviticus 4:1-5:13 Leviticus 6:24-30 2 Corinthians 5:21	Male and female of herd and flock, or turtle-doves, young pigeons, one-tenth deal of fine flour.	All the fat on Court Altar and blood poured at bottom of Altar.	Blood applied to horns of Court Altar– bullock burned outside Camp.
	Trespass Offering	Leviticus 5:13-6:7 Leviticus 7:1-10 Colossians 3:13, 14 1 Peter 2:24		(On Day of Atonement, the blood of the Sin-Offering was applied to horns of Altar of Incense and carried into Holy of Holies; see Leviticus 16.)	

The Five Principle Offerings of the Tabernacle Services
(second half)

Symbolism	Messiah in the Five Offerings
Offerer presents his life to Jehovah. *Consecration*	Messiah is the Ox (*bullock*) pulling us out of sin. He is the *Lamb* bearing away our sin. He is the *Dove* of Heaven who makes us as if innocent of sin. He presented Himself to the Father, to do His will.
Offerer presents his life for service to Jehovah in thankfulness. *Service*	Messiah is the *Fine Flour*–gives us His righteousness. He gives us the *Oil* and *Frankincense* (the Holy Spirit) for our service. He is the righteous Servant of Jehovah.
Offerer in fellowship and communion with Jehovah. *Fellowship*	Messiah is *Peace* with God (reconciliation). He is the bond of fellowship between God and man.
Offerer is forgiven as a sinner. *Redemption* (for the sinner)	Messiah is made *Sin* for us; He is our atonement. He atoned for the GUILT of sin.
Offerer is forgiven for the sins he has committed. *Redemption* (for the sin)	Messiah paid the penalty of sin; He forgives our *Trespasses*. He atoned for the DAMAGE of sin.

Test Questions

1. What materials were used for the Altar of Sacrifice and what is the significance of each?
2. What was the measurement of this Altar?
3. What do the measurements of this Altar tell us which make it distinct from all other articles of furniture of the Tabernacle?
4. What does the Altar of Sacrifice symbolize? Give a similar outstanding symbol, made of the same material as this Altar, to which Christ referred in a prophecy of His own death. Give Old and NT references.
5. What do the four horns on the Altar represent? What significance are the cords tied to these horns?
6. What does the metal on the wood tell us?
7. How many instruments were there for service at the Altar and what did they represent?
8. What was prophesied in the commandment that the ashes of the sacrifice were to be carried to a clean place outside the Camp of Israel? Give the reference that tells of the fulfillment.
9. Describe the Grate and Network for the Altar. Explain the "compass" and its literal meaning.
10. Compare the measurements of the Mercy Seat and the Altar Grate. Explain the significance.
11. (a) Why was the Altar "hollow with boards" at God's commandment? Give spiritual significance. (b) What are the two "deaths" of Christ? Give Scripture reference where this is foretold.
12. (a) On what side of the Altar were the sacrifices slain? (b) Compare with Scripture showing this side of the Altar as the place of judgment. (c) Name the Five Great Offerings.
13. Draw from memory a diagram which shows the cross formation in the Tabernacle furniture.
14. By the blood shed at the Sacrifice Altar what was God teaching the Children of Israel?
15. What truth is outstanding to you in this section?

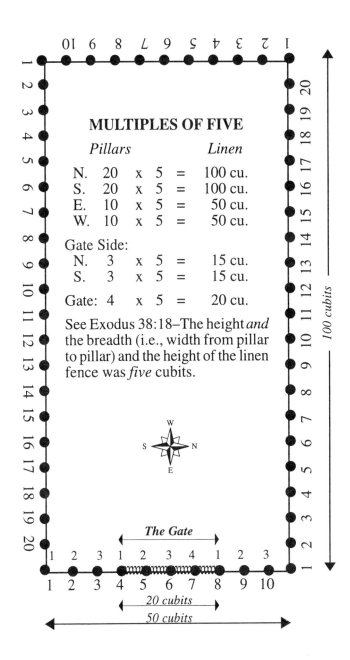

SIXTY PILLARS OF THE COURT
Exodus 27:9-18

The Court Fence

Verse Nine

> *"And thou shalt make the court of the tabernacle: for the south side southward there shall be hangings for the court of fine twined linen of an hundred cubits long for one side:"*

The "hangings" of the Court was a curtain which enclosed the dwelling place of God, the camp of Israel (man's dwelling) on the outside and the Tabernacle (God's dwelling) on the inside of it. This shows the Linen Fence as a "go-between" for the children of Israel, prophesying of the Lord Jesus Christ who is the Mediator between God and man.

The court curtain was also a protection for the Holy Sanctuary in the desert. It kept the Sacred Building and the Holiness of God from intrusion, from unlawful approach. Although a "mediator," the linen enclosure was also a "separator," a barrier to the tribes of Israel encamped around it. God, who Himself is righteous, pure and holy, demands purity and righteousness on the part of man for him to be able to stand before Holiness. But the natural man does not meet these requirements, therefore man is shut out from the presence of God (Exodus 19:21-24).

The "hangings" of fine twined linen tell of the righteous humanity of the Lord Jesus Christ. No other one was righteous but Christ as He walked among men. He is the righteousness of God. He lived such a perfect life that no man could attain to it. It was a barrier, shutting man out from God's presence even as the linen fence of the Court.

This wall of linen was not only a mediator, protector, and a barrier, closing God in and shutting man out, but it was also a fine-line marker. It distinguished the tents of Israel from the Sacred Tent of Jehovah. Here, beyond this line, on the inside was Holiness, on the other side was worldliness. Christ lived in this "marking line." He was separated from the world to the Holiness of God, and those that are in Christ Jesus are to walk the same: the world on the outside, while they are closed in with God. The Christian is to be clothed with the righteousness of the Lord and to walk in Him. Though he is in the present world, he is to be separated and different from the world. The Lord commands this:

"... *come out from among them, and **be ye separate**, saith the Lord, and touch not the unclean thing; and I will receive you, And will be a Father unto you, and ye shall be my sons and daughters, saith the Lord Almighty"* (2 Corinthians 6:17-18).

The believer in Christ is expected to be distinguished, to be different from all those on the world's side of the "line" that when he is looked upon by them, his very appearance will tell them that he belongs to a Holy God.

Verse Ten

"And the twenty pillars thereof and their twenty sockets shall be of brass [copper] ... ."

The ancient Hebrew language did not have punctuation marks. The construction of this verse according to the Hebrew text is: "The pillars thereof shall be twenty, their sockets twenty, of copper."

The sockets were to be of brass (copper), but it was not plain as to what material God wanted the twenty pillars to be (cf. Exodus 38:10, 11, 17, 19). Also notice that when it was recorded for what the (brass) copper was to be used, there was *no mention of the pillars.* This is found in Exodus 38:29, 31. Brass (copper) was to be used for the Altar, sockets, pins, etc. The pillars represent the Church, unknown to the world, standing on copper sockets. The copper, symbolic of judgment for sin, is not above or around these pillars; judgment is past. The Church is judged already in Christ and *standing* in the desert upon this foundation because God met the sin question for her through Christ on the Cross.

[verse ten continued] *" ... the hooks of the pillars and their fillets shall be of silver."*

The hooks of silver held the fillets of silver. The fillets united each pillar to another. The Church of Jesus Christ throughout the world is joined with the silver of redemption.

Verse Eleven

"And likewise for the north side in length there shall be hangings of an hundred cubits long, and his twenty pillars and their twenty sockets of brass; the hooks of the pillars and their fillets of silver."

The pillars each stood in a copper socket, were *joined* by *silver*, and held up the fine linen fence by silver hooks. They were not seen on the outside, but the linen they upheld was displayed to all those in the tents of Israel surrounding the Court. The Church does not display herself, but the righteousness of Christ, to the world. She walks in "white" before men, "perfecting *holiness* in the fear of God" (2 Corinthians 7:1).

Verse Twelve

> *"And for the breadth of the court on the west side shall be hangings of fifty cubits: their pillars ten, and their sockets ten."*

The width of the Tabernacle court was 50 cubits, the length 100 cubits, making it a rectangle, two perfect 50x50 squares.

Verse Thirteen

> *"And the breadth of the court on the east side eastward shall be fifty cubits."*

Pentecost and the Year of Jubilee are emphasized in the measurement of *50* cubits.

Verses Fourteen and Fifteen

> *"The hangings of one side of the gate shall be fifteen cubits: their pillars three, and their sockets three. And on the other side shall be hangings fifteen cubits: their pillars three, and their sockets three."*

Each side of the Gate measured 15 cubits. There were three spans of five cubits (between the pillars); and the height and breadth were to be the same measure. The fine linen (without the colors) was to measure (in cubits) 30 on the east, 100 on the south, 50 on the west, and 100 on the north amounting to *280* cubits for the *white* Fence, minus the Gate (with the colors). It is interesting to note that in Physiology the various periods of gestation are commonly a multiple of *7*, either of days or weeks. With the human species it is (9 months) *280* days, or 40x7. The pure white curtain which surrounded the Court (Earth), a symbol of God's righteousness, speaks of Christ who was the Child *born* of a woman, made under the Law. His righteous *humanity* is "pictured" in the *280* cubits of *'fine twined linen'*.

Verse Sixteen

> *"And for the gate of the court shall be an hanging of twenty cubits, of blue, and purple, and scarlet, and fine twined linen, wrought with needlework: and their pillars shall be four, and their sockets four."*

The linen fence was not only a mediator, protector, barrier, separator, and a marker, but it also provided a way of access to the Court. The Lord has not shut us out completely from His presence. That He demands holiness is true; that He demands righteousness on the part of man in order to come to Him, is certain, but He has provided an entrance into the Throne Room, into the Holy of Holies. This provision of God is found at the east side of the Fence, the Gate. Christ was not only man's barrier *from* God by His perfect life, but He was also the way *to* God, the Gate of access to His Holiness, by His sacrifice on Calvary.

In God's directions concerning the three entrances of the entire Tabernacle structure, He begins with the Veil on the inside of the sacred building. Man begins from the outside, the Gate. This Gate was to be hung on four pillars. "Four" tells of the Universal Christ; He is the Gate who "hung" upon Golgotha that "whosoever" in the four corners of the earth could come to God by *way* of Him.

There was only one Gate to the Court which surrounded the Holy Tent. It was for each and every one of the people of God, as they were represented by their priests, the Levites. The only means of access whereby a visitor could approach the Tabernacle was from the East, from the direction of the rising sun, where the tribe of Judah was. They could not come in any other way. There is only one way of salvation for all mankind. Jesus is the Way. No man can come to the Father except by Him (John 14:6). He is the Son (Sun) in the East who came from the Tribe of Judah.

This entrance was wide, for "whosoever" and low, easy access. (The Door is the same Christ manifested in a different capacity.) It was made as a curtain. Why was it a curtain? We do not find a curtain difficult to enter. It is not like a wooden door which requires a little effort, a little strength to push open. All one must do with a curtain in order to enter in is to lift it aside very easily. And so it is with the salvation which the Lord has provided. The strong or the weak, the young or the old can come in through the "curtain." The Lord has made it so that even a little child can understand the way to God.

Now then, a curtain is lifted *silently*. It is thus with the Divine transaction in a human heart. The results or reaction of the born-again experience might become "noisy" with different persons as to their individual characteristics of expression when coming in contact with God, but the transaction itself takes place *silently* in the heart.

Then, as the priest would lift the curtain and come in, he would be completely inside the court. He would come in through the side of this "hanging" and it would fall behind him in a sharp, dividing line. He was not halfway inside and halfway outside the Gate, as it would be in the case of a wooden doorway, but he was completely inside the court of salvation surrounded by the white linen walls. Thus it is with us when we come to God. We enter through the "riven side" of the "Hanging," the Lord Jesus Christ. We are not halfway in the world and halfway in Christ. We are complete. When we come to Him and receive Him, we are enclosed by Him. All the way around us is the fine twined linen wall–His righteousness.

In the days of the Israelites they could come in through the Gate only by their representative priests. But now we come in through our precious Lord Jesus. The Gate was made of needlework. This was embroidery on one side of the curtain. In order to see these beautiful colors and design clearly a person had to come inside. It is so in salvation. As an individual stands on the outside, Christ is not beheld in His beauty and His loveliness, but as he steps in through the way of salvation he can then see Him as represented in the beautiful colors designed with needlework on the inside of the curtain entrance.

The Gate, Door and Veil

In the three entrances of the Tabernacle we see Jesus, the Way (Gate), the Truth (Door), and the Life (Veil). The number "three" represents God, the Trinity. God's fullness is summed up in Christ as shown in these three doorways. *"For in him dwelleth all the fullness of the Godhead bodily"* (Colossians 2:9). Only through Him can we approach the fullness of spiritual life.

The gate was 20x5 cubits equaling 100 (see Exodus 27:18 for height of the Court Fence). Here is *one hundred percent salvation* the Lord has purchased for all who will come to Him. It was low and wide, extending (as it were) its arms to "whosoever." Breadth or width indicates great liberty of access. The door was 10x10 cubits equaling 100 also (Exodus 26:16 tells that the *height* of the Boards was also the *height* of the Veil). The Lord has *one hundred percent fellowship* for His own. The curtain was, however, higher and narrower than the Gate. Height means a greater, more enlarged spiritual experience. There is a narrower walk with God, an enlarged and higher plane of living. It is through the sanctifying of the Spirit of God for fellowship and service with Him.

Some Christians stop after entering the Gate of salvation. They live selfishly, keeping silent concerning their salvation, becoming stagnant by not allowing the "rivers of living water" to flow through them to others. Their lives are not fruitful; they do not grow. They remain unhealthy babies in the Kingdom of God. There is no burden for the lost; there is no fire of holy zeal, no testimony, no light for sinking souls. They have only entered the Court, and have failed to explore further into the depths of divine grace!

After entering the Holy Place through the Door, the priests would minister to the Lord at the Golden Lampstand, the Altar of Incense, and the Table of Shewbread. They would partake of and participate in these typical objects showing their close relationship with their God on behalf of the people. Those who enter into the Holy Place with God receive more light, food, and worship. Here the Christian grows in the knowledge of the Messiah for He is "the Light of the world." He is "the Bread which came down from heaven." He is the Great Intercessor. Here one can partake of the very life of God and continue to grow into the stature of the Messiah, which is the will of God concerning each of His own.

Next, the priests would approach the Veil which was the entrance to the Holy of Holies. It was also 10x10 cubits as was the Door, but it was more beautiful. The design of the cherubim was added to it. In Scripture, the cherubim, were guardians of God's Holiness, the Executors of His Righteousness. The Gate and the Door, were made of needlework which was embroidery of color and design on only one side of the material. The Veil was made of "cunning work" which indicates that the design and colors were woven through and through the material so that it was seen on both sides. 10 multiplied by 10 equals 100. God offers *one hundred percent of **His glorious Holy Presence*** to those who desire it, for He has purchased it for them with His own precious blood! There is a more beautiful walk with God: It is ***the way of Holiness***. Without Holiness, no man shall see (understand and know) God.

Through the Veil in the Holy of Holies was the Ark of the Covenant upon which were the golden cherubim with their wings touching and between these cherubim was the Shekinah or Divine Presence. Here in the Holy of Holies, the High Priest ministered directly with God by placing the blood of the sacrifice upon the Mercy Seat in behalf of the Children of Israel for their sins.

Beyond the Court, beyond the Holy Place, there is a deeper walk with God. In the days of Christ there were three classes of people who followed Him: First, the *crowds* (multitudes) who thronged around Him. These had entered the Court to see the miracles, the loaves and the fishes. He rebuked them because they labored for the *"meat which perisheth,"* they were attracted by that which their five natural senses could understand. They were interested in material blessings, that which they could receive to gratify the flesh. They followed Him not because they loved Christ for Himself, but for what He could give them.

Then there were those who followed on past the Court to enter the Holy Place, the Room of fellowship and service. These were *disciples* (apostles) who ministered to Him, with Him, and for Him. They partook of all He provided and revealed concerning Himself. They were actively engaged in His service.

Next, there were the three disciples of the *"inner circle,"* Peter, James and John, who entered the Holy of Holies. They beheld Him transfigured on the Mount. They saw the Shekinah!

John had an experience on the Island of Patmos in which he saw the Lord in His coming majesty, holiness, and justice. He dwelt with God *between the cherubim*! This is our inheritance in Christ, if we will only believe it. It is where the hidden, secret things of God are revealed, where we meet Him face to face!

Under the First Covenant, the Israelites were restricted concerning the Temple, for they were only allowed through the Gate (the first entrance), into the Court. They were shut off from the Holy Place by the curtain called "The Door." Only the priests, the sons of Aaron, were allowed through this entrance. But even the priests were shut off from the Holiest Place by the Veil. One man (beside Moses), the High Priest, was allowed through the Veil into the Holy of Holies once a year, and at that time he could not enter without blood!

But these restrictions were changed–done away with in Christ who fulfilled the Old Covenant and established the New.

> *"Jesus, when he had cried again with a loud voice, yielded up the ghost* [spirit]. *And, behold,* **the veil** *of the temple was rent in twain from the top to the bottom; and the earth did quake, and the rocks rent"* (Matthew 27:50-51).

When Christ died at three in the afternoon it was the time of the evening sacrifice in the Temple. The priests were in the Holy Place in front of the Veil engaged in their duties when this happened. The Veil was parted and they could now see into the secret of the Holy of Holies. They could enter in!

Man did not tear the Veil. According to Josephus, the great Jewish historian, this Curtain was four inches thick and 30 feet square (twice the size of the Veil in the Tabernacle), higher than a man could reach and stronger than a man could tear apart. It was said (by this same Josephus) that a team of oxen tied to either side of it and pulling in opposite directions could not tear the Veil apart! Nothing else in the building was shaken or marred in any way. The Curtain did not fall, for the gold hooks above (on the pillars), held it. Divinity rent the Veil yet Divinity also held up the Veil. It was the will of God to bruise Him (Isaiah 53:10). Christ said of God, the Father: *"Thou hast brought my soul to the dust of death"* (Psalm 22:15). Yet God also gave Christ power to be raised again, Hallelujah! The Veil in Herod's Temple was torn in the middle in two equal pieces still hanging from the gold hooks. It was rent from the top down to the bottom, not jerked apart by some one from below. It was torn by an invisible hand from *above*! From Heaven God came down; from the "heights" God ripped the Veil to the "depths." Now the Holy of Holies is opened, not only to the High Priest, but to everyone who has come to Christ and is cleansed. God, the Father is no longer shut off from us. Jew and Gentile who have come to the Lord Jesus are no longer barred from God, but can now come past the door, past the Veil into the Holiest Place and dwell between the cherubim with God!

> *"Having therefore, brethren, boldness to enter into the holiest by the blood of Jesus, By a new and living way, which he hath consecrated for us, through the **veil**, that is to say, his flesh; And having an high priest over the house of God; Let us draw near with a true heart in full assurance of faith, having our hearts sprinkled from an evil conscience, and our bodies washed with pure water"* (Hebrews 10: 19-22).

Verse Seventeen

> *"All the pillars round about the court shall be filleted with silver; their hooks shall be of silver, and their sockets of brass [copper]."*

The pillars of the Court were connected together with silver rods. "Filleted," in the Hebrew text, is "joined" or "to set (in) love." The silver half shekel from which these fillets were formed is a symbol of redemption through the blood of the Lamb. The Church is united together in the love of God expressed through Christ who provided salvation by His own blood.

Not only were the rods to be of silver, but the hooks and capitals also (Exodus 38:27, 28). These chapiters or capitals show forth the beauty of redemption in each child of God (1 Peter 3:3, 4). We notice that the hooks, fillets, and sockets were not measured, nor the height of the pillars. Redemption is not measured, neither is God's judgment for sin given an estimate, and there is no limit to the heights man can attain as he is adorned with the loveliness of Christ!

Notice that silver was above the fence and copper below. Redemption from above is supplied because of God's judgment for sin on earth below. "God's justice rests upon the ground where man walks; but its head is crowned with the silver of redemption."

Verse Eighteen

> *"The length of the court shall be an hundred cubits, and the breadth fifty **every where**, and the height five cubits of fine twined linen, and their sockets of brass."*

The original text is rendered "fifty by fifty" everywhere. God emphasizes Pentecostal significance in the very beginning of the Tabernacle. It was after the Children of Israel left Egypt (50 days later) that the plan for the Sacred Building was given to Moses on Matthew Sinai. (The Greek word for "fiftieth" is "Pentecost.") "Fifty" is the prominent number everywhere in the Court measurements of the ancient Sanctuary in the desert. It prophesies of the infilling of the Holy Spirit in the Holy One of Israel (of whom the Tabernacle is a type) as also in believers who are Tabernacles of God in this wilderness world. Fifty days after Christ was resurrected from the dead "when the Day of Pentecost was fully come (the Fiftieth Day had arrived)," the Holy Spirit who desires to "dwell within" His redeemed people, came from Heaven even as Christ promised. *"And they were all filled with the Holy Ghost and began to speak with other tongues as the Spirit gave them utterance"* (Acts 2:4).

In order to make the Court "fifty by fifty" everywhere (Exodus 27:18–Hebrew text) as God had commanded, the length of 100 cubits would have to have been halved. This Court was a perfect rectangle, 100x50 cubits. Halving it would have made it into two perfect 50x50 squares. In the center of one–the Altar of Copper (a symbol of the Cross). This shows that God does all things consistently and in order; placing the Altar to the side or beyond the center would have shown imbalance to the full design. The same is true of the second 50x50 square. In its center–the Ark of the Covenant, representing God's power and glorious presence.

In redemption there are two separate and distinct experiences. One centers around the Cross and has to do with salvation from sin. The other centers around the Presence of God and has to do with service and witness for Christ. In the first we are dead to sin and in the second we are alive unto God. In the first we meet with God and in the second God meets with us. The first is for the sinner, the second is for the saint. Salvation from sin is experienced when we enter through the Gate of the Court and meet God at the Cross. God is *with* us. Witnessing and working for God occurs when God meets with us at the Throne of grace. God is *within* us (in the sense of *dwelling*). Pentecost is an integral part of the Tabernacle, symbolized in the two 50x50 squares of the Court (Ezekiel 36:26, 27). This does not mean that a person fails to be a recipient of salvation by not entering the second 50x50 square, for the moment he enters the court gate and meets with God at the Copper Altar, he becomes a child of God by the regenerating power of the Holy Spirit (see Diagram "Fifty-by-Fifty Everywhere," the following page).

The wall was too high; no one could see or climb over it. No one can climb over God's grace on his own good works. *"He that entereth not by the door* [the Gate of the Court] *into the fold of the sheep, but climbeth up some other way, the same is a thief and a robber"* (John 10:1).

The height of the linen fence was five cubits, which was also the measure of the distance between each pillar (Exodus 38:18). *Five* surrounded the Holy Tabernacle: By the grace of God the spirit of man (represented in the Holy of Holies) is "furnished" with *five* senses: faith, hope, love, reverential fear of God and true worship. God supplied the soul of man (represented in the Holy Place) with *five* senses: reason, imagination, affections, memory and conscience. Man's body (represented in the Court) is graced with *five* senses: sight, hearing, taste, smell and touch (see diagram, page 1). God graced His Creation with *five* manifestations of His creative power found in the first two verses of Genesis: "In the beginning"–*Time,* "God created"–*Force,* "the heavens"–*Space,* "and the earth"–*Matter,* "And the Spirit of God moved"–*Motion.*

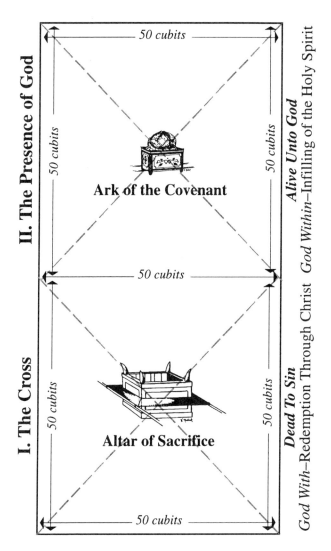

FIFTY-BY-FIFTY EVERYWHERE

100x50 cubits–One Rectangle–One Redemption
Two perfect 50x50 squares–Two Phases of One Redemption
   I. 50 – Year of Jubilee–Slaves set free.
   II. 50 – Day of Pentecost–Freed slaves, God's Habitation.

Verse Nineteen

> *"All the vessels of the tabernacle in all the service thereof, and all the pins thereof, and all the pins of the court, shall be of brass* [copper].*"*

The Tabernacle was held together by brass (copper) pins. God planned even the little things and they were to be made perfectly "according to the pattern." God is interested in the smallest detail of our lives and is concerned that these details coincide with His great plan for us.

Another word to be used for these pins is "nails." The word, "pin," *yathed* is translated "nail" or "tent pin" in Judges 4:21 and 5:26. In Isaiah 33:20 and 54:2 it is given as "stake." These nails were hammered down into the sand, cords were tied to them and attached to the Tabernacle curtain and the linen fence. The curtains and pillars were pegged down to the sand because of the cords and copper pins. "The (Bedouin) tent was held in position by ropes of the same material (goats' hair) tied to pegs driven into the ground by a mallet (Judges 4:21, 26)."[56]

Christ is described as "a nail in a sure place" (Isaiah 22:22-23; cf. Revelation 3:7). He holds us in righteousness; He is our Anchor; He has been judged for our sins, as symbolized in the copper. With the cords of love He holds us straight in the desert. Our feet are in the copper sockets (our sins have been judged), and we are held by the ropes of God's promises and crowned with His salvation (silver caps).

Notice that these pins, in order to hold the Tabernacle, Tent, and the Court Fence, had to be hammered down deep in the sand. The Lord Jesus sunk down into death; He descended, was hammered down below the earth. We are identified with Him in His death. *"I am crucified with Christ..."* He was buried and we are identified with Him in His burial. (Baptism in water is a symbol of burial.) He was judged for our sins; we are judged in Him. He was made sin for us that we might be cleansed. He was identified with us in our sins that we might be identified with Him in His righteousness.

In order for the cord to be tied to it, the head of the nail had to extend *above the ground.* Christ not only died but He *rose*

---

[56]George M. Mackie, *Bible Manners and Customs*, p. 89.

from the dead. We are identified with Him in His resurrection for we rise with Him and walk in newness of life. The nail that is seen above the earth, as it were, is looking up into Heaven. The believer is identified in Christ ("the Nail") "looking for that blessed hope" (Titus 2:13), with his face ever toward Heaven and the return of his Lord.

The cords, fastened to the nails, had the power of holding and the power of drawing. God's love binds us with cords to a pin that is in a *"sure* place." *"I drew them with a cords of a man, with bonds of love"* (Hosea 11:4). God has, through Christ, drawn us to Himself and He has the power to hold us, to keep us from falling, and to present us faultless before the presence of His Glory with exceeding joy (Jude 24)! *"Cast thy burden upon the Lord and he shall sustain thee: he shall never suffer the righteous to be moved"* (Psalm 55:22).

> He will hold me fast,
> He will hold me fast.
> 'Cause my Saviour loves me so,
> He will hold me fast.

Verse Twenty

> *"And thou shalt command the children of Israel, that they bring thee pure oil olive beaten for the light, to cause the lamp to burn always."*

Immediately after directions for the "little things," God gives the commandment to bring the oil. Even the minutest detail of the Sanctuary is associated with this lubricant. Everything in God's Dwelling Place is important to the Holy Spirit!

"Pure beaten olive oil" (Exodus 27:20; 29:40) was the finest in quality. Leaves, twigs, and dirt having been removed, the olives were beaten to pieces, and crushed and put into a basket, and the oil was allowed to flow out of itself. It was a sort of first fruit obtained before the pulp was placed under the press."[57]

From the "crushings" of the Lord Jesus, the fragrance of the Holy Spirit was produced for others. The oil (Holy Spirit) for the "lower lights" was poured out by Him after the "beatings" of Calvary.

---

[57]*Westminster Dictionary of the Bible*, John B. Davis, editor, p. 436.

The Jewish people today remember the "perpetual light" in their celebration of Chanuka (*Hanukkah*) on Kislev 25 (coincides with December). It was on this Feast of Dedication that Jesus walked in the Temple and the Jews inquired of Him if He was the Christ (John 10:22-24). They were remembering the oil which (according to tradition) was miraculously supplied for the "burning lamp" after their deliverance from their enemy, Antiochus Epiphanes.[58] If only they had known that Christ was their Light and the Supplier of the Oil of Heaven! Today they observe the Feast of Hanukkah not knowing that Christ is ready to pour the oil of His love and grace into their souls. He is ready to reveal Himself as their long-awaited Messiah whom God has anointed with His holy oil. He would also anoint them with the Holy Ghost and power if they would desire Him.

There was to be a continual supply of oil to keep the lamp "to burn always" (see also Leviticus 24:1-4). Paul admonishes believers to be filled with the Spirit (Ephesians 5:18). The idea here (from the Greek text) is to keep on being filled with the Spirit. Continually the "lamp" is to be shining for God.

Verse Twenty-One

> *"In the tabernacle of the congregation without the veil, which is before the testimony, Aaron and his sons shall order it from evening to morning before the LORD: it shall be a statute for ever unto their generations on the behalf of the children of Israel."*

Rashi says "from evening to morning" means that "sufficient oil was to be poured into the lamp to enable it to burn from evening to morning, the amount varying with the duration of the night. The Rabbis declared that half-a-log (a unit of measure) sufficed for the long nights, and the same measure was used for the shorter nights, what was left over being drained off (*Soncino Chumash* on Exodus 27:21).

Some commentators write that the Lampstand burned all night and was relighted. Others state that it burned from "even" (3 p.m.) until midnight or a little toward sunrise. In Psalm 134:1 we read about the servants of the Lord *stand* (are employed to minister) in the Sanctuary *by night*. Is this so they were to keep the light burning?

---

[58]See *Apocrypha, I and II Maccabees.*

A Song of degrees. Behold, bless ye the LORD, all ye servants of the LORD, which by night stand in the house of the LORD (Psalm 134.1).

2 Chronicles 13:10-11 states the lamps were to be lighted *in the evening.* Exodus 30:7-8 states they were "dressed" in the morning, lighted in the evening. Leviticus 24:3 tells that the lamps were "ordered" (taken care of) from evening (first) to morning. It was supposed that sometimes the priests allowed the light to go out at night (see 1 Samuel 3:3), then relit it in the morning.

The lamps were to be taken care of at the same time as the morning and evening sacrifices, the burning of the incense, the care of the shewbread, and the pouring of the drink offering (the wine). Therefore it was decided that the lamps were to be lit "at even" (3 p.m.), and again relit in the morning (the third hour or 9 a.m.).

The wicks, representing humanity, had to be trimmed daily, and the oil supplied. Though anointed, we must be cleansed of the char and ashes that accumulate in our lives. The wicks produce the char and ashes–not the Oil. The hindrance is never in the Holy Spirit, but in ourselves.

Let us ask our great High Priest to come with the Golden Scissors (Holy Spirit) and trim all things "foreign" to God from our lives so that we can shine more brightly for Him!

Test Questions

1. Explain why the Fence can be considered as a mediator.
2. Give spiritual application of the fact that the pillars held up the linen Fence.
3. Of what material were the pillars made? Explain with Scripture and give significance.
4. Give the number of pillars on each side (N. S. E. W.), and the sum of all the pillars of the Court Fence, including the Gate.
5. In what did these pillars stand? Give symbolism.

6. Of what were the hooks and fillets of the Court Fence made? For what were they used? Give symbolic meaning.
7. What was the length of the Court curtain, excluding the Gate? Give significance of this measurement.
8. What five things was the Court Fence to the Children of Israel?
9. Of what material and colors was the Gate?
10. Where was the Gate located and what does this tell us?
11. Explain "wrought with needlework," of which the Gate was made. Give the spiritual application.
12. How many pillars held up the Gate?
13. (a) Give the measurements of the Gate, Door, and Veil. (b) What were the similarities and differences in the Gate, Door and Veil?
14. What joined the pillars to each other? Give the symbolic meaning.
15. What was above, on the pillars? What did this represent?
16. (a) Give measurement of the Court Fence-width and length. (b) What was to be the measurements of the Court "everywhere" as in the original text and what does this represent?
17. Describe the cords and pins of the Court and give the symbolic meaning.
18. (a) Of what does the continual supply of oil in the "burning lamp" remind us? (b) How and when were the lights to be dressed and lighted? (c) Who was appointed by God to take care of the lamps and of whom are they typical?
19. (a) What does the cleansing and trimming of the wicks in the lamps tell us? (b) Of what is the wick a symbol? the Oil?
20. What truth was outstanding to you in this section?

CHAPTER FOUR
EXODUS 28

The Tabernacle Priesthood

We cannot enter this subject in detail here but, since the Tabernacle Study would be incomplete without the service of the priests, we will consider it very briefly.

Verse One

> "And take thou unto thee Aaron thy brother, and his sons with him, from among the children of Israel, that he may minister unto me in the priest's office, even Aaron, Nadab and Abihu, Eleazar and Ithamar, Aaron's sons."

The meaning of the names tell a story: *Aaron*–"Very high," *Nadab*–"Willing," *Abihu*–"My father is he," *Eleazar*–"Help of God," *Ithamar*–"land of palm." Christ is very high, and He is willing to obey His Father and God helps Him to be Victorious.

God instructed Moses that his brother, one of his own flesh and blood, was to be High Priest in Israel. This is a beautiful prophecy of the Lord Jesus Christ. He partook of our humanity, that is, He was born into the human family, a part of us, chosen and called of God to be our High Priest.

The sons of Aaron were also to be taken from among the Israelites that *he* might serve in the priest's office. There is an implication here that Aaron was able to minister only if his sons were with him. He did not perform his priestly duties without his sons and they did not attend to the service of the priesthood without him. They were *one*.

When an individual receives Christ as his Saviour, he is given the power to become a *son* of God. Being born into the family, he is permitted to minister as a priest *with* the great High Priest. We (with Israel, 1 Peter 2:9) are a *chosen* generation, a holy and special people, a *royal **priesthood*** who do not serve as priests without Him. He does not minister without us. We are His hands, His feet, His representatives on earth.

> "And no man taketh this honour unto himself, but he that is called of God, as was Aaron" (Hebrews 5:4). Only those who

are in the "heavenly family" can be priests, not man-appointed priests but *the called of God* (see Ephesians 4:1-2; 2 Thessalonians 2:13-15). They must be sons of His own "flesh and blood." They cannot buy the priesthood, but must be *born* into the priesthood.

"That he may minister unto me"–not unto men but to God (Ephesians 6:6-7; Colossians 3:22-24). He does not minister to please men but he serves according to God's desire that he might bring the Divine approval: "This is my beloved Son" (we are sons in the Son) *"in whom I am well pleased"* (Matthew 3:17; 17:5), and at the end of this earthly life on the "Golden Shore" to hear those blessed words from the Master: *"Well done, thou good and faithful servant"* (Matthew 25:21). *"... they shall come near to me to minister unto me and they shall stand before me to offer ..."* (Ezekiel 44:15).

One of the primary duties of the priests was to offer the sacrifices. We as believer priests are also to offer *acceptable* spiritual sacrifices of *praise* continually to God with which He is well pleased (1 Peter 2:5; Hebrews 13: 15; also see Psalm 27:6).

Let us not be as those who stop in the outer court and kneel at the Cross (Altar of Sacrifice) to accept Christ as *Savior,* but fail to go on into the Holy of Holies and meet God at His Throne, (Ark of the Covenant) to accept Him as **Lord**! There were *four* sons of Aaron. Four is the universal number; it represents "whosoever." It is also earth's number, signifying man's weakness and helplessness. The four sons *with Aaron* equal *five* (grace). How significant this is of Divine strength added to, and made perfect in weakness–omnipotence combined with the impotence of earth.

GRACE

"Grace means *favour*.
a) Favour shown to the miserable we call *mercy*.
b) Favour shown to the poor we call *pity*.
c) Favour shown to the suffering we call *compassion*.
d) Favour shown to the obstinate we call *patience*.
e) But Favour shown to the unworthy we call *GRACE*."[59]

---

[59] W.E. Bullinger, *Number in Scripture*, p. 135.

Verse Two

> *"And thou shalt make holy garments for Aaron thy brother for glory and for beauty."*

The priest was not only to be chosen and called, but he had to be properly clothed. The High Priest, as well as his sons, (see verses 4-5, 39-40) had to wear white linen garments close to his body (also verses 40-43; Exodus 29:5, 29; 31:10; 39:1-2; Leviticus 8:7,30; Numbers 20:26, 28). These were to be holy garments. Linen represents righteousness, and therefore can be called "holy" (see Leviticus 16:4, 32; also Revelation 3:4, 5 and 19:8). Believer priests are to "worship the Lord in the beauty of holiness" and to serve Him only, as they are dressed in His righteousness (Psalms 96:9; 132:9).

Levites were commanded that they should not wear anything that would produce sweat (Ezekiel 44:15, 17, 18). Sweat is caused from physical energy, indicating the work of the flesh instead of the Spirit. In other words, they were not to minister to God through their own natural energy, but by the supernatural energy from above. It is *"not by might, nor by power, but by my spirit, saith the Lord of hosts"* (Zechariah 4:6).

What those Old Covenant priests wore as a covering on the outside, the priests of the New and Better Covenant should wear on the inside! We who are the sons of God are to be "covered" by the fine twined linen of Christ's righteousness, and are to minister to Him, not in the energy of the flesh, but in the power of the Holy Ghost!

Verse Three

> *"And thou shalt speak unto all that are wise hearted, whom I have filled with the spirit of wisdom, that they may make Aaron's garments to consecrate him, that he may minister unto me in the priest's office."*

Those who were to make the garments of consecration were to be wisehearted, filled with the wisdom of God. All that was concerned with this clothing was to be anointed of the Holy Spirit. Only those with Divine enablement in the New Covenant are to be associated with "holy things" in the service of God!

Aaron was required, not only to have his sons with him in order to minister, but he was to wear particular garments as he served in the Sanctuary. He had to be clothed according to Divine prescription. Thus it is with you and me, who are sons of God. The "spiritual clothing" He has provided must cover us before we can serve Him acceptably in the priest's office.

Verses Four and Five

> *"And these are the garments which they shall make; a breastplate, and an ephod, and a robe, and a broidered coat, a mitre, and a girdle: and they shall make holy garments for Aaron thy brother, and his sons, that he may minister unto me in the priest's office. And they shall take gold, and blue, and purple, and scarlet, and fine linen."*

Notice in God's directions concerning the vestments of the High Priest that He began with the breastplate and ended with the fine linen. The breastplate is symbolic of the glory and wisdom of God–the fine linen, His righteous humanity. First, Heavenly Majesty is displayed; God begins from Himself; He then comes to display His righteousness on earth.

There were three parts of the "holy garments" of linen: The mitre, the "broidered coat" with the linen girdle, and the breeches ("drawers" Exodus 28:42).

> "The coat represents holiness of heart. The linen girdle represents holiness of service. The mitre represents holiness of thought. The undergarment represents holiness of the flesh."[60]

Altogether there were eight parts for the High Priest's clothing:

(1) Breastplate with Urim and Thummim.
(2) Shoulder stones.
(3) The Ephod.
(4) The Blue Robe with the "curious" girdle or "embroidered" belt.
(5) The Broidered Coat (The Linen Coat) and (linen belt) Girdle of Needlework.
(6) The Mitre (linen bonnet).
(7) Golden Crown.
(8) The Linen Breeches.

---

[60]Dr. Arthur Petrie, *Typology in the Tabernacle*, p. 25 (unpublished notes).

Eight is the number representing a New Beginning, Resurrection, and Eternity. Our Lord High Priest is the Antitype of this glorious dress and He offers to believer-priests a New Beginning, Resurrection Power, and Eternal Life.

> "Had I an angel's raiment fair
> With heavenly gems unpriced,
> That wondrous garb I would not wear
> My *robe* is Christ."

(Composed by the Pietists of 300 and 400 years ago; see Romans 13:14; Galatians 3:27.)

THE HIGH PRIEST OF ISRAEL

Verse Forty

God began His directions for the Glory garments with the Breastplate. However, because of man's approach and manner of dressing we begin with the *linen* garments.

> *"And for Aaron's sons thou shalt make **coats**, and thou shalt make for them girdles, and bonnets shalt thou make for them, for glory and for beauty."*

Verse Forty-Two and Forty-Three

> *"And thou shalt make them linen breeches to cover their nakedness; from the loins even unto the thighs they shall reach: And they shall be upon Aaron, and upon his sons, when they come in unto the tabernacle of the congregation, or when they come near unto the altar to minister in the holy place; that they bear not iniquity, and die: it shall be a statute for ever unto him and his seed after him."*

Verses Thirty-One and Thirty-Two

> *"And thou shalt make the robe of the ephod all of blue. And there shall be an hole in the top of it, in the midst thereof: it shall have a binding of woven work round about the hole of it, as it were the hole of an habergeon,[61] that it be not rent [torn]."*

Over the fine twined *linen* breeches and coat the High Priest wore another garment. This robe could only be put upon a person already wearing the fine linen. It was put on *from above* and always worn as a symbol of office, authority, and dignity. Christ is the very righteousness of God symbolized in the coat of linen, and He is the King; therefore, He could wear the Robe! We who are the sons of God wear the garments of salvation, dress up in Christ's righteousness; therefore we can be clothed "from above" with His heavenly dignity. He is the King-Priest; we are the children of the King, a *royal* priesthood.

It is not stated of what material this robe was to be made, only that it was to be of *blue,* Heaven's color, representing the Lord who came from Heaven. It tells of His heavenly origin and destiny, and of ours. We are God's people who have our "BA" degree, "Born from Above," Born Again!

---

[61]*Habergeon*–"coat of mail," an armored plate to protect neck and breast. The neckpiece of the blue robe was to be as strong as this coat of mail.

God did not give directions for a seam in this Robe, no beginning and no end. Our Lord is from everlasting to everlasting (Psalm 90:2). He has the "power of an endless life" (Hebrews 7:16). Those who are in Christ wear this "spiritual dress" of Eternity for He promises His sons, *"... because I live, ye shall live also"* (John 14:19), and He declared, *"... whosoever liveth and believeth in me shall never die"* (John 11:26).

Around the neck of this garment was a "linen corslet" ("binding of woven work," *tacharah* which implies "white" or "linen") which made it impossible to rend, for the rending of it was forbidden (Leviticus 10:6). Notice that, in fulfillment of this commandment and prophecy (Psalm 22:18), the Roman soldiers did not divide Christ's robe among themselves as was the custom, but gambled for the *entire* garment instead (Mark 15:24; John 19:24). God had also commanded that the people of Israel rend their hearts and not their garments (Joel 2:13). Christ's robe was not rent, but His heart was torn, broken for the sins of the world.

His heart was "melted in the midst of his (body)" (Psalm 22: 14). "Melted"–"to liquefy." This signifies that the heart had broken (was ruptured) for only in this way could it become as liquid "in the midst" of Him (see also Psalm 69:20). In John 19:34 the original text is "... there *gushed* out blood and water." (Compare with Psalm 105:41, water *gushed forth* from the Rock!) In prolonged, intense agony and suffering, a great amount of lymph (watery fluid) is formed within the walls of the pericardium (the sac which surrounds the heart) adding to the lymph already encased there. With the rupture of the heart, the blood also enters this sac, extending it greatly. When the Roman soldier pierced the side of Jesus, blood and water *gushed* forth since the pericardial space had been entered. The blood would not seem to gush forth from a dead body, yet it is pressure that causes this. Christ was indeed dead at the time of the incident. Crucifixion would not *by itself* have killed Him in so short a time. The only explanation is that Christ had died of a *broken heart* (according to the prophecy in Psalm 22:14), and when the outside wall of the pericardium was pierced from below, the force of gravity caused the blood and water, which had greatly extended the sac, to *gush* out of the opening made by the spear.

Caiaphas rent his garment when Jesus stood before him. The penalty under the Law was death, for disobedience to the commandment stated in Leviticus 10:6. Unconsciously Caiaphas testified, by rending his robe, that he had "died" and was no longer the High Priest in Israel. Jesus is the true High Priest! No man could take Christ's life from Him. He laid it down of Himself. The robe was kept *whole;* it could not be torn. And no one can take our life in Christ from us!

Verses Thirty-Three, Thirty-Four and Thirty-Five

> *"And beneath upon the hem of it thou shalt make pomegranates of blue, and of purple, and of scarlet, round about the hem thereof; and bells of gold between them round about: A golden bell and a pomegranate, a golden bell and a pomegranate, upon the hem of the robe round about. And it shall be upon Aaron to minister: and his sound shall be heard when he goeth in unto the holy place before the LORD, and when he cometh out, that he die not."*

Upon the skirts or hem of the seamless robe of blue were alternating pomegranates and bells. The blue, purple, and the scarlet which are blended in this fruit upon breaking, prophesied of the bruising, the crushing of Christ. Also, in the pomegranate there is a multitude of seeds which signify fruitfulness. The bell, which was of gold, had a tongue in it. This tells of testimony (tongue), *Divine* testimony (gold). It rang clearly because there was a pomegranate between each bell. The pomegranate was made from a woven material (perhaps linen; the Septuagint says it was cotton) of blue, purple and scarlet, and acted as a pad between each bell. The softness prevented the bells from clanging together and producing discord. Our Lord Christ wore the *spiritual* fruit and bells all around the hem of His seamless garment as He walked upon the earth (hem near the earth). He had a clear, ringing testimony which was backed up by the fruit of His life. So it should be with Christians who wear the spiritual robe of blue. It is not by our speaking, or by our preaching, neither by the miracles we perform in the Name of Jesus, or the gifts of the Spirit operating through our lives that we are known. But the Lord said, *"By their fruits [karpos,* 'fruit' as plucked] *ye shall know them"* (Matthew 7:16, 20). The Talmud states it this way:

"They say to fruit–bearing trees, 'Why do you not make any noise?' The trees reply, 'Our fruits are sufficient advertisement for us'."[62]

The New Covenant priest is to wear the bell with the pomegranate, not one without the other, in order to bring a clear, ringing testimony with the fruit of Divine love to the world. This is strikingly portrayed for us in Paul's first letter to the Corinthians, where there are two "power" chapters, and between them the "fruit" chapter: The 12th chapter is the "bell," the testimony of God's power; the 13th chapter is the "pomegranate" or *fruit* of Divine love, and the 14th chapter is another "bell," or testimony of the power of God. It is interesting to note that 1 Corinthians 13 is the only chapter of the writings of Paul in which he does not mention the Lord Jesus, yet He is there; He is *love*! The pomegranate and the bell, not one without the other; Sound and Fruit, preaching and practice. The Gifts of the Spirit must operate with and by Divine Love!

> "With golden bells the priestly vest
> And rich pomegranates bordered round,
> The needs of Holiness expressed,
> And called for fruit as well as sound."[63]

On the Day of Atonement, the High Priest would take off his glorious garments in the Holy Place. To make the sacrifice he wore only the "holy" coat of fine twined linen (with the mitre), and the linen undergarment (the linen breeches).[64]

> "The High Priest's dress was *all white* when he entered the Holy of Holies, whereas in the Tent of Meeting it was blue, purple, scarlet and gold; but this is only an apparent difference. White is the sum of the other colors. Let a ray of white light be split up by a prism and this will be evident; or paint a disc with blue, purple, etc. and cause it to revolve quickly and it will appear *white.*"[65]

The Jewish Rabbis' apparel on their Day of Atonement (*Yom Kippur*) is taken from this Tabernacle custom. On that day, according to tradition, their fathers wore the *Kittel,* a long white robe which was the ancient Jewish national garment. It is still

---
[62]*Bereshith Rabbah*, 16, 3.
[63]Charles T. Potter, *Christ and Christian Experience in the Tabernacle*, Cover Imprint.
[64]See Leviticus 16:4, 23, 32-33 (Ritual for the Day of Atonement).
[65]W.P. Partridge, *Object Lessons in the Tabernacle*, p. 57.

worn on special ritual occasions, especially at the Seder of Passover (*Pesach*). The Rabbis teach that:

> "When people appear before a human judge, they wear black, somber clothing because they fear the possible verdict, but when Israel appears before the Divine Judge we wear white, since we have great confidence in God's mercy and faith in His forgiveness!"

All year long, until this day, the bells on the High Priest's robe of blue would tinkle clearly (because of the pomegranate pad between them) and the Children of Israel would know that he was ministering before the Lord for them. But on this solemn day, the bells were silent. When he would put on again his garments for glory and beauty after the ritual was completed (Leviticus 16:23), the bells would ring out to God's people that the sacrifice had been accepted by God on their behalf, and that their High Priest was still alive!

Our great High Priest, the Lord Jesus Christ, laid aside His "glory garments" to make the sacrifice of His own life. When He hung between Heaven and earth, unwanted by both, the bells were silent; no Divine voice was heard. Forty days after His resurrection He ascended to God, presented the tokens of His sacrifice before the Mercy Seat (in keeping with the ritual) and ten days later poured out the Gift of the Holy Spirit upon His waiting disciples.

Now we can understand the admonition of Christ to Mary on the occasion of His appearance to her after His resurrection (John 20:17). Why did Jesus tell her not to touch Him? Christ is the Anti-type of the High Priest in Israel who performed the ceremonies on the Day of Atonement exactly as he did. Great care was taken to guard against the entrance of any unclean person into the Sanctuary (see Numbers 19 and Leviticus 16:17). No one was permitted to remain there while the High Priest officiated in the Holy of Holies on that great Day. No unclean person could touch him and he could not touch anyone for fear of defilement. When the blood had been applied to the Mercy Seat, and every detail had been carried out as God had commanded, thus receiving His approval and acceptance, the High Priest could then be "touched" by hands and congratulated for his work which had been accomplished (cf. Leviticus 16 with Hebrews 8:1-6; 9:6-14).

*According to a **tradition*** of the Jews, so awful was the presence of Holiness in the Holiest Place–and they were so fearful that the Priest who entered within might not be approved by God–that a long rope was tied to his ankle which extended into the outer court, as he walked into the Holy Room beyond the Veil. After a certain time, if he did not appear to the people, he was pulled from the Room by this rope. It was assumed that he was struck down in death because he did not follow correctly the directions for the ceremony. They knew that the death penalty fell upon the one who disobeyed God's prescribed order for the Day of Atonement, and they did not dare enter the Holiest Place to secure the body of the Priest. Instead, they used the rope, by which the corpse was pulled out from the presence of God. (It is not on record that any High Priest in Israel ever died in the Holy of Holies.)

As soon as Christ rose from the dead, He had to immediately enter the Holy of Holies. That is, He had to ascend straight to God, and present there the *tokens* of His sacrifice on Calvary, to complete this important Day's ritual. The reason He gave to Mary for not wanting her to touch Him[66] was that He "had not yet ascended to the Father." He had not entered the Holy of Holies to complete the ritual; therefore, He would not allow anyone to touch Him, as was the case according to the commandment of God to the earthly High Priest of the Tabernacle service for the great Day of Atonement. When He entered the Holy of Holies and concluded the ceremony at the Mercy Seat in Heaven (which could have lasted only a second), He returned and met His friends on earth, who could then "touch" Him (*held* His feet) and "congratulate" (worshiped) Him (Matthew 28:9) for the work He had done!

After offering the sacrifices, the Israelites waited for the sound of the bells which indicated their High Priest had put on his garments for glory and beauty again and, therefore, was alive because God had accepted the sacrifice. Thus it was that 120 disciples in the Temple at Jerusalem knew that Christ, their High Priest, lived in the presence of the Father when they heard the *sound* from Heaven. The Divine testimony (golden bells) rang clearly through the disciples, showing them that their Christ

---

[66]John 20:17–"touch"–*hapto*, "to fasten to," "cling to," "lay hold of."

was alive, continuing His life and work through them (pomegranates–reproduction) by the operation of the Holy Spirit (golden bells).

Verse Six

> *"And they shall make the ephod of gold, of blue, and of purple, of scarlet, and fine twined linen, with cunning work."*

Over the robe of blue the High Priest wore the Ephod (*ayphod*, "a girdle" from *ahphad*, "to gird," "bind on," "put on"), which was a short garment from the neck down to the knees, sleeveless, made with embroidery of "cunning work" something like the Veil. The colors and design were woven through and through the material of fine twined linen. Added to these colors and for the first time mentioned, was a gold metal thread (Gold beaten into thin slates and cut into wires–Exodus 39:3) intertwined throughout the garment, significant of the Divinity of the Lord Jesus. The "cunning work" symbolizes the Holy Spirit, who was responsible for the glorious "weaving" of Christ's two natures–God and man. It also testifies concerning the work of the Holy Spirit, which was manifest in Christ throughout His earthly life and ministry. Following the "arrangement" of gold is the blue, signifying the heavenly character of our Lord Jesus. He could say of Himself, *"No man hath ascended up to heaven, but he that came down from heaven, even the Son of man which is in heaven"* (John 3:13; see also 1 Corinthians 15:47).

The believer wears the Ephod with the beauty of the "colors" woven into the linen, which is intertwined with the "thread of gold," for he is a partaker of the Divine nature; he is born of heaven. The "cunning work" is in his priest's garment, for he ministers to God only as he is empowered by the Holy Spirit, even as was Christ.

Verse Eight

> *"And the **curious** [Hebrew rendering is "embroidered"] girdle of the ephod, which is upon it, shall be of the same, according to the work thereof; even of gold, of blue, and purple, and scarlet, and fine twined linen."*

This was similar to a belt which served to gird the body and to hold the Ephod closely to the garment of fine linen (see Leviticus 8:7). The glory and power of Christ is "combined" with His righteousness. His humanity and Divinity are "held together" by the *work* of the Holy Spirit. This is also applicable to New Covenant priests.

The embroidered Girdle represents service. It was to be made with the same work as was in the Ephod. Though He is Divine, yet Christ took the form of a servant, girded Himself with a towel and served His disciples (John 13:4, 5). God's righteous Servant was equipped with power to minister (see Psalm 18:39; Isaiah 52:13; 61:1; Mark 10:45) and did not serve until after the "cunning work" of the Holy Spirit was "woven" into His "curious girdle." Believer-priests are to receive and "put on" the same garments of ministry!

Verse Nine

> *"And thou shalt take two onyx[67] stones, and grave on them the names of the children of Israel:"*

God carefully and purposefully chose the stones which He desired to be placed in the garments of the High Priest. The cutting and setting of those gems was to be carried out according to the pattern Moses saw on the Mount. He must have seen them in Heaven, even as John saw them on the Isle of Patmos. Those stones were dug out of the earth, created by God as a very "part" or expression of Himself.

As we understand it today, gems are formed from water percolating through rock masses, which picks up mineral deposits, settling in rock crevices, and then crystallizing through heat and constant pressure. "Rock Hounds," finding these unattractive earth particles, put them into a rotating drum which contains a chemical to take off the rough places. In this way they are polished and their color and design brought out. After about a hundred hours of a tumbling process, these common-looking rocks come out from the tumbler as precious gems. The Egyptians, from whom the Israelites received these gems before leaving Egypt, must have had some similar process of "developing" these stones. (Bezaleel was given wisdom to cut and set them–Exodus 31:1-5; 38:22.)

---

[67]Onyx = *shoham*, from an unused root meaning "to shine with the lustre of fire;" see Job 28:16, *the precious onyx.*

Thus did our Lord Jesus come to earth, dug out of the earth's deposits, was found to be unattractive by those who did not believe on Him, tumbled (as it were) in the drum of earth's sufferings, and The Rejected Stone is the Precious Gem of Heaven. So, with the believer in Christ–unattractive to the world, tested and tried in earth's tumbler, polished to be a jewel in the Master's Crown, beautified with His very own loveliness, a gem "upon His shoulders and on His heart."

The stones were *engraved* with the names of those who were redeemed out of Egypt; nothing could erase them. God will never forsake His own (Isaiah 49:15, 16; John 10:27-29; Romans 8:35, 39).

Verses Ten, Eleven and Twelve

> "Six of their names on one stone, and the other six names of the rest on the other stone, according to their birth. With the work of an engraver in stone, like the engravings of a signet, shalt thou engrave the two stones with the names of the children of Israel: thou shalt make them to be set in ouches ["settings," encasings] *of gold. And thou shalt put the two stones upon the shoulders of the ephod for stones of memorial unto the children of Israel: and Aaron shall bear their names before the LORD upon his two shoulders for a memorial."*

The stones were secured on the shoulders of the High Priest. Christ bears His redeemed upon His shoulders, which is the place of courage and strength (Isaiah 9:6). He promises, *"I will strengthen thee; Yea, I will help thee"* (The Lord is our *Help* Psalm 121:2; 124:8.) "Yea, I will uphold thee with the right hand of my righteousness" (Isaiah 41: 10). The ministry of New Covenant priests is to bear one another's burdens (Galatians 6:2), the strong bearing the "infirmities" of the weak (Romans 15:1). We are admonished to pray for one another and to strengthen one another in the Lord (James 5:16; Luke 22:32).

Not only does the shoulder signify courage and strength, but it is the place that represents leadership or government, and is open, or in public view. Christ leads His people; they are Divinely governed. His ministry is to His people, open and public.

There was a certain arrangement and a certain stone to be placed on the High Priest's shoulders. Six names of the sons of

Israel were engraved in an onyx stone on one shoulder and six names of the sons of Israel were engraved in another onyx stone on the other, *according to* **birth.**

The names associated with the stones were a very part of them, for they were engraved there permanently. Each of the names had the same kind of stone–no difference. Each of us who are sons of God, born into God's Kingdom of Priests, are the same. We are equally recognized in Christ "according to our new *birth*," each engraved on the same kind of stone, encased in gold, brilliant, flashing with the lustre of the fiery Holy Spirit. We are lifted high upon the shoulders of our great High Priest, borne up above earthly ties and boundaries to a place in the heavenlies!

There is a precious truth told in the meaning of these names of which we cannot write in detail (it is inexhaustible), but we will just center on the first and last names which includes them all. "According to birth" tells us that since Reuben was the firstborn of Israel (Jacob), his name was engraved first on the shoulder stone. (Hebrew is read from right to left.) "Reuben" means "Behold (or see), a Son." Does this not direct our attention to the Greater Son, our Lord Jesus Christ? The angels announced His *birth* in Bethlehem; the prophet Isaiah declared of Him, *"A child is* **born***, a son is given."* God informed the disciples concerning Christ: *"This is my beloved* **son***, in whom I am well pleased."* And who of God's people can forget this most precious verse, *"God so loved the world that he gave his only begotten son."* **"Reuben! Behold a Son!"**

The last name on the shoulder stones was *Benjamin*. Remember the story of his birth? Because she was dying Rachel named him *Benoni*, "Son of my Sorrow." But Jacob named him *Benjamin*, "Son of My Right Hand." The Lord Jesus was born into this world and fulfilled the first name for Benjamin; He was a *"man of* **sorrows** *and acquainted with grief." "He was despised and rejected of men."* He suffered, bled and died, the Son of Sorrow. Benjamin was the only son named by his father, Jacob. "Son of My Right Hand" signifies an exalted, an honored place, in an equal position. Christ gave His life (one sacrifice for sins forever) and is *seated* on the right hand of God in an exalted, honored place. The Father God says of Him, **"Benjamin!"** *"Son of My Right Hand!"*

Through the regenerating power of the Holy Spirit we are born of God and given the right to be the *sons* of God. Our Christ, the Greater Son, rejoices in the presence of the angels when a sinner receives Him, and it is as though all heaven rejoices with Him when they see this take place. It can then be said of this sinner: *"Reuben!" "Behold, a son!"*

After this new birth, there is joy and yet there is sorrow for the dying souls of men as we enter into "the fellowship of His sufferings." God promises that if we suffer with Christ, we shall also reign with Him in "glory." We can only wear the golden crown at last if we were able to wear its "thorny rim" first. Sons in the Son will be exalted to the position that He promised: *"To him that overcometh will I grant to* **sit with me in my throne***"* (Revelation 3:21). He will say to us in that day, *"****Benjamin****"! "Son of My Right Hand"*!

Verses Fifteen, Twenty-One and Twenty-Nine

> *"And thou shalt make the breastplate of judgment with cunning work; after the work of the ephod thou shalt make it; of gold, of blue, and of purple, and of scarlet, and of fine twined linen, shalt thou make it. And the stones shall be with the names of the children of Israel, twelve, according to their names, like the engravings of a signet; every one with his name shall they be* **according to the twelve tribes***. And Aaron shall bear the names of the children of Israel in the breastplate of judgment upon his heart, when he goeth in unto the holy place, for a memorial before the LORD continually."*

Aaron bore the names of the Israelites upon his chest as he went into the Presence of God. Jesus, our High Priest, bears our names on His heart continually before His Father (Hebrews 7:25; 8:34).

The precious stones in the breastplate of the High Priest were the same as those mentioned by John in the Revelation on Patmos, concerning the foundation walls of the celestial city (Revelation 21:19). As the names of the 12 tribes of Israel were engraved on the stones in the High Priest's garments, so the names of the 12 apostles are inscribed on the wall gems of the New Jerusalem.

As the heavens are an expression of the Creator, His attributes and power, so is the earth. Out of the dust of the earth (or "fine earth" ready to be cultivated), God formed man. Out of the earth, and from the same materials which make up the earth, came the stones which shone forth in the garments of "Aaron," and will shine in the Holy New Jerusalem! They reflect the glory, power, and nature of God Himself.

Precious stones are composed of the same elements which exist in coarser rocks or common earth. The diamond is composed of that which is found in any piece of ordinary charcoal. The silex which, with some mixtures of common iron, forms the jasper, amethyst, chalcedony and agate, is the basis of all sand upon the seashore, as well as most of the solid rock of the globe.

Most of the stones listed in the Glory garments of Aaron and in the New Jerusalem are of a very hard substance, colorful and glittering in appearance. They are common earth particles, cut and polished, precious, brilliant, beautiful, transparent and without flaw.

Christ is the Stone "cut out of the mountain without hands" (Daniel 2:45); He came from God; He was cut out of the mountain and set in His honored place. He is the Tried Stone (Isaiah 28:16), the Chosen, Elect and Precious Stone, the Living Stone (1 Peter 2:4,6). He is the Stone with the Seven Eyes (Zechariah 3:9 with 4:10 and Revelation 5:6), the Perfect, All-Seeing, All-Knowing God.

It is striking to note that in the High Priest's Breastplate, the *Sardius* gem was mentioned *first* and the *Jasper,* **last**. However, in Revelation 4:3, where God's appearance is described, this order is reversed. The first and last of anything includes all in between; therefore, these two stones incorporate *all* the precious gems of the New Jerusalem in describing our wonderful God and Saviour, as well as describing His people who have been given all things in Christ!

By all the foregoing we can conclude that, the precious stones of the Glory garments and the New Jerusalem represent the Lord Jesus Christ in every phase of His life, power, and ministry. Further, that these stones are also applicable to each believer who is a partaker of the Divine nature.

The stones were set into the breastplate, each one *surrounded by gold* (Exodus 28:20). *Ouches* mean "to set." There was a setting of gold for each stone. These represent the redeemed children of God filled with that same wisdom from above and endued with His power and glory having his own particular beauty and function, yet each one reflecting some ministry of Christ. We are identified with Christ. He is the Living Stone; we are living stones. He is the Precious Stone; we are precious stones. He is the Rejected Stone; we are rejected stones. He is the Chosen, the Elect Stone; we are Chosen, the Elect of God!

On the breastplate[68] there were different and various colored stones with the names of Israel *according to their **tribes***. Here we see unity combined with diversity. Each name had its own particular stone. Each stone had its own peculiar color, glory, and beauty. The redeemed of Christ are all set within the Body, united with one another, yet having various ministries.

The names engraved on the stones were in the same arrangement as that of the Camps of Israel around the Tabernacle and the order of the march through the wilderness, *according to their **tribes***. The names engraved upon them were associated with that particular stone as though descriptive of that tribe. Being engraved tells us of permanency, and the faithfulness of God to all His promises involving each tribe.

The first gem was Sardius, the color of which was red ("Sardius," *odem*, "red"), and engraved upon it was the tribal name "Judah," which means "praise" ("Praise of Jehovah"). God always puts ***praise*** first. Christ partook of flesh and *blood* (red); He came from the tribe of Judah, He who is the personified Praise of God. First the redeemed of the Lord come to God with praise because they are born of Him who is from the Tribe of Judah. Judah's Camp was located on the east side of the Tabernacle near the Gate of the Court, where the sun rose, and toward which the Tabernacle faced. The redeemed of the Lord enter the Gate into salvation's court with praise to Him who is the Sun, who rises "with healing in His wings."

The last stone on the Breastplate was Jasper and upon it was the name *Naphtali*, which means "wrestling" (inferring that this wrestling was for certain *rest* and victory). The story in this name, as it was associated with the stone in which it was

---

[68]*Hoshen* from an unused root prob. meaning "to contain," "to sparkle," "a pocket" (as holding the Urim and Thummim) or "rich" (as containing gems). The Septuagint gives it as *logeion* or "oracle."

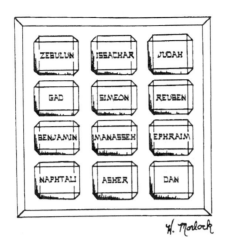

THE BREASTPLATE OF DECISION

STONES OF THE BREASTPLATE

Judah	= Sardius		Ephraim	= Ligure
Issachar	= Topaz		Manasseh	= Agate
Zebulun	= Carbuncle		Benjamin	= Amethyst
Reuben	= Emerald		Dan	= Beryl
Simeon	= Sapphire		Asher	= Onyx
Gad	= Diamond		Naphtali	= Jasper

The Names engraved *according to their tribes* in the *Breastplate of Decision* tell a beautiful story of Christ and His people. May the Holy Spirit open the reader's spiritual understanding to see these precious truths!

Following is the list of names *according to birth* engraven on *The Shoulder Stones:*

Left Shoulder		*Right Shoulder*	
Gad	= "A Troop"	Reuben	= "Behold (See) a Son"
Asher	= "Blessed" (original is 'Happy, very Happy')	Simeon	= "Hearing"
Issachar	= "Hire" or "Reward"	Levi	= "Joined"
Zebulun	= "Dwelling"	Judah	= "Praise"
Joseph	= "Fruitful"	Dan	= "Judging"
Benjamin	= "Son of My Right Hand"	Naphtali	= "W*rest*ling"

engraved, is likened to Christ in His wrestlings upon the earth, to destroy the work of the enemy for the rest and victory promised to His people. It tells of the children of God who wrestle not against flesh and blood, but against the powers of darkness, the wickedness of Satan, and who have overcome him in the name of Christ.

It is striking to notice that the appearance of God (Revelation 4:3) is likened to the first and last stones of the Breastplate of Judgment (in reverse). Since names are to be engraved on each stone, telling of permanency as well as describing the precious Gem of Heaven and His people, this reversed order of the gems, as John saw them, presents another glorious truth: *Naphtali* (on Jasper); we have *wrestled* and have the victory because of Christ. *Judah* (on Sardine or Sardius); we are entered into rest–we are home at last–to *praise* Him forevermore!

In Aaron's garments, represented in the stones, we see a double function of the redeemed people as they served in the priesthood. Theirs was a "shoulder" as well as a "heart" ministry. The shoulder, which is the place of strength, courage, and leadership, is open and public. The breast, being over the heart, signifies love and affection and is secret, private. Thus did our great High Priest function, and thus should believer-priests function today–with a "heart and shoulder" ministry.

The office of the High Priest called for compassion on the ignorant and on them that were out of the way (Hebrews 5:1-6, 10). The fulfillment of this was in Christ, who was "moved with compassion" many times in His earthly ministry. He is continuing this compassion through His sons, believer-priests in the New Covenant, who minister **with** Him in the priest's office.

Verse Thirty

> *"And thou shalt put in the breastplate of judgment the Urim and the Thummim; and they shall be upon Aaron's heart, when he goeth in before the LORD: and Aaron shall bear the judgment of the children of Israel upon his heart before the LORD continually."*

We notice that there was no command of God to *make* the Urim and the Thummim, only to *nathan*, "put in" or give them into the breastplate, *i.e.*, into the *pouch* of the breastplate. The same words ("put in") were used for the Law to be in the Ark of the Covenant, with the idea that it was to be covered completely. So this informs us that the Urim and Thummim were to be put inside the "doubled over" pouch of the breastplate–covered, even as the Law was, inside the Ark. There was no use of Urim and Thummim (so named) after the reign of David. At the time of the return from exile, there was no priest with Urim and Thummim (Ezra 2:63; Nehemiah 7:65).

No one knows for certain what Urim and Thummim were, and there is much speculation concerning them. Some translators give these two Hebrew words as "Lights and Perfections." In the Septuagint or Greek version of the OT it was given as "Manifestation and Truth."

The first time the word "perfect" (*tamiym* from *tamam*," "to complete") is found in the Hebrew Bible it is used to speak of a **walk** or life (Genesis 6:9, *tamiym*–"complete," "entire," "without blemish," "perfect," "integrity," "truth").

The last occurrence of this word in the Pentateuch plainly refers to the Lord Jesus: *"He is the rock. His work is **perfect**"* (Deuteronomy 32:4). The first and last occurrences of words or subjects in Scripture are always important indicating a deeper meaning that is otherwise overlooked. It is very striking in this connection, that the words "without blemish," with references to the Passover Lamb, and the sacrifices in Leviticus and Numbers, is also translated as the word "perfect" and is very similar to the word ***thummim*** (*tamiym*)!

The first word of this combination (Urim-Thummim) is the plural of Ur, which is translated Light. God is the Creator of Light. The Lord Jesus is the Light of the World, who manifests the Father of Lights (James 1:17). He makes known the counsels and purposes of God. The mind and will of God can be perfectly revealed by Him and communicated by Him to His saints.

These two words are considered to be plurals of majesty, the singular "light" (which is a metonymy, meaning *what is brought to light,* i.e., *guilt*[69]), and "perfection" (a metonymy for moral perfection, *i.e.*, innocence). The phrase "black-balling" arose from a person being given a black stone due to a guilty

---

[69]Ephesians 5:13: *"Whatsoever doth make manifest is light."*

verdict at trials in ancient times. (See 1 Samuel 14:41–"Give a perfect lot," "Give perfections," *i.e.*, "Thummim:" "Give clear manifestation:" Urim; "Give or show the *innocent*.")

Only Christ is the *perfect **walk***, the *perfect **work***, the *light*, the *truth*, the *innocent* One who was made as *guilty* that the guilty might be declared *innocent* by believing on His Name!

The Hebrew text shows the first letter of *Urim* is the first letter of the Hebrew alphabet (א). The first letter of the word *Thummim* is the last letter of the Hebrew alphabet (ת)and each of these words is preceded by the combination of the first and last of the Hebrew alphabet. This is the Name of the Messiah written many times but hidden in the OT and carried forward into the Greek as "Alpha-Omega" (ΑΩ). "Alpha-Omega" are the first and last letters of the Greek alphabet. Christ called Himself by this name in Revelation 1:8, 11; 21:6. Christ is the First, the Last; He is the Urim and the Thummim. Urim first, the Divinity of our Lord, He is the Creator of Light which reveals. Thummim–Perfections, the Humanity of our Lord. His perfect humanity; He is the unblemished Lamb and undefiled High Priest!

God commanded that the Urim and Thummim were to be put into the breastplate. This implied the doubled pouch of the breastplate, since the Hebrew word for "put in" indicates that it was *covered* by material of some kind ("put *into*" is more correct). We find this same indication in Proverbs 16:33 *"The lot is cast into the **lap*** [Hebrew, *bosom*]." *Bosom* here is put for the clothing, or the covering over it (cf. Exodus 4:6-7). In this same verse, the word for lot is *goral*, a "stone." Too, "the disposing is of the Lord" translates correctly as "the *judgment* or *decision* ... is of the Lord" from which comes the name "Breastplate of *Judgment*." Numbers 26:56 mentions the *lot* as though it were a person who spoke, "The *mouth* of the lot," or "according to the lot" as translated. Other references to the lot are found in Joshua 18:11, "came up," "came forth." Joshua 19:1, "came out," Joshua 19:17, that is, the lot came up, forth, or out of the bag, the breastplate pouch of the ephod.

The "lots" or "stones" in the breastplate pouch were used or cast as dice (hence "Sacred Dice"), and by their fall somehow revealed the Divine will or judgment. Support of this theory is found in the book of Samuel where casting of lots is twice referred to in close association with seeking revelation through Urim and Thummim (1 Samuel 10:19-22; 14:37-42). Casting of lots was known among the Hebrews and other peoples of antiquity. It was common practice to use black and white stones, casting them on the ground to decide matters, and also as a form of gambling (dice, *black* dots on *white*). This no doubt was taken from the sacred lots, the custom of standing before Urim and Thummim to determine the mind of the Lord in important matters. Also, in ancient times it was the custom for a white stone to be given to one who had returned from the battle, having won a victory.

The "prophecy of the stones" is fulfilled in heaven! The names of the Israelites, the redeemed, are in the stones. The names of the 12 apostles are in the wall gems of the New Jerusalem (Revelation 21:19). Yes, the sacred lots will be there, too. A white stone with a new name will be given the redeemed (Revelation 2:17). He will be fully acquitted, declared innocent before all the hosts of heaven. He has won the victory through the Testimony of the Lamb!

The Priest's Consecration by Blood Application

On the *ear* for *Hearing* the Word of the Lord.
On the *thumb* for *Work* or *Service*.
On the *toe* for *Walk* or *Conduct*.

Consecration of the Priests

Before being clothed, the priests had to be cleansed (Exodus 29:4) by the water of the Laver, symbolic of the Holy Spirit (water) and the Word of God (laver; see section on "The Laver"). The Royal Priesthood of believers needs to be immersed in the Spirit and the Word in order for them to be effective witnesses for God. We are to be *living epistles* (full of the Spirit and God's Word), to be read correctly by all men (2 Corinthians 3:2). Jesus Christ Himself was "washed" and baptized with the Spirit in the Jordan before He began His ministry (Matthew 3:16). He, who is the Incarnate Word, taught by this "cleansing" and "immediate" clothing (equipment for service), even for Himself, that those who would follow Him should be recipients of the same.

After the priests were clothed, a ram was slain and its blood applied to them for their consecration (Exodus 29:19, 20; Leviticus 8:22-24). The tip of the right ear, the thumb of the right hand, and the big toe of the right foot received this blood application. This symbolized that the *hearing* of the priests (ear), their *service* (thumb of the hand), and their *walk* (toe of foot) were dedicated to God.

So it is with believer priests in the New Covenant. When we are born of God, we are cleansed and consecrated by the blood of the Ram, Christ Jesus, to *hear* God's voice, to *minister* to Him, and to *walk* in His Way.

After the blood was applied, the priests (as well as their clothing) were to be "sprinkled" with the blood from the Altar and the Anointing oil (Exodus 29:21; Leviticus 8:30; also Leviticus 14:14-18). So, individuals who have now been cleansed by the blood of Christ (Ephesians 1:7; Hebrews 9:12) are to be anointed of the Holy Spirit that they, as priests of God, might minister with Him in the priest's office. First the blood, then the oil. It is to be observed that Aaron was anointed with oil *before* the blood was applied, while his sons were not sprinkled with oil until *after* the blood was applied. In like manner, Christ was first anointed with the Holy Spirit *before* the blood of His sacrifice was shed, but we receive salvation through the blood before we become candidates eligible to receive the Holy Spirit baptism (oil). The reason for this is that Christ, who is the antetype of Aaron, had His own righteousness intact, as compared to us, who need to be redeemed (bought). First, salvation from sin, then the Baptism with the Holy Spirit follows.

The Order of the Camp and Priest's Duties

Immediately upon anointing the priests, their work in the Tabernacle began. Duties were assigned to them according to their tribes and the location of their tents surrounding the Court Fence (see Numbers 2 and 3). Each one was given his particular portion to care for and to minister in the Holy Sanctuary.

God does all things decently and in order concerning organization and discipline. The Tabernacle was the center of the Camp of Israel. The encampment of Israel extended to a circuit of 12 miles, composed of 2,500,000 people (Numbers 2 and 3:14-38). There was a reserved space "far off about the Tabernacle" (Numbers 2:2), between the first line of the tents of Levi and the encampment of Israel, which was for the nation to assemble before Jehovah for worship and instructions. God dwelt there, and He desires to dwell in the very center of our lives.

The Tribe of Levi was separated from the rest of the tribes, for they were to do the service of the Tabernacle (Numbers 3:6-13; see Leviticus, which is also called *The Priest's Handbook*). The Levites belonged to the Lord and were to be separated from the Camp of Israel in their consecration (Numbers 8:14). The Levites had been commanded to dwell in their tents, all around the Tabernacle, between the rest of the tribes and their God. They were to preserve the Israelites from His wrath (Numbers 1:53) through their appointed mediatorial service. They were comprised of three families: The sons of *Gershon*; the sons of *Kohath*; and the sons of *Merari* (Numbers 3:17).

The Gershonites camped on the *west* in front of three tribes of Israel: Ephraim, Menasseh, and Benjamin. The Kohathites were on the *south* in front of the tribes of Reuben, Simeon, and Gad. The Merarites were on the *north* in front of the tribes of Dan, Asher, and Naphtali. Moses, Aaron and his four sons who were of the family of Kohath, pitched their tents on the *east* directly in front of the Tabernacle, and before three tribes of Israel: Judah, Isaachar, and Zebulun.

The Encampment Around the Tabernacle

Total number in the 12 tribes was 603,550 males from 20 years old and upward, plus 22,000 Levite males from a month old and upward (Numbers 2:32; 3:39).

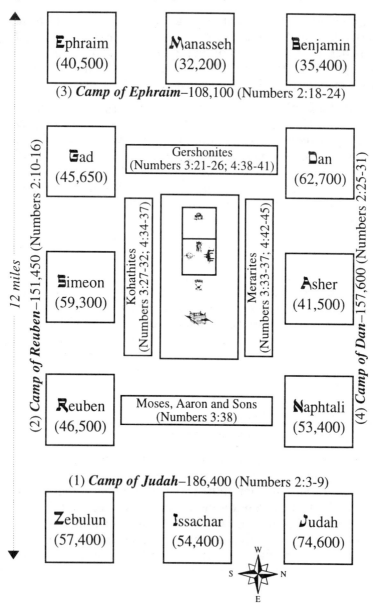

The Tribes of Israel

The Tribes of Israel are now interspersed among the nations of the world even as prophecy declares. For 2,000 years their genealogical records were perfectly accurate. Whenever a child was born among them, his name, family, and tribal ancestry was immediately put down in writing (see 1 Chronicles 5:17; 9:1; Nehemiah 7:5). If one would claim any inheritance as a priest, his genealogy must be proved (Ezra 2:61-62). When Christ was born it was set down in the Temple that He was of the Tribe of Judah, the son of Abraham. His lineage was never doubted. Twenty times in the NT it is written that He was the son of David and this, of course, was according to the prophecy of the coming Messiah of Israel. In 70 AD the Temple at Jerusalem was destroyed and the genealogical records with it, *making it impossible for any Jew today to know his tribal ancestry.* The 12 tribes are scattered over the face of the earth, but are kept distinct and separated, known as Jews, Israelites, or Hebrews (cf. Paul's statements concerning himself in Acts 21:39; 22:3; Romans 11:1; Philemon 3:5). But one day a certain number of these people will be brought together by God Himself, and it will be *according to their tribal divisions,* for God alone knows each name, family, and tribe to which they belong (Revelation 7:4-8).

In connection with this there was an interesting fact reported by the New York Times from Jerusalem in 1957. This fact concerned the genetic characteristics of the Jewish people from 72 different nations, living in Israel. Some of their ancestors came from the Orient and left "Palestine" soon after the destruction of Jerusalem in 586 BC, more than 2,500 years ago. All these widely separated groups from different parts of the world revealed a definite likeness in *fingerprint characteristics*!

Duties of the Levites

The Gershonites had charge of the coverings of the Tabernacle, hangings for the door of the Holy Place, the curtains, the hangings of the court and the cords for these curtains and hangings, **The Soft Things** (Numbers 3:25, 26). Two wagons and four oxen were given to transport those things while traveling (Numbers 7:7).

The Merarites had charge of the boards, bars, pillars, sockets and pins, and the cords for the pillars, **The Hard Things** (Numbers 3:36-37). Four wagons and eight oxen were given for the transporting of these.

The Kohathites were entrusted with the Ark, the Table, the Lampstand, the Golden Altar, the Copper Altar, the vessels of the Sanctuary, and the Veil, **The Precious Things** (Numbers 3:31). They had to carry everything upon their shoulders (Numbers 7:9).

On their journeys, the Tribes of "Jeshurun" marched in relation to the Tabernacle (Numbers 10:17). *Jeshurun* means "upright one" (Isaiah 44:2). It is "a name of endearment" used in poetry for the nation of Israel with reference to the moral character which it was created to exhibit (Deuteronomy 32:15; 33:5, 26; Isaiah 44:2)."[70]

The Camp of Judah marched first, then the families of the Gershonites and Merarites, carrying the Tabernacle in six wagons; next came the Camp of Reuben and, following this, the Kohathites with the vessels of the Sanctuary; then the Camp of Ephraim, and lastly, the Camp of Dan, three tribes in each Camp.

The Twelve Tribes were the **Warriors;** the Levites were the **Workers;** and innermost of all was Moses, Aaron and his four sons, the **Worshipers.** There are these three classes of God's people today, yet God calls each of His own to be all three in one!

When the Tabernacle was *prepared for the march* we see a wonderful prophecy of the Christian:

"1. The Holy Things were covered and taken away. So the soul and its powers are first withdrawn from the body by death.
2. As the curtains and the coverings were taken off and folded up–So the skin and the flesh of our bodies are pulled off and consumed.
3. As the boards of the Tabernacle are disjointed and pulled apart–So shall our bones and sinews be parted.

---

[70]John B. Davis, *The Westminster Dictionary of the Bible.*

4. As the disjointed and dissolved Tabernacle was afterwards set up again–So shall our bodies be joined together again in the resurrection (1 Corinthians 15:51-54)."

—Adam Clarke

The true priests of God are "Company **C**." "We **C** Jesus," for by God we have been:

Levites Erecting Walls of Tabernacle

- **C** hosen ("Take ... Aaron thy brother and his sons with him,"9 Exodus 28:1);
- **C** alled ("from among the children of Israel," Exodus 28:1);
- **C** ommitted ("that he may minister unto me," Exodus 28:1);
- **C** leansed (by the water in the Laver, Exodus 30:17-21);
- **C** lothed (with holy garments, Exodus 28:2);
- **C** onsecrated (by the blood application, Exodus 29:19,20);
- **C** hristed ("anointed" with the anointing oil, Exodus 29:21);
- **C** onformed (see Leviticus, which is also referred to as *The Priest's Handbook*);
- **C** ommissioned (Duties assigned, Numbers 1:49-54).

As we, the Royal Priests in the New Covenant, march through Earth's Wilderness, let us truly be called out from the world, cleansed, clothed, consecrated and commissioned, with the Anointing Oil upon us. Let each one perform his assignment as God has given it to him, each one bear a true testimony of the "precious things," as did the sons of Kohath, witnessing in thought, word, and deed that we are Tabernacles of the Most High God. Let us show forth His power, presence, and miraculous Life!

I'VE BELIEVED THE TRUE REPORT

(Hymn by C.P. Jones)

I've believed the true report,
Hallelujah to the Lamb!
I have passed the outer court,
O glory be to God!
I am all on Jesus' side,
On the Altar sanctified,
To the world and sin I've died,
Hallelujah to the Lamb!
I'm a king and priest to God,
Hallelujah to the Lamb!
By the cleansing of the blood,
O glory be to God!
By the Spirit's pow'r and light,
I am living day and night,
In the holiest place so bright,
Hallelujah to the Lamb!
I have passed the outer vail,
Hallelujah to the Lamb!
Which did once God's light conceal,
O glory be to God!

But the blood has brought me in
To God's holiness so clean,
Where there's death to self and sin,
Hallelujah to the Lamb!
I'm within the holiest pale,
Hallelujah to the Lamb!
I have passed the inner veil,
O glory be to God!
I am sanctified to God
By the power of the blood,
Now the Lord is my abode,
Hallelujah to the Lamb!

(Chorus)
Hallelujah! Hallelujah!
I have passed the riven Veil
Where the glories never fail.
Hallelujah! Hallelujah!
I am living in the presence of the King!

Test Questions

1. What was the first requirement for the High Priest of Israel?
2. Give other qualifications for the priests listed in this section.
3. What truth is illustrated by the fact that the material the priests wore was not supposed to produce sweat?
4. Who made the garments of the priests? What does this tell us?
5. (a) List the eight parts of the garments of the High Priest. What does this represent? (b) What does the seamlessness of the blue Robe teach us? (c) What is the significance of the binding around the neck, that it could not be torn?
6. Briefly describe the Ephod and the "Curious" Girdle. Of what is the Girdle symbolic?
7. How many stones were there on the shoulders of the High Priest? What kind of stone were they?
8. How many stones were there to be on the Breastplate? How were they arranged?
9. What does the "shoulder" signify? The "breastplate over the heart"?
10. What is the meaning of the words Urim and Thummim? How were they made? Where were they to be placed?
11. How is the Urim and Thummim connected with "lots"? Explain with Scripture.
12. Whom did the stones of the breastplate and shoulders represent *according to birth* and *according to tribes*? Whom do they represent today?
13. Explain the "shoulder" and "heart" ministry of the Tabernacle priests.
14. What was the High Priest's garment over the "coat of linen"? Describe it and give some NT applications to Christ and the believer.
15. Describe the hem of the robe and give its significance. Apply to believer-priests today.

16. In what book and chapters of the Bible written by Paul do we find the bells and pomegranate fruit in a spiritual sense? Explain.

17. On the Day of Atonement, what did the High Priest do with his garments for glory and beauty? Give Scripture reference. Compare to Christ's Day of sacrifice.

18. Before being clothed, what was required of each priest who was called of God?

19. (a) Explain the ritual of the blood consecration and the oil for anointing. Give its meaning for New Covenant priests. (b) Of what is the ear, thumb, and toe symbolic?

20. (a) Name the twelve tribes of Israel and their Camp location. (b) Give Camp location of Moses, Aaron and his four sons. (c) Describe the order of encampment of the priests. Give their names and their duties. Be able to draw diagram of Camp Order.

21. List the order of the priests in their march through the wilderness.

22. Compare the Christian to the dissembling and erecting of the Tabernacle.

23. (a) List "Company C." (b) What is the duty of believer-priests in their march through this Wilderness World?

24. What truth was outstanding to you in this section?

CHAPTER FIVE
EXODUS 30

The Altar of Incense

Verse One

"And thou shalt make an altar to burn incense upon: of shittim [acacia] *wood shalt thou make it."*

Only the sons of Aaron were to burn the incense (see 2 Chronicles 26:18). After God's commandments concerning the priests, He gave instructions for the Golden Altar which was vitally associated with their ministry. However, directions had to be given for the Altar in the Court outside, before instructions could be given for this Altar within the Tabernacle Building. There was a reason for this order. First, one had to meet with God at the Copper Altar before he could meet with God at the Golden Altar. The First Altar suggests the work of Christ done on earth, and is for the sinner (Hebrews 9:13-14). The Second Altar is a reminder of the Lord's present ministry, and it is for the saint (Hebrews 9:24; 1 John 2:1). The Court Altar: Jesus *died* at Calvary. The Holy Place Altar: Jesus *lives* for us as our High Priest at the Throne of God.

Incense, which was to be offered on this gold-covered structure was used as a symbol of prayer. David referred to it as such when he talked to God, "Let my prayer be set before thee as incense (Psalm 141:2; see Isaiah 6:3,4; the smoke–incense), and in the case of Zacharias we see the same, for "the multitude ... were praying without at the time of *incense*" (Luke 1:10; see also Revelation 8:3-4).

This Altar was to be made of acacia wood, telling again of the humanity and humiliation of the Lord Jesus. He, who is God, humbled Himself, became man; God was manifest in the flesh. It is said of Christ,

"... it behoved him to be made like unto his brethren, that he might be a merciful and faithful high priest ..." (Hebrews 2:17).

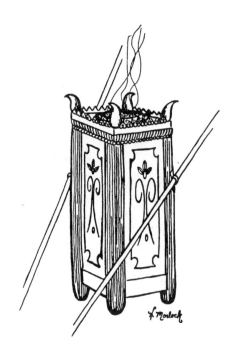

The Altar of Incense

Verse Two

> "*A cubit shall be the length thereof, and a cubit the breadth thereof; foursquare shall it be: and two cubits shall be the height thereof: the horns thereof shall be of the same.*"

Being the highest *measured* article of furniture in the Sanctuary Building, this Altar stresses prayer as the highest form of activity of the Christian. It is "communion" with God, the true source of life and power. (Three articles of furniture in the entire Structure were *not* measured: The Cherubim on the Mercy Seat, the Golden Lampstand, and the Laver.)

This Vessel for the Incense is seen to be reaching up beyond the other furniture toward the Mishkan curtain above, the ceiling most symbolizing the Lord Jesus Christ. Prayer unites us to Him as no other spiritual activity.

The measurement of *two* (cubits) in the height of this piece of furniture portrays *union* and *agreement* with God by the Holy Spirit in prayer. "Likewise the Spirit also helpeth our infirmities:

For we know not what we should pray for as we ought; but the Spirit 'Himself' maketh intercession for us ... according to the will of God" (Romans 8:26, 27). Christ was in agreement with the Father in all His prayer life and thus it should be with His redeemed people.

We also learn through the significance of the number "two," of the promise God has given to His own (even *two*), to agree in prayer and "it shall be done" (Matthew 18:19).

This Altar was foursquare, its four horns (no mention here of *four* horns, but implied; see Revelation 9:13), as it were, pointing to the four corners of the earth. God gives commandment and desires that *all* nations and peoples *everywhere* praise Him (Psalm 117:1; Romans 15:11).

The horns of either side of this foursquare Altar speak of the power and strength of God (the ability of the Holy Spirit) offered to the saints in the four quarters of the globe. This is the way to pray effectively and to praise Him sincerely: in the Holy Spirit (Ephesians 6:18; Jude 20).

Verse Three

"And thou shalt overlay it with pure gold, the top thereof, and the sides thereof round about, and the horns thereof; and thou shalt make unto it a crown of gold round about."

Here (in the gold) the divinity of Christ is represented. The gold beautified the wood even as the Divinity of Christ glorified His humanity. The Golden Altar prophesied of the Lord Jesus, who is Prayer Personified. He is the Prayer, the Intercessor, the Mediator between God and man, our High Priest, the One on earth who brings us into Heaven (Hebrews 4:14-16; 10:19-20).

The crown on the Incense Altar signified authority, Kingship, a finished work. Our great High Priest is also the King who "finished" the work of redemption on Calvary. Prayers are answered on this basis.

First we come to the Court Altar presenting ourselves there as a "living sacrifice" (Romans 12:1). After the fire of God falls upon us we proceed to the Golden Altar placing this "coal of fire" upon it where it is surrounded by the Crown. Here the Crown holds the "coal of fire" from falling. We are kept from falling to the ground as we remain "fired" with the Spirit of prayer!

Verse Four

> *"And two golden rings shalt thou make to it under the crown of it, by the two corners thereof, upon the two sides of it shalt thou make it; and they shall be for places for the staves to bear it withal."*

The rings signify God's love "shed abroad in our hearts by the Holy Ghost" (Romans 5:5), which prompts us to pray. Notice in the Ark of the Covenant and in the Shewbread Table there were *four* rings as there were in the Altar of Sacrifice. But in the Altar of Incense there were only *two* rings. In the verses of Scripture regarding the rings of the Ark, the Table and the Altar of the Court, God specified the number very plainly as *four*. In the building of the Tabernacle (chapter 36) we also see that the builders observed God's commandment and cast four rings for each article of furniture, but when God instructed them concerning the rings of the Golden Altar He only specified *two*. When the Israelites made the Altar of Incense it was recorded that they made *two* rings for it, one ring in one side and another ring in the second side.

The Golden Altar was carried through the desert by the staves through the two rings. Whenever the priests would step down in their journey through the wilderness, the furniture with the *four* rings which they were carrying would go down with them into the place where they stepped (in the same forward leaning position). When they would walk up an incline, then these pieces of furniture would go with them in the same position as they were because of the staves through the *four* rings. (Christ is with his people up mountains of difficulty and down into valleys of decision.) But not so with the Altar of Incense, which portrays Christ in a different sense to His people. It is typical of prayer and His prayer life. When the priests would step down or climb up, this Altar would remain the same–on the same level as always–it would not tip forward as they would be walking down, nor tip backward if they were walking up. No doubt there was some kind of a "stop" by the rings (for all the furniture) to keep the Altar from sliding on the poles (staves) for it remained level because of the *two* rings on the *two* sides which gave it perfect balance. The Lord Jesus Christ in His earthly life was always praying, praying without ceasing, no variation, no wavering, no unsteadiness. He was always the same. The Lord Jesus was a prayer Warrior, the great Intercessor; He prayed in His life as He walked upon the earth, prayed, all night many times, before great decisions were made, and with His last dying breath He prayed, *"Father, forgive them for they know not what they do"* (Luke 23:34). Even now He is praying, interceding for His saints at the right hand of God. He is our Example, our Pattern. As He was in the world so are we to be. We are to pray in faith and in the power of the Holy Spirit even as He. Oh, how our cry should be, even as it was for the disciples of old, "Lord, teach us to pray" (Luke 11 :1)!

Verses Five and Six

> *"And thou shalt make the staves of shittim [acacia] wood, and overlay them with gold. And thou shalt put it before the veil that is by the ark of the testimony, before the mercy seat that is over the testimony, where I will meet with thee."*

The Veil, before which this Golden Altar stood, was a barrier to the priests and to all the people of Israel. No one could go beyond it, only the High Priest on the Day of Atonement, and Moses, any time, at God's appointment (Exodus 25:22). Every time the High Priest would go into the Holy of Holies he would first pass this Altar. There is only "one mediator between God and man, the Man, Christ Jesus" (1 Timothy 2:5). No other individual upon the earth can gain access for us beyond, into the Holiest of All. We must go through Him to enter the Throne Room of God. The Golden Altar was the closest piece of furniture to the Holiest Place (Hebrews 9:3, 4). In the preceding passage the Golden Censer is considered by some commentators to be referring to The Altar of Incense. "Censer," from the Greek word *thumiaterion*, "a place of fumigation" ("to burn incense"), i.e., "the altar of incense." However, according to the Jewish *Mishna* (used in the days of Christ) the Censer was of *gold* which the High Priest used *only* on the Day of Atonement. He used the *copper* censers (firepans of the Sacrifice Altar) all year long until this special day. The Golden Altar (if not referring to the Golden Censer) is not mentioned here by name but is implied since the Golden Censer must receive the incense from it before the High Priest entered within the Veil (see Leviticus 16:12-13 with Exodus 30:36).

Notice in this passage (Hebrews 9:3, 4) that the "tabernacle" was where pieces of furniture were placed but when the Golden Censer is mentioned, it is spoken of in a different manner–not as though it had been a permanent object in the Holiest Place ("where *was*") but as though the ritual of the Day of Atonement "made" the Holiest *have* it ("which had"). By the oneness of the Golden Altar and Censer in the service of the Day of Atonement, and the fact that this chapter is dealing with "better" things–does this not show that the blessed Holy Spirit directs our attention to the fact that the *better* Day of Atonement has been fulfilled in Christ–that He is the Golden Censer filled with the Heavenly Incense now in The Holiest Place as our representative and interceding for us? It reminds us that prayer is the closest of all our activities to that of heaven. The location of this piece of furniture also signifies that the deepest essence of prayer is the putting away of the self-life.

Notice that the Altar of Sacrifice in the Court came first, and then this Altar in the Holy Place. The sacrifice had been offered on the First Altar before the incense was kindled on the Second Altar. Sin must first be dealt with and put away before the cloud of incense can rise. We must die to sin and self or there will be a hindrance to the spirit of prayer. *"If I regard iniquity in my heart, the LORD will not hear me"* (Psalm 66:18).

Verses Seven and Eight

> *"And Aaron shall burn thereon sweet incense* [Exodus 30:34-38] *every morning: when he dresseth the lamps, he shall burn incense upon it. And when Aaron lighteth the lamps at even, he shall burn incense upon it, a perpetual incense before the LORD throughout your generations."*

When Aaron offered up the sweet incense before the Lord each morning and evening, he dressed the lamps at the same time. The light shone brightly upon the cloud of incense as it ascended to God. Thus is the light of our lives in Christ to shine, and the "incense" of our worship, prayer, adoration, and thanksgiving to ascend acceptably to God as we allow our High Priest to "dress the lamps."

It was to be a "perpetual" incense, a fragrance continually ascending to the Lord (cf. 2 Thessalonians 5:17). Morning and evening the High Priest took coals from the Sacrifice Altar to kindle afresh the fire upon the Incense Altar. This teaches us that there must be definite and frequent seasons of prayer on the part of the New Covenant priest (2 Thessalonians 5:16-18). Jesus, our blessed Lord, not only prayed now and then, but He prayed regularly. His whole life was punctuated and filled with prayer. He was the sinless Son of God and yet it was necessary for Him to come to His loving Father and open up His heart to Him. He fulfilled the "perpetual" incense ascending to the Father and is our Example to follow!

Verse Nine

> *"Ye shall offer no strange incense thereon, nor burnt sacrifice, nor meat offering; neither shall ye pour **drink offering** thereon."*

Drink offerings accompanied many of the sacrifices (Exodus 29:40-41). At set feasts (Leviticus 23:18, 37); free will offerings (Numbers 15:4, 5, 7, 10, 24); continual burnt offerings (Numbers 28:7-8); The Sabbath (Numbers 28:9-10).

There are those who have a set, stereotyped form of prayer, man-made prayers, the kind that God forbids. They approach God with "strange fire" which, to Him, is as vain, repetitious and meaningless phrases (Matthew 6:7; cf. Luke 11:1-4). Their hearts have no contact or fellowship with God. Christ rebuked the Pharisees for enlarging the borders of their garment (the fringes and ribbon of blue in the four quarters of it, Numbers 15:38) and agreed with Isaiah in his description of the Jewish custom of kissing these fringes before their prayers, *"These people draw nigh to me with their mouths and honor me with their lips* [kiss the fringes] *but their hearts are far from me"* (Matthew 15:7, 8).

All prayer is to be "by Him" (Hebrews 13:15), through Him and to Him. The Lord said to offer no strange ("foreign") incense or death would be the result. It is only as we accept the "Righteous Incense" He has prepared and come to Him with heartfelt prayers that we can enter into the Holiest.

We notice that the incense was put on *burning coals*. This fire on the Altar drew forth the sweet odor of the frankincense. The fire of God makes a "burning heart" bringing forth the fragrance of the Holy Spirit in our lives and in our prayers. It is not our *position* in prayer, but our *disposition*, not *ritual*, but *reality,* nor our *altitude*, but our *attitude*, neither is it the *length*, but the *strength* of our prayers that are effectual in the sight of God. True prayer is "praying with the Spirit." And it is necessary that one be *filled* with the Spirit in order to "pray with the Spirit" (1 Corinthians 14:15; Ephesians 5:18-20).

> "What would be the effect on the priest's garments, of their remaining any time in the Holy Place? There were no doors nor windows, the place was full of incense continually burning; there was the smell of the frankincense from the Table of Shewbread, and the sweet olive oil from the Candlestick. Would they not 'smell of the Sanctuary'? Would not their clothes indicate where they had been, for in no other place could the same incense be found? And if real believers have been worshipping the Lord in spirit and in truth, will they not have the 'savor of Christ' about them, and will people not 'take knowledge of them that they have been with Jesus'?"[71]

The sacrifice, meat (meal) offering, etc. already had been given in the Court. There were *five* great offerings in the ritual of the First Altar. Grace had been extended there and man cannot add to that work. Christ is the Sacrifice who already has been given to us. Once and for all He laid down His life upon Calvary's Copper Altar. It is on the merit of His finished work that we offer our prayers, not on any additional work of our own. Every carnal method or means of sentiment on our part to excite worship does not meet with God's approval, but all is to be centered on Christ.

Our prayer pattern is Jesus. He prayed, not for Himself, but for others (John 17:9,20). It was *after He was anointed of the Holy Ghost* that His prayers were recorded in Holy Writ. The Holy Spirit enabled Him to be the Great Intercessor and thus it is to be with those He has redeemed.

<pre>
          O for a passionate passion for souls
              O for a pity that yearns!
          O for the love that loves unto death,
              O for the fire that burns!
        O for the pure prayer–power that prevails,
            That pours itself out for the lost!
         Victorious prayer in the Conqueror's Name,
                O for a *Pentecost*!
</pre>

–Amy Wilson Carmichael

---

[71] W.P. Partridge, *Object Lessons in the Tabernacle*, p. 39.

THE HIGH PRIEST ENTERING THE HOLIEST

Verse Ten

> *"And Aaron shall make an atonement upon the horns of it once in a year with the blood of the sin offering of atonements: once in the year shall he make atonement upon it throughout your generations: it is most holy unto the LORD."*

Before the High Priest could go in beyond the Veil, he had to put the blood of atonement upon the horns of the Golden Altar (The Altar of Incense). This blood came from the sacrifice that was laid up before God on the Copper Altar in the Court. The only way that the High Priest could come in beyond the Veil was through this means. Only on the basis of the blood atonement can we come to God and be heard. Because the precious blood of Christ was shed upon the Cross we can now have access into the Holy of Holies.

The Lord Jesus Christ gave us an example of true prayer by His story of the Publican and the Pharisee who went up into the Temple. The Pharisee prayed *with himself*, telling God how good he was, that he wasn't as other men were, and that he tithed and fasted. He was offering strange incense to the Lord. He thought he was very spiritual and could be heard on this basis. But the Publican recognized himself as a sinner who could only approach God through the blood atonement. He did not even so much as lift his eyes to Heaven when he offered his prayer to God. He smote himself upon his breast in his repentant, humble attitude and said, "God, be merciful to me, a sinner." One can sense his thinking, "God, I recognize the blood upon the horns of the Altar of prayer and on the Mercy Seat as the way Thou hast ordained for forgiveness of my sins. God, You are my Mercy Seat.[72] You are my Propitiation, my Propitiary. God, be 'mercy-seated' to me, a sinner." He acknowledged God's mercy through the *blood of atonement* and went away justified. Each individual must recognize this as the only way to come to God.

Verses Eleven and Twelve

> *"And the LORD spake unto Moses, saying, When thou takest the sum of the children of Israel after their number, then shall they give every man a ransom for his soul unto the LORD, when thou numberest them; that there be no plague among them, when thou numberest them."*

Immediately after the Lord had commanded the application of the "sacrificial" blood on the horns of the Golden Altar, He gave directions for the ransom price which each Israelite had to give for the work of the Sanctuary. Each one had to have this atonement money before he could be numbered or else the plague would be visited upon him. No one could be numbered with the Children of Israel unless he met this requirement. David sinned greatly by numbering the people without the atonement money (see 2 Samuel 24 and 1 Chronicles 21). His failure to collect the half shekel of silver resulted in the death of 70,000 men of Israel! So it is with those who would be in the heavenly family today, those who would be a habitation of God. So is it with those who would escape the wrath of God upon them and His judgment for sin; they must have this same redemption price.

God promised that no *plague* (from *negeph*, "an infliction (of disease)" would come upon them if they gave a "ransom for

---

[72] Old Testament word *"Kapporeth"* ("Kapporas") translated as "Mercy Seat." New Testament word is *"hilasterion"* or *"propitiation;"* see Romans 3:25; 1 John 2:2; 4:10; (Exodus 25:10-22–Mercy Seat).

their soul." This connects *physical* healing with *spiritual* healing in the atonement provided at the Altar of Calvary. Isaiah prophesied of this, "Surely our diseases did He bear."[73] The fulfillment of this verse of Scripture is written in Matthew's gospel:

> *"When the even was come, they brought unto him many that were possessed with devils: and he cast out the spirits with his word, and **healed all that were sick:** That it might be fulfilled which was spoken by Esaias* [Isaiah] *the prophet, saying,* **Himself took our infirmities, and bare our sicknesses"** (Matthew 8:16-17).

Verse Thirteen

> *"This they shall give, every one that passeth among them that are numbered, half a shekel after the shekel of the sanctuary: ... shall be the offering of the LORD."*

In our present day coinage (before inflation) this half shekel of silver would amount to about 32 cents.[74] This was paid literally as well as spiritually by Christ (Matthew 17:24-27).

The mere *death* of Christ was not the complete atonement! It had to be approved of God before it could be the Mercy Seat or Propitiation for sin. This death, however, was the preparation, material and groundwork for the full atonement. The two goats upon which lots were cast on that Day, were types of atonement's *essence* and *effect.* One was *slain* and one sent out *alive.* The first goat's blood was a "cover up" of the people's sins as applied on the Mercy Seat. The second goat, by the imposition of hands of the High Priest, took the *atoned-for sins* far off from the people, that is, removed or erased them. But the "scapegoat" was not introduced until *after* the first goat had been slaughtered and its blood accepted as an atonement in the Holiest (Leviticus 16:8-10). Thus it is with Christ, the Antitype of those two victims used on *Yom Kippur* (Day of Atonement). He *died* (for the people's sins, "the essence"), but He is *alive* ("the effect"), completely satisfying the demands of the Law. His resurrection and ascension to Heaven, to appear in the Presence of God for us, had to be accomplished before *all* the requirements of the case were met. Both His death and resurrection had to occur before it became *complete* atonement!

---

[73] Isaiah 53:4 (Isaac Leeser's trans.) Isaiah 53:5, "By his stripe was healing granted unto us." *Stripe*–"bruise," (the black and blue mark itself), "blueness," (cf. 1 Peter 2:24), "By his *stripe* ..."
[74] Finis J. Dake, *Dake's Annotated Bible*, p. 96.

After the first Passover in which the blood of a lamb was shed and applied for redemption and deliverance, the Lord commanded Israel to redeem their firstborn (Exodus 13:13) in remembrance. Today Jews observe what they call *Pidyon Haben* ("Redemption of the Son") in which they substitute five silver dollars for the half shekel which they give to their Rabbi. Oh, if only the eyes of these dear Jewish people would be opened to behold the Lamb of God who takes away the sin of the world! Oh, that they might accept Him, the Ransom for their soul, and have in Him the "half shekel of the Sanctuary" to present to God at His commandment!

Verse Fourteen

> *"Every one that passeth among them that are numbered, from twenty years old and above, shall give an offering unto the LORD."*

Not only the OT, but the NT mentions offerings and tithing to the Lord. It is surprising how much Christ had to say about money and property. One verse in every six in Matthew, Mark, and Luke is on this subject. In 16 of the 36 parables of our Lord, He dealt with the right or wrong use of money. This matter is not foreign to the gospel of Christ.

The tithing plan was first revealed to God's ancient people, the Israelites (Leviticus 27:30-32). It received the endorsement of Christ and His apostles in the NT. And it has been transferred to the gospel age as God's plan for His people today. Ministers of the Sanctuary were supported by this giving on the part of the people (see Numbers 18:20-24 and this God-ordained plan was carried forward into the NT, 1 Corinthians 9:13-14).

Verse Fifteen

> *"The rich shall not give more, and the poor shall not give less than half a shekel, when they give an offering unto the LORD, to make an atonement for your souls."*

The price was the same; rich and poor alike could not deviate in the amount of this redemption money. All are equal in God's sight and He has the same precious Ransom for each one. Ability, talent, personality, possessions, natural goodness or good looks is not required by God. The Lord Jesus gave the Ransom price, the half shekel of the Sanctuary, as He hung upon the Cross. There it was–the precious flow of His life's blood–the same "atonement money"–was poured out for rich and poor alike!

Verse Sixteen

> *"And thou shalt take the atonement money of the children of Israel, and shalt appoint it for the service of the tabernacle of the congregation; that it may be a memorial unto the children of Israel before the LORD, to make an atonement for your souls."*

This was a memorial, the silver piece that went into the silver foundation for the boards and into the silver hooks and fillets of the court fence (see Exodus 38:25-28). It was a reminder of the atonement provided for them when they were slaves in Egypt. They were never to forget that a lamb died in their stead and its blood was struck upon the doorposts of their houses to redeem them from death, as well as to deliver them out of the land of bondage.

The Church of the Lord Jesus Christ has a memorial of "Atonement Money" which is appointed by God for her service before Him. Always she must remember her redemption, her deliverance from the bondage and death of "Egypt's land." It is through the blood of God's innocent Lamb.

Test Questions

1. What is the significance: that the instructions for the Golden Altar were given *after* the instructions given for the Copper Altar?

2. For what purpose was the Golden Altar made?

3. Of what is this Altar (with the *Incense*) a symbol, pertaining to the Christian life, and what do the measurements signify in this respect?

4. Give at least three titles of Christ that are represented in the Golden Altar.

5. Name three features of design in the Golden Altar and give the significance of each.

6. Where was this Altar located? Give type and the significance of this position.

7. (a) Who was to do service at this Altar? (b) When was it to be done and how often?

8. How was the incense on the Golden Altar "caused to ascend"?
9. What were the restrictions concerning the incense upon this Altar? Explain its significance.
10. How are we enabled to pray *effectively*?
11. Explain the effect upon the Priest's clothing as they ministered in the Holy Place, and give the spiritual meaning.
12. What was the ritual involving this Altar on the Day of Atonement? Explain its significance.
13. Explain the Golden Censer in the Holiest (of Hebrews 9:4) with the Golden Altar before the Veil.
14. What did the "atonement money" represent and who was to pay this?
15. How is physical healing associated with the atonement by the "half-shekel of the sanctuary"?
16. To whom was the tithing plan first revealed? How was this plan carried forward in the NT?
17. Explain the equality of rich and poor who give "the ransom price," and apply spiritual significance.
18. For what service was the silver in the Tabernacle to be used? Give Scripture reference.
19. Of what was the half-shekel price a reminder?
20. What truth was outstanding to you in this section?

The Laver

Verses Seventeen and Eighteen

> "And the LORD spake unto Moses, saying, Thou shalt also make a laver of brass [copper], and his foot also of brass [copper], ..."

One other article of furniture is thus mentioned in connection with another (the Table of Shewbread with the Ark of the Covenant). The Laver was closely associated with the Altar of Incense (Exodus 30:1), suggested by this word "also." Not one without the other. The Laver for cleansing had to be appropriated, before the Golden Altar of prayer and praise could be approached. The priests had to be clean before there could be any fragrance of worship to God.

The copper of the Laver was obtained from the Jewish women who donated their looking glasses to the service of the Lord. In Exodus 38:8. the word "assembling," in the original text is "assembling by troops" as an army (cf. Psalm 68:11), "The Lord gave the Word, great was the company of those that published it." The Hebrew word for "company" tells us it was a *feminine* army, an army which assembled by troops.

> "*Women* served at the door of the Tabernacle (1 Samuel 2:22, RV) as did the Levites (Numbers 4:23; 8:24). They probably came at stated intervals, as did the Levites and priests (Deuteronomy 18:6; Luke 1:8, 23), to render various kinds of service; see Exodus 15:20; Judges 21:21; Psalm 68:25."[75]

---

[75]John D. Davis, *Westminster Dictionary of the Bible*.

"One must not forget the great women of the OT, nor of the Talmud, nor the fact that the pages of Josephus are crowded with references to women, and to their conspicuous part of the time."[76]

The Laver (*kiyor* implies something round, "to wash in"), a symbol of God's Word. The Jewish women donated their copper looking glasses for the building of it therefore "implying" that the *Word of God* (the Laver) was "published" by **women**![77] They were willing to give up their prized possessions which they had taken for a "spoil" from the Egyptians before they left the land of bondage. These looking glasses revealed to them their natural beauty. How they delighted to see their reflection in those highly polished copper mirrors! Copper is a symbol of judgment for sin; they judged their outward appearance there. But they gave up that outward judging for the spiritual when they turned over those mirrors for the work of the Tabernacle. The copper looking glasses were then used in the construction of the Laver for the washing of the priests. In other words, the women gave up the desire for natural beauty, the outward adorning, in preference for that beauty which comes from within (1 Peter 3:3-5). "Man's mirror shows and judges spots on the outward appearance but God's Mirror reveals and judges the blemishes of the heart."

The looking glasses of Egypt tell us of the intense desire of mankind to appear beautiful, outwardly, to impress others and attract attention to self, but this is all changed when redemption is applied to the soul. Then the primary, highest, and most important desire is the adorning of the inner man, that the beauty of the Lord of hosts shines forth from their life, and attracts the attention of onlookers to Him who is Altogether Lovely.

> *"O the unsearchable riches of Christ!*
> *Who shall their greatness declare?*
> *Jewels, whose luster our lives may adorn,*
> *Pearls that the poorest may wear."*

Both the Hebrew and Greek words applied to "laver" indicate a receptacle containing water which is used for "washing." Twice in the NT this term refers to a spiritual washing or cleansing. Paul spoke of Christ having cleansed the Church "by the laver

---

[76]H.G. Enelow, *A Jewish View of Jesus*, p. 102.
[77]See Appendix III, *God's Word and Women Preachers*, p. 222.

of water by the word" (Ephesians 5:26, "laver," *loutron* from *luou*, "to wash"), and again of God having "saved us, through the laver of regeneration and renewing of the Holy Spirit" (Titus 3:5). We are born again, regenerated by the incorruptible seed, the Word of God (the Laver) through the power of the Holy Spirit (the water in the Laver).

The Laver is a symbol of the Word (James 1:22-25) which is God's Mirror into which we look and judge ourselves (see Hebrews 4:12; "discern" comes from the Greek word, *kritikos* meaning "critic" or "judge"). There we see our own reflection and there also we see the remedy provided for our cleansing.

The Copper Altar has already been built, and it is for the sinner. The Laver is for the saint. We meet God first at the Cross and are cleansed by the blood of the Lamb, then daily we come for cleansing by the Water of the Word. The Altar is for "saving" us and shows us what *Christ* is. The Laver is for "keeping us saved" and shows us what *we* are. At the Altar we learn that what Christ *has done* meets the need of the sinner. At the Laver we learn that what Christ *is* meets the need of the Christian. We are *safe* because of the Blood (Copper Altar); we are *sure* because of the Word (Copper Laver).

There were no measurements for the Laver, neither for the water within. God's Word cannot be measured, neither can the Holy Spirit, who gave the Word, be measured in His work of regeneration and cleansing. He is God's immeasurable Gift to all who will believe.

The "foot" was the foundation upon which the Laver stood. All the foundations of the Tabernacle furniture picture Christ; there is no other foundation! Again and again it is written: "the Laver and his foot." The Word of God stands upon Christ and is upheld by Him. These are inseparable, not one without the other.

> [verse eighteen continued] *"... to wash withal: and thou shalt put it between the tabernacle of the congregation and the altar, and thou shalt put water therein.."*

The Laver was located at the *door* of the Tabernacle. It was a basin at the threshold of the building. (The Hebrew word for "basin" and "threshold" is the same in Exodus 12:22.)

The copper of this basin was highly polished so that the Door and the Copper Altar, between which it stood, were reflected in it. The Word of God, as a mirror, reveals the Cross (Sacrifice Altar) and the Door (Christ), by which we enter into fellowship with God.

The Copper Basin was situated before the "tabernacle of the congregation" or the Holy Place, where the Table of Shewbread was. This showed that there was an experience of cleansing before feasting. Children are not to be dirty when they come to the table; they are commanded to *wash* first. No believer is entitled to come to the Breaking of Bread at the Table in the Holy Place without *self*-examination. *"But let a man examine himself, and so let him eat ... for if we would judge ourselves, we should not be judged"* (1 Corinthians 11:28, 31).

The priests could not wash themselves with the Laver itself. There was to be *water* therein which points to a great spiritual truth. This is what cleansed them and fitted them for their tasks. The only water the sons of Israel had in the desert was that which gushed forth from the smitten rock (Exodus 17:6). Remember how Moses was commanded of the Lord to strike the rock (which Moses did) and water came forth for the thirsty Israelites (see Numbers 20:8, 11). The second time, Moses was to *speak* to the rock, but he struck it twice instead. For this sin of disobedience Moses was not permitted to enter the promised land with the Children of Israel. Christ, the Rock, was *struck* **once** and ever after we need but to *speak* to Him for our supply of spiritual drink! *"And* [our fathers] *did all drink the same spiritual drink: for they drank of that spiritual Rock that followed* [went with] *them: and that Rock was Christ"* (1 Corinthians 10:4). The Lord Jesus is the Rock of Ages. It was only after this Rock was struck on the Cross, rose from death, ascended up into Heaven, that there was poured out "spiritual drink" (the Holy Spirit) for His people!

Verse Nineteen

*"For Aaron and his sons shall wash their hands and their feet **thereat:**"*

Notice this little word "thereat." It does not say that they shall wash their hands and their feet *therein*(inside of)–but *thereat* (at the side of or near it). The Hebrew text tells us that it is "out of" or "from," implying that the water was taken out of the Laver to be used for the washing of hands and feet. With smaller basins they were to take the water out of the larger Basin and wash themselves at the side of the Laver. If one priest had cleansed his hands and feet *in* the Laver, the water would have become polluted for the next priest. The Word of God is not defiled by man's imaginations, doctrines, or by his opinions and explanations.

> "To deny the Word of God is to deny the basic foundation of all law, for all law is based on Blackstone, and Blackstone bases his law on the moral ethics of the Word of God."[78]

The Word of God is clear, pure and clean. It is illumined to our hearts by the Holy Spirit undefiled. We wash *thereat*. The Laver, as the Word of God, gives us a reflection of ourselves whereby we can judge ourselves, but it also contains the water whereby we can wash. The Lord Jesus said to His disciples, *"Now are ye clean through the **word** which I have spoken unto you"* (John 15:3). We also read that the Lord Jesus gave Himself for His Church that He might cleanse it by the *water* of the Word (Ephesians 5:26). David declared, *"Wherewithal shall a young man cleanse his way? by taking heed thereto according to thy word"* (Psalm 119:9). Concerning His disciples, the Lord Jesus requested the Father to: *"Sanctify them through thy truth: thy **word** is truth"* (John 17:17). David refers to the washing (at the Laver) as an illustration of innocence (Psalm 26:6).

We notice that the priests were to wash their *hands* and their *feet*. God's people are to be a *clean* people. *"Who shall ascend into the hill of the LORD? or who shall stand in his holy place? He that hath **clean hands**, and a pure heart; ..."* (Psalm 24:3-4). Our *work* (hands) and our *walk* (feet) are to be cleansed by the Water of the Word. No one can live in the filth of sin and expect to live in fellowship with God (Psalm 26:6; 51:2, 3, 7; Psalm 119:9; Isaiah 1:16; Galatians 5:19-21; 1 Corinthians 6:9-10; 1 John 1:6; 2:4-6; 3:10; 4:10, 20; 5:16-17)! The priests did not stand off from the Laver only to look at it, or admire it. They did not speak of its beauty, attractiveness, or usefulness, but they obeyed the commandment of the Lord concerning it. They used the water that the Laver contained. We do not stand off from the Word of God and admire it, talk at length about it;

---
[78] Jack MacArthur, Litt. D., (Tract) *God's Answer to the Skeptic*.

neither do we approach it, study it, know its history, its characters and all its miracles; nor quote chapters from it, and expect that all this cleanses us! The Laver does not wash us, nor the water that it contains. To be effective, *it must be applied.* Self-examination (self judgment) is not merely thinking about it, but applying the water of the Word to our *hands*–which speaks of *our actions*, and to our *feet* (which speaks of *our walk*). We are not only to believe God's Word by receiving it, but we are to serve God's Word by observing it. We are to be *doers* of the Word, not only hearers.

Verses Twenty and Twenty-One

> *"When they go into the tabernacle of the congregation, they shall wash with water, that they die not; or when they come near to the altar to minister, to burn offering made by fire unto the LORD: So they shall wash their hands and their feet, that they die not: and it shall be a statute for ever to them, even to him and to his seed throughout their generations."*

Even though the priests had met God at the Altar of Sacrifice and had been cleansed of their sins, yet ever afterward there was daily defilement that had to be washed away. Even after we have been cleansed of our sins on acceptance of the Lord Jesus Christ as our Saviour, we must keep on being cleansed by the Word of God daily, in order that we may walk with God and have fellowship with Him. The words of our Lord, *"... He that is washed needeth not save to wash his feet, but is clean every whit: ..."* (John 13:10) is an example of this. Christ fulfilled the service of the priest, not in washing His own feet, but in washing the feet of another (John 13:14). In our Lord's time people returning from the public baths found it necessary to wash their feet which had become soiled from walking through miry streets. So the Christian has been cleansed once for all, but in walking through the world he often contracts defilement, and therefore needs daily cleansing.

In the old country there was a special sidewalk for the Jews to walk on who were coming home from the Temple. So the priests of God are to walk in a special way after they are "washed," for the Lord will not have fellowship with uncleanness. It is necessary that believer-priests *bathe* in the Word every day. *"Let us draw near with a true heart in full assurance of* *faith, having our hearts sprinkled from an evil conscience, and our bodies **washed with pure water**"* (Hebrews 10:22). Aaron's sons died, not only because they offered strange fire in the Holy Place, but they also neglected to wash at the Laver before their entrance and service there. God has provided a "beauty bath" for His "royal priests" and it is expected that they "wash" in the Word of God before they perform any service to Him.

We criticize those who never avail themselves of the opportunity to wash their physical bodies, and consider them obnoxious to our sight and smell. But what a stench in the nostrils of God are His children who never give themselves a "spiritual" bath at the Laver! The Word of God is here for us that we might be able to be cleansed thereby. *"If we confess our sins, he is faithful and just to forgive us our sins, and to **cleanse** us from all unrighteousness"* (1 John 1:9).

There was a possibility that these priests of God could die, which in a spiritual sense was separation from God, spiritual death. If you and I, who are called to be kings and priests, do not continually wash with the water of the Word, we will suffer the penalty for this disobedience even as the Tabernacle priests did when they disobeyed. We will die–spiritually. Separation from God takes place when we fail to cleanse ourselves according to God's commandment. Continual failure on our part in this respect will lead to the "second death." It is mentioned in Exodus 30:20-21 *two* times: "thou shalt die." There are *two* deaths even as there are *two* births. Someone expressed it so very true: If a person is born only once, he will die twice, but if he is born twice, he will die only once (cf. Revelation 2:11, 20:6, 20:14, 21:8)!

The Old Covenant priest was required to wash each time, before he could perform a service. This was "a statute forever." Similarly, New Covenant priests continually apply the Water of the Word, which is required for a state of continual holiness, a continual communion with God (Philemon 3:12-14; 1 Corinthians 9:24-27; 1 Timothy 6:17-19).

"In Revelation 15:2 we find the last mention of the Laver in the Bible. It is in Heaven, described as 'a sea of glass'. The Redeemed stand on it, no longer to wash therefrom, but to be ever reminded of the source of their purity. They *stand on the sea* and sing of the Lamb. In Heaven the Altar and the Laver are never forgotten. The Altar bears witness 'Without the shedding of blood ... ,' the Laver testifies, 'Without holiness no man shall see the Lord'."

Test Questions

1. Explain the significance of the location for the Golden Altar with that of the Laver.

2. Who donated the copper for the building of the Laver? Give Scripture reference. What is the spiritual significance of the copper looking glasses?

3. What does the laver symbolize? The water?

4. Explain the significance for the location of the Copper Altar in relation to that of the Copper Laver.

5. (a) Where was the Laver located? (b) Who was to use it? (c) When was it to be used, and for what purpose?

6. What was the penalty for failure to wash at the Laver?

7. (a) Explain the word "thereat" in connection with the water in the Laver. (b) What is the symbolism in the application of water to "hands" and "feet"?

8. What is the measure of the Laver? Give spiritual application to your answer.

9. Give references and write out the portion in the NT where the term 'laver" is used in Greek for a spiritual washing or cleansing.

10. What truth was outstanding to you in this section?

The Anointing Oil

Verses Twenty-Two and Twenty-Three

> "Moreover the LORD spake unto Moses, saying, Take thou also unto thee principal spices, of pure myrrh five hundred shekels, and of sweet cinnamon half so much, even two hundred and fifty shekels, and of sweet calamus two hundred and fifty shekels,[79] [here, shekel, according to medical language, equals nine drops; five hundred shekels would then be 4,500 drops].

In most cases it was uncertain as to what those Bible spices really were, but it has been concluded that they are comparable to many of the spices of today, with different names.

The Tabernacle Study began with the desire of God to dwell *within* His people by the filling of the Holy Spirit. It now ends with the anointing oil and the glory cloud filling the finished Sanctuary.

The Lord instructed that the Tabernacle with all its features be built, and every detail of the services, as well as the clothing of the priests, were to be made "according to the pattern" Moses saw in Heaven when he was on Matthew Sinai. And this was done as God commanded. There were the beautiful colors, the shining gold, silver and copper, the articles of furniture all set in their places, but the whole structure was inoperative. The priests were all dressed in their linen garments, the High Priest in his beautiful and glorious vestments, the sacrifices were at hand for the Altar, the water was in the Laver, etc., but nothing supernatural occurred until the directions for the anointing oil were carried out and everything received this ointment. Then, and only then, did the Holy Spirit begin to move in His Holy Habitation!

The first of the spices was *myrrh*. Myrrh is a gum which comes from the stem of a low, thorny, ragged tree of the *terebinth* family growing in Arabia and East Africa. It is a bitter plant from which sweetness can be obtained after it is bruised. The word is taken from the Hebrew, *mor*, which means "to drop on from a container above," in other words, it is distilled. It was to

---

[79]Shekel, a weight, sometimes a coin, sometimes translated as "pieces." Silver or gold shekels have come to mean money today.

be pure, the best of the myrrh which exuded spontaneously from the bark. (The inferior myrrh comes more abundantly by splitting the bark.) Myrrh was used as a perfume, as a medicine for deadening pain (Mark 15:23), also for correcting secretions, on the dead (John 19:39-40), as a modifier of other medicines, and for purification (Esther 2:12). Through the power of the Eternal Spirit, Christ gave Himself freely. He was made sin or "bitter," but from His bruising came forth the sweetness of the Holy Spirit. He was dead, His body anointed with myrrh; He is our purification (Hebrews 9:13-14). His life He gave was sweet to God, sweet to the saints, and His life is a healing medicine for those who are sick in spirit, soul, or body.

We notice in the Record that, during six of the 12 months for Esther's preparation and purification to be among the number who were to stand before the King, she was rubbed down daily with this spice (Esther 2:12). It was Esther, the one who gave forth the fragrance of myrrh, who was chosen to be his Bride. As we stand before King Jesus, the holy anointing oil with the sweet smell of myrrh should be upon our garments of salvation. Freely we are to give ourselves, even as He freely gave–die to self–for "Except a corn of wheat fall into the ground and die, it abideth alone: but if it die, it bringeth forth much fruit" (John 12:24). We are daily to apply this anointing oil, to purify ourselves even as He is pure, as we prepare for the marriage of the Lamb!

The second ingredient was sweet cinnamon which is a bark of a small evergreen tree of the laurel family ("cinnamon," "to erect," "cinnamon bark" as in *upright* rolls). Cinnamon comes from a tree growing in Ceylon and on the islands of the Indian Ocean. It is largely used for flavoring since the odor is sweet and the taste agreeable. As a medicine it is a stimulant and cordial. The tree was an evergreen; so our Lord was ever the unchanging One whose leaf did not wither in time of drought or cold. The fragrance, no doubt, counteracted the stench of the butchering, burning, and cooking of animals in the Tabernacle court. Though the Cross of Christ revealed an ugly and awful death, yet there was the fulfillment in it of the burning, scorched flesh of all the Old Testament sacrifices, which were acceptable to God on behalf of the people because of the "cinnamon fragrance" which accompanied them.

We are admonished to present our bodies as a living sacrifice upon God's Altar which is our reasonable service (Romans 12:1). And though there is sin, death, and decay included in this offering, yet by the application of the cinnamon this is all counteracted and we become a sweet-smelling savor in the nostrils of God (2 Corinthians 13:14).

Cinnamon has a warm, sweet, pleasing, and peculiar aroma. Christ, with the Holy Spirit, the "Divine Cinnamon," resting upon Him, gave forth that feeling of warmth which was sweet, pleasing and peculiar. This is the case with all those whose lives have been anointed with the Cinnamon.

The third ingredient was sweet *calamus* which grows in Arabia and India (Song of Songs 4:14; Ezekiel 27:19). Sweet calamus is a fragrant cane whose root is highly prized as spice. The root word means "to stand upright," hence, "a cane," or "reed." It usually grows in miry soil. The more this bark is beaten, the sweeter is its fragrance. How like the Christ who grew in the mire of this world "upright" and fragrant to God. He was beaten, humiliated, spit upon, and nailed to the Cross of Agony, yet He prayed on behalf of His persecutors, "Father, forgive them for they know not what they do." We are to be as He was. "Love your enemies," and "Pray for them that despitefully use you," etc., were His commands. The more we are persecuted, the sweeter we are to be, by the enablement of the Holy Spirit, the Heavenly Calamus.

Verse Twenty-Four

"And of cassia five hundred shekels, after the shekel of the sanctuary, and of oil olive an hin:" [Here the shekel is a weight after the weight of the atonement money.]

There were four principal spices with oil. In the four "corners" of the earth God anoints His own with the Holy Spirit. *"The promise is unto ... even as many as the Lord our God shall call"* (Acts 2:39).

The fourth spice was *cassia*, which grows in various parts of the East. The word is thought to be derived from the root meaning "to split," and refers to the rolls of bark being split. This word is mentioned in Ezekiel 27:19 and Psalm 45:8. It is said to resemble cinnamon and to be of the same family, but less fragrant. It was used for flavoring, and as a medicine. It was a bitter medicine, but one which purged and healed all who received it. This aromatic bark comes from a shrub which grows only on great heights of around 8,000 feet. As this plant flourished where other plants could not grow, so we see at Calvary's height the perfection of Christ in His faithfulness. In the place of His sacrifice for sin there was yielded a "peculiar" fragrance such as from no other death. Coming from the heights of Calvary is the Holy Spirit who elevates the receiver to heavenly places, above the elements of the world.

Four spices were to be combined with a hin (six quarts) of pure olive oil (see section on *The Golden Lampstand* and *The Burning* Lamp). Besides other meanings, the four spices tell of trials and blessings:

"Myrrh, pure: shekels 500 = *Bitter;*
Sweet Cinnamon: shekels 250,
Sweet Calamus: shekels 250,
Cassia: shekels 500 = *Sweet.*
1,000 Sweet = much blessing,
500 bitter: some trials for Christ and believers."[80]

For their exhibition, the "vehicle" of these four ingredients was the Olive Oil, a symbol of the Holy Spirit. All true witness to the grace and excellency of Christ must be in and by the Holy Spirit. The spices are dry apart from the oil.

Oil is also a lubricant which is used to heal and energize, as well as to aid in giving light and fire. This is characteristic of the Holy Ghost in the life and ministry of Christ and believers.

Verse Twenty-Five

"And thou shalt make it an oil of holy ointment, an ointment compound after the art of the apothecary: it shall be an holy anointing oil."

The holy anointing oil was a different oil than that which was used for the lamps. Though the lamps were filled with pure olive oil for light, yet the holy ointment had to be applied as God directed. After Christ was baptized of the Spirit at the River Jordan, this anointing upon Him became evident. It was for special services, by the Gifts of the Spirit working through Him,

---

[80]W.P. Partridge, *The Tabernacle*, p. 51.

on behalf of the people. It was prophesied by Isaiah concerning this unction from on High:

> *"The Spirit of the Lord* [the pure Olive Oil] *is upon me, because He hath anointed me* [the anointing Oil] *to preach the gospel to the poor; he hath sent me to heal the brokenhearted, to preach deliverance to the captives, and recovering of sight to the blind, to set at liberty them that are bruised"* (Luke 4:18; cf. Isaiah 61:1-2).

Believers are baptized with the Holy Spirit (the pure Olive Oil), and through the Gifts and Fruit of the Spirit (the anointing Oil) work for God in specific and special occasions on behalf of the people (1 John 2:20; 2 Corinthians 1:21). As we abide in Him this will become operational as the appointment demands (1 John 2:27).

The ointment was to be a compound after the "art of the apothecary," the "manufacture" of perfumes by such a man talented to do so. Only the Holy Spirit can combine "Holy Spices" with "Divine Oil" in proper proportion and make the spiritual application to our lives. He is the Heavenly Apothecary who compounds the Holy Ointment.

In studying the ingredients for the holy anointing oil we have discovered several similarities which speak to us symbolically of the Person and work of the Holy Spirit:

1. All four spices were imported from another country. This other country represented Heaven. The Holy Spirit is sent from Heaven.
2. They were not only fragrant but were used in healing as a medicine. The "Anointing" breaks every yoke of bondage.
3. They brought forth fragrance upon being bruised or crushed. Christ was crushed, the fragrance of the Holy Spirit came from Him, and so with us.
4. They grew at great heights and were erect plants, standing upright. The Holy Spirit is from *above*.
5. They were all mixed with the oil. The *work* of the Holy Spirit comes from the Holy Spirit.
6. They were to be mixed by an apothecary, an artist in the manufacture of perfumes. The spices are the works or acts of the Holy Ghost; the apothecary is the Holy Spirit Himself.

7. All the mixture was called holy. God, the *Holy* Spirit, is the one who compounds this mixture.
8. They were all combined into *one* measure of oil. The Gifts and Fruit come from *one* Holy Spirit.
9. They were all called *principal* spices. All the works, fruit, and gifts of the Spirit are principal spices.
10. Moses was to use this anointing oil on the Tabernacle and all that pertained to it. Moses is a type of Christ who sends the Holy Spirit to us.

Verse Twenty-Six

"And thou shalt anoint the tabernacle of the congregation therewith, and the ark of the testimony,"

The ancient habitation of God was finished and set up in the midst of the camp of Israel. However, it was not operative until after the holy ointment had been applied! The True Tabernacle, Christ Jesus, was born in the midst of Israel, yet did not begin to manifest God's presence openly until after the Anointing Oil was poured upon Him at Jordan. The Ark of the Testimony was placed in the Holy of Holies, but the *Shekinah* did not dwell between the cherubim until it had received the holy compound. Just so, Christ did not reveal Himself as the Holy Ark which carried the Testament in His heart, where the Shekinah "dwelt within," until He was baptized of the Spirit and received the Holy Spices. How important it is that these tabernacles of clay, believer-priests, receive Divine Anointing Oil!

Verse Twenty-Seven

"And the table and all his vessels, and the candlestick and his vessels, and the altar of incense,"

The Table which held the showbread had to be anointed. Christ, the Table of the Lord, who held the bread for the hungry, received this Holy Oil. Thus should believers who carry the Bread of Life be anointed of the Holy Spirit.

The Lampstand which had already been filled with olive oil for the light, then received the application of the Divinely appointed ointment. The Oil of Heaven was poured into the Holy Lamp, the Light of the World, and ever afterward He manifested the power and presence of God in His miraculous life and ministry. Thus it is with the lesser and "lower" lights. By the baptism of the Holy Spirit (the filling of the pure olive oil) into the lamps (our bodies which are the Temples of the Holy Ghost), we are enabled to shine effectively for Him. By the application of the Holy Ointment (the evident *operation* of the Holy Spirit), we continually allow Him to shine through us.

The Altar of Incense, which is symbolic of prayer, also needed the Oil of anointing. It was prophesied that Christ, our great Intercessor, our High Priest forever after the order of Melchizedek, was to be anointed with the Holy Spirit (Isaiah 61:1). Similarly, believer-priests need this endowment to be effective prayer warriors in His Kingdom!

Verse Twenty-Eight

> *"And the altar of burnt offering with all his vessels, and the laver and his foot."*

Before the Sacrifice could be offered up to God the Copper Altar was to be anointed with oil. Divine approval of our "living sacrifice" upon His Altar follows the application of the Holy Anointing Oil!

The Laver and also "his foot" were to receive the Holy Compound. The Word of God must be accompanied by the Holy Spirit to be effective. Christ, the Living Word, performed His service and lived His life in the power of the Holy Spirit. We are to be "living epistles," with the Oil of Heaven upon us, to be read correctly by all men.

Verse Twenty-Nine

> *"And thou shalt sanctify them, that they may be most holy: whatsoever toucheth them shall be holy."*

Thus the furniture and the vessels with them were all anointed before their function in the Tabernacle. They were sanctified before the Lord to be used for His glory. They were set apart for God's service by this Holy Ointment. The holy furniture typifies Christ and those who are in Him.

Verse Thirty

> *"And thou shalt anoint Aaron and his sons, and consecrate them, that they may minister unto me in the priest's office"* (cf. Leviticus 8:30).

It was after the anointing of the Laver that God gave this commandment concerning Aaron and his sons. They had been called, chosen, cleansed, clothed, consecrated by the blood and oil, and commissioned, yet they had to be *anointed* as well! The Laver was for their "washing," yet they were to be empowered for service. The Word cleanses New Covenant priests for their ministry to God, yet they are to be filled with the Holy Spirit to be effective witnesses *of* Him.

Anointing was the seal of God's consecration of the priests to His service. Without his anointing a priest missed the chief qualification for his office. David said, concerning the Lord as his Shepherd, *"Thou anointest my head with oil."* He compared it to the shepherd's application of oil to the sheep of his flock. We are the sheep of His pasture and need the anointing oil upon our lives.

Verse Thirty-One

> *"And thou shalt speak unto the children of Israel, saying, This shall be an holy anointing oil unto me throughout your generations."*

This holy ointment was to be used freely in every generation only upon the priests (ministers) of God (Exodus 29:7, 21; Leviticus 10:7). Israel pictures the Church, who is to be empowered by the Holy Spirit. The Church (as was prophesied of Israel) is a "chosen generation," a "royal priesthood" and, therefore, needs the Oil in order to minister before God. We can only present the Lord (which is the most important service of our ministry) as He empowers us from above!

Verses Thirty-Two and Thirty-Three

> *"Upon man's flesh* [the **natural man's** flesh] *shall it not be poured, neither shall ye make any other like it, after the composition of it: it is holy, and it shall be holy unto you. Whosoever compoundeth any like it, or whosoever putteth any of it upon a* **stranger***, shall even be cut off from his people."*

God's Kings were also anointed with oil (1 Kings 1:39), but this was not the same as for the priests. This "anointing oil" was particularly to be used for the priests in the Tabernacle. It was not to be used for anyone who was not a priest, or who did not know the Lord, *i.e.*, the *natural man*.

Only God could compound a holy anointing oil for His people. It was not manufactured through the brilliance of man's mind. Human intelligence has nothing to do with the enablement of Divine power. This anointing oil was holy, even as God is holy and is only to be poured upon His people to whom he has given His holiness. It was not to be imitated by any man, neither to be poured upon one who was a stranger to God. God alone made it and only He is able to anoint His own.

Verse Thirty-Four

> *"And the LORD said unto Moses, Take unto thee sweet spices, stacte, and onycha, and galbanum; these sweet spices with pure frankincense: of each shall there be a like weight:"*

Stacte is supposed to be the gum of the storax tree found in the East. *Onycha* comes from a sweet smelling shell found on the shores of the Red Sea and the Indian Ocean. It is said to increase the fragrance of other perfumes, and to be the basis of perfumes made in the East Indies. *Galbanum* is juice of a shrub growing in Arabia, Persia, India and Africa. *Frankincense* is the most important of the aromatic gums and is regarded by itself as a precious perfume (Song of Solomon 3:6; 4:6, 14). It comes from a tree that grows abundantly in India (Song of Solomon 4:14). The word *pure* used here refers to the free flowing and liberal giving forth of its odors. It is useful as a medicine and an antidote to poison. Very striking indeed is the prominence of the number *five* in this spice: The frankincense flower has *five* petals and stamens; the fruit is *five*-sided, and there are *five* species of the plant!

All three spices were for the holy perfume of the Incense Altar. All were obtained from some kind of life form which gave of itself. The stacte oozed forth spontaneously from a growing tree; the onycha came from a crab in the depths of the Red Sea which gave up its life; the galbanum spice came from crushed leaves; the frankincense came from a tree which was pierced. How like the Holy Spirit's work through the great High Priest and our Example in serving God; for He was as the stacte, spontaneous in worship; He is as the onycha, sincere in the depths of His heart; as the galbanum, broken and contrite; as the frankincense, the One who was pierced! All worship must be through ***Him*** who gave up His life that we might come into the Holiest Place with God!

All the ingredients were of equal weight and measure. The work of the Holy Spirit is equally given. All of it is important. He does not do one kind of work above another.

Verse Thirty-Five

"And thou shalt make it a perfume, a confection after the art of the apothecary, tempered together, pure and holy:"

The perfume was to be made according to the work of the apothecary, even as was the anointing oil. Only the Holy Spirit knew how to combine all these spices with the frankincense, so that it was pure and holy, for use in the Sanctuary.

Verse Thirty-Six

"And thou shalt beat some of it very small, and put of it before the testimony in the tabernacle of the congregation [the Altar in the Holy Place], *where I will meet with thee: it shall be unto you most holy."*

Some of this combination of spices was set apart from the rest for a special ministry. This was beaten "very small," to be used on the Day of Atonement, and was called "most holy." For the ritual on that Day, the High Priest took a golden censer full of burning coals of fire from the Copper Altar into the Court to the Golden Altar before the Veil. Then the beaten incense was put upon the coals so that it would ascend as a smoke to cover him and the Mercy Seat, to protect him from the "awful" holiness of God, that he "die not"(see Leviticus 16:12, 13).

The High Priest not only had to bring the blood of the sacrifice into the Holy of Holies, but he also had to be enveloped by the fragrant spices, which were "beaten small" and placed upon coals of fire from off the sacrificial Altar. He could not approach God, could not come into His presence without the proper "equipment." Christ fulfilled the ministry of the High Priest who, by the perfume of the Holy Spirit, presented (the tokens) of His own precious blood at Heaven's mercy seat. So you and I, the priests of God, must enter into the Holy of Holies. In essence we take with us the precious blood of the Lamb as we are enveloped by the fragrance of the Holy Spirit. This is the way we come into the presence of God that we "die not."

Verse Thirty-Seven

"And as for the perfume which thou shalt make, ye shall not make to yourselves according to the composition thereof: it shall be unto thee holy for the LORD."

This perfume was not to be made by man for self, for the gratification of the flesh, to use extravagantly, but it was "holy," therefore it was for the worship of our holy God. We do not enter God's presence through carnal means, or use methods dreamed up by man. We do not worship God in a manner that pleases the flesh, for God is Spirit and seeks those to worship Him in spirit and in truth. It is by the Holy Ghost, the "composition most holy" that is *made for the Lord,* by which we come into His Holy Presence.

Verse Thirty-Eight

"Whosoever shall make like unto that, to smell thereto, shall even be cut off from his people."

The warning was given for anyone who would dare try to make a similar perfume, to even have the same fragrance. That one who presumed to turn aside from God's designated regulations for an approach to Himself would have no part with Him or with His people. There is only one way of worship: It is God's way. Man may plan this service in the Holiest of All; he may have great influence in his methods and words of prayer and praise; he might have a beautiful ritual in the church, but if he comes to God, or endeavors to bring the people to God by any other way than by God's way, his efforts are in vain, for it is *"... Not by might, nor by power, but by my spirit, saith the LORD of hosts"* (Zechariah 4:6).

CONCLUSION

Five times God described the Tabernacle and that which pertained to it (Exodus 25-30; 35:4-29; 36:8-39: 1-32; 39:33-41; 40:1-33). God's grace, symbolized by the number *five*, is pictured throughout the construction of this Holy Edifice in the wilderness The True Tabernacle, the Lord Jesus Christ, is the manifested Grace of God. New Covenant believers, who are God's Holy Habitation through the Spirit, picture God's grace and reflect His glory in this world.

In the fifth description God gave of the Tabernacle Structure we find these words *seven* times: "As the Lord commanded Moses" (Exodus 40: 19, 21, 23, 25, 27, 29, 32). This Sanctuary was *perfectly* (7) built because of the *perfect* obedience of Moses who was a type of Christ. Christ carried out every detail of God's instructions concerning His Tabernacle *perfectly*. He was obedient to the commandments He received of His Father. So it should be with "sons in the Son" who delight to do the will of God, *perfect* in obedience to His every command.

"*So Moses finished the work*" (Exodus 40:33). The words of our incomparable heavenly "Moses" (Jesus), "*It is finished,*" tell us that all the Old Covenant was fulfilled in Him. Christ finished the work on earth which His Father gave Him to do. The believer must also be true to the task given him by God, that is, fill his place in the Divine plan for his life. Then he can say at the end of the race, even as Paul:

> "*I have fought a good fight, I have **finished** my course, I have kept the faith: Henceforth there is laid up for me a crown of righteousness, which the Lord, the righteous judge, shall give me at that day: and not to me only, but unto all them also that love his appearing*" (2 Timothy 4:7, 8).

"*Then a cloud covered the tent of the congregation, and the glory of the LORD filled the tabernacle*" (Exodus 40:34).

The Holy Tent was now completed. After it was anointed with the holy anointing oil, the Presence of the Lord was manifested in a pillar of cloud *over* it and His glory filled it *within*. And so it is with the Church today, "*In whom ye also are builded together for an **habitation of God** through the Spirit*" (Ephesians 2:22); for as the *Shekinah* was "within" the Tabernacle of old, the Spirit of God is within those who are redeemed. The believer's body is the holy temple of God (1 Corinthians 6:19)!

There were seven weeks (49 days) of services in the Tabernacle after it was set up (Numbers 10:11). It was then God's will to move on, for the cloud was taken up (Numbers 9:22). They had no other guide. It was on the *fiftieth day* they moved on. Yes, *Pentecost* moves; *Pentecost* is active, dynamic and powerful. Those who are led by the Holy Spirit (the Pillar of Fire and Cloud) are those who *move* with God!

The Glory of the Lord was *with* the Wilderness Tabernacle in the Pillar of Cloud *above* it and was *within* after the Cloud *filled* it (Psalm 105:39; Nehemiah 9:12). This pillar of cloud by day and pillar of fire by night never left the Camp of Israel from the time they came out of Egypt until they crossed Jordan and entered into Canaan. This Pillar of Cloud is "above" the believer, a Tabernacle in this wilderness world; God is *with* him, and by the Baptism of the Holy Spirit, the Glory Cloud fills him; God "dwells" *within*. Oh, that the children of God would fulfill His desire and command: *"Let them build me a sanctuary that I might dwell **within** them"* (Exodus 25:8, Hebrew text).

FILL ME NOW

Hover o'er me, Holy Spirit,
Bathe my trembling heart and brow;
Fill me with Thy hallowed presence,
Come, O come and fill me now.
Thou can'st fill me, gracious Spirit,
Though I cannot tell Thee how;
But I need Thee, greatly need Thee,
Come, O come, and fill me now.
I am weakness, full of weakness,
At Thy sacred feet I bow;
Blest, divine eternal Spirit,
Fill with pow'r, and fill me now.
Fill me now, fill me now.
Jesus, come and fill me now;
Fill me with Thy Holy Spirit,
Come, O come and fill me now.

–Hymn by E.R. Stokes & John R. Sweney

Test Questions

1. Name the five ingredients for the Anointing Oil and give the chief characteristic of each.

2. What do each of these ingredients represent, singly and collectively, and what are their symbols?

3. Explain "art of the apothecary" and give the spiritual significance.

4. What was the first article of furniture to be anointed with the holy anointing oil? Explain the significance.
5. List the furniture in order, as they were anointed with oil.
6. After the anointing of what article of furniture were Aaron and his sons to be anointed? What does this teach us?
7. What was the chief qualification for the office of priest?
8. (a) What were the restrictions regarding the anointing oil? (b) What is the meaning associated with these restrictions?
9. List similarities of the ingredients for the anointing oil.
10. Name the three sweet spices for the holy perfume. Give the meaning of each.
11. With what ingredient were these three spices combined?
12. Explain this "confection tempered together" and give its spiritual significance.
13. (a) Explain the "beating small" of some of the "confection." (b) Where was this portion to be placed? (c) What was the purpose of this "most holy" portion of the perfume?
14. For whom was this perfume to be made?
15. What was the restriction concerning this holy perfume and what was the penalty for disregarding it?
16. List the five places in Scripture where God described the building of the Tabernacle.
17. Explain the words: "As the Lord commanded Moses" as applied to Christ and believers.
18. What is brought to your attention by the phrase "And Moses finished the work"?
19. What occurred after the Tabernacle was completed and anointed? What does this teach us?
20. What truth was outstanding to you in this section?

(The following composition was written by one of my students who was in my Tabernacle Study class at Seattle Bible College. On March 14, 1968 he had completed the assignment I gave to the class to write a 500-word composition about the Tabernacle.)

CHRIST IN THE TABERNACLE
by Harold Turner

I come over a hill and look upon an enclosure. There is a fence, a linen fence surrounding a Court. In the Court there is a tent or building. Odd, but in itself this building is not attractive, yet I am–for some strange reason–as if by a will other than my own, drawn toward this building.

As I near the enclosure, I desire much to enter in, I notice that where I stand there is not a way in. The linen fence is about seven and one-half feet tall and extends from the ground upward. I search the entire side of the enclosure and see that here there is no way in so I begin to walk around the enclosure. As I go I count the posts upon which the fence hangs. I notice that there are sixty of them. There were twenty on the North and South sides, the sides being about one hundred and fifty feet in length. Along the West end, as I went by, I counted ten pillars there. Each of the pillars was set firmly in copper sockets so that I could not enter by any side. I neither could go over the top for the tops of the pillars were adorned with silver and so high that I could not get over. There were silver fillets that kept the linen fence from sagging and all kept me from entering, or rather my own limitations kept me out.

I continue walking and at last I come to the east side or end of the enclosure. I had just begun to think that there was no way in when I turned the corner and found a Gate! It was a beautiful gate but I knew that it was more beautiful for that it led me to the inside of the enclosure. It was also linen but different in that it had colors of blue, purple and scarlet in needlework upon it. But as I said: it is of no use unless one goes through it so I found the opening, located on the North side of the Gate and entered into the enclosure. I have this right for I am a priest of the living God! I became a priest as I entered the Gate.

(This is an account of an experience I underwent about thirteen years ago and not the experience of a man thousands of years in the past.)

I learned as I walked round and round to try to find a way in that I could not. My Lord was too righteous for me to enter into fellowship with Him. The fence was indeed "too high." The pillars that upheld it were too deeply imbedded in judgment. The capitols that topped the pillars were made of silver and I had no redemption money. But when I saw the Gate in all His heavenly glory, Who had become a Son of Man that I might become a Son of God, Who became a Servant though He is a King; when I saw Him and knew that He was my redemption price, I took Him and entered into the Tabernacle through His bleeding Side!)

As I enter I see the awful price that had to be paid so that I may be cleansed and enter the Holy Place. The smoke from off the Altar of Sacrifice stings my eyes; The blood causes a stench that would nearly turn one's stomach; the Altar is three cubits high and five cubits square; upon it a sacrifice is burnt. All I see here is horror.

(Christ became sin for us that we who are sinners might be made righteous. He became sin, even the Father could not look at Him, and the very ugliness of what He became; it was not His sin that put Him on the Cross but mine, is what makes me a child of God.)

I still stumble under the knowledge of what my sin necessitated but I am still drawn onward. I pass and stop at a Laver. This is made of copper (as was the Altar of Sacrifice) and is filled with water. Around the base of it are mirrors [highly polished copper] and in them I see that, while at the first Altar I was cleansed and imputed righteousness by the Father, I still have dirt upon me that must be taken off. Water is poured from the Laver and I am cleansed as is evident when I examine myself by the mirrors in the base of the Laver.

I desire to enter into prayer and because God is righteous I must be clean as I go to Him. I could not help but pass the Laver with its "mirrors" which showed me that I needed cleansing. Rather than be as the man mentioned in James 1:24 who "beholdeth himself and goeth his way, and straightway forgetteth what manner of man he was: I would be as he that "looketh into the perfect law of liberty, and continueth therein" (James 1:25). The Laver then shows me that I need to be cleansed. It is the Word of God.

Alas, "the letter killeth, but the Spirit giveth life." As the Spirit is poured upon me in sanctifying power I am separated from the world, for while copper is a type of judgment, water always gives life.

Another curtain confronts me as I go on. It, too, is blue, purple, and scarlet but boldly, for I am pure, I step through the Door to the Holy Place.

Here I see light shine from a golden Lampstand and I see a Table with bread upon it. All this is part of this room which is a place of prayer. Another Altar is here. This one is Golden. All things in this Holy Place are Golden. Incense burns and smoke rises from the Altar and ascends up past a most beautiful Veil.

The Veil is made of linen and upon it in cunning work are cherubim in constant guard lest any should pollute the Holy of Holies in which the Glory of God dwells. I can go no further.

Here is where a comparison ends also. For as I enter the Holy Place there is no longer any Veil of God's righteousness separating me from the presence of God. Not that God is less righteous, but as Christ's flesh was torn for me, the Veil was torn down in the temple thus opening the way for the wonderful communion that we have in Him.

Here in this place I receive wisdom and guidance as the Light of the World sheds forth His glory. Here I receive food as the Bread of Life is given to me.

Here I see a purer incense burn and the prayers of Christ rise as He says: "Forgive them for I bought them with my blood." God in turn looks at me and sees Christ in my stead.

With the Veil torn asunder, I am directly at the Mercy Seat pleading the precious blood of the Lamb and putting my petitions before my Heavenly Father.

After all, why should I be ashamed to come here, I am a son of God!

APPENDIX I
Notes on Typology and Symbolism

Typology is the science of types in the Bible and must be understood before one can properly understand the Word of God.

God has given a series of pictures (or types) in the OT which the NT refers to and explains.

The Typology of the OT is the *alphabet* of the NT. One cannot correctly or clearly understand the doctrine or teaching of the NT until he knows his Alphabet!

Types run through the entire Bible and are not, as some suppose, a very small part. **The Bible is full of types!**

> "The typical part of the Bible is just as important as the historical, biographical, prophetical, poetical, doctrinal, or practical parts. All are necessary to a complete Bible, and the study of all essential to a mind well stored with the truth of God."[81]

Why Pursue a Study of Types?

It is a neglected subject because many feel that types are *difficult*. Others say types are all imaginary and uninteresting. Some say they are not necessary. Some, on the other hand, go overboard to the extreme and make everything a type, and this causes confusion. There is a danger of misinterpreting types in relation to doctrine; therefore, many stay away from it and close the door to a beautiful and wonderful study.

I. DEFINITIONS OF TYPES AND SYMBOLS

    A. Type
        1. A type is a person, thing, or event in the OT, designed to represent or prefigure some person, thing or event in the NT. The one in the OT is called a Type; the fulfillment in the NT is called Antitype (*antitupon*, Greek).
        2. A type is a "shadow of that which is to come."
        3. Types are OT illustrations of NT truths.

---
[81]Downie, *Harvest Festivals*, p. 14.

      4. Types are the shadows. The fulfillment of the type (or antitype) is the substance.
- B. Symbol
  1. A symbol is a species of type by which some thing or some act is represented by another or similar act which is considered suitable to serve as a resemblance or representation.
  2. A symbol is an illustration of that which already exists.
- C. Types and Symbols
  1. Generally speaking, the Type is prefigurative, the Symbol illustrative of what already exists.
  2. Some things, such as the Passover and the Tabernacle, were both symbols and types. They commemorated something and they prefigured something else.
- D. Shadow and Substance
  1. "Trace any shadow with the light before you, and you will arrive at the substance." (Slemming)
  2. The SHADOW is behind you–not clear–maybe? When the SUBSTANCE arrives you are no longer "hazy" about the shadow and not interested so much in the "shadow" anymore. The ONE that cast the shadow is here and you are taken up with HIM!
- E. Kind of Types (or Symbols)
  1. Persons
  2. Ceremonial Institutions
  3. Offices
  4. Events
  5. Actions (also Colors, Numbers, Names)

II. WHY IS THE STUDY OF TYPES IMPORTANT?

- A. The Bible contains them.
- B. They throw light on the great precepts and doctrines revealed in the NT.
- C. The Holy Spirit places types in Scripture.
- D. Jesus Himself constantly referred to them.
- E. Paul said they were examples for our learning.
- F. Typology is another evidence of the essential unity of the Bible.

III. REASONS FOR STUDYING TYPES
  A. God Sets Great Value On Them
    1. His Spirit designed them and He will lead us to understand them.
    2. The Holy Spirit placed types in the Scriptures (Exodus 26:33 with Mark 15:38) and that is one reason why the study of types is important.
    3. Notice Hebrews 9:8 *"The Holy Ghost thus signifying* [setting forth by object lesson or type] *that the way into the Holiest of all was not yet made manifest, while as the first Tabernacle was yet standing."* This statement **clearly shows** that the Holy Ghost, through the study of the Tabernacle, is imparting spiritual truths by **types**!
  B. Christ Thought Much of The Types
    1. Again and again He referred to them, showing how they pointed to Himself (Luke 24:44).
    2. Jesus used types as a method of teaching:
       a. John 1:51–He claimed to be the antitype to *Jacob's Ladder*.
       b. John 3:14,15–He referred to Himself as the antitype to the *brazen serpent* written in the OT.
       c. John 6:35–Here Jesus teaches that He, Himself, is the antitype to the *Manna* in the wilderness, etc.
  C. The Types Speak of Christ
     Christ said to the Jews, *"Had ye believed Moses, ye would have believed me, **for he wrote of me**."* It was mostly in the **types** that Moses wrote of Christ.
  D. The NT Writers Accord to Types a Very High Place in Their Writings
    1. 1 Corinthians 15:4 *"Christ rose again the third day, **according to the scriptures**"* [the Old Testament].

> Leviticus 23:11 tells of the waving of the sheaf the third day after the lamb is sacrificed: "the morrow after the sabbath." *The very day of the **Resurrection** is foretold!* It is the resurrection of Christ who is as the Sheaf of Firstfruits "waved before the Lord."

    2. Paul used types as a method of teaching:
       a. Romans 5:14–Paul mentions *Adam* as a Type of Christ.

b. 1 Corinthians 5:7–He speaks of the *Passover* as a Type of Christ.
   c. 1 Corinthians 10:4–He refers to the *Rock*, as a Type of Christ.
   d. Colossians 2:16, 17–He talks of the shadow of things to come, of which the body or antitype is Christ Jesus.
3. The writers of the NT were students of the OT and alluded over and over again to types and shadows.

Paul the Apostle wrote 1 Corinthians 10: 11, *"Now all these things happened unto them* [Israel] *for ensamples* [object lessons or types] *and they are written for our admonition"* [exhortation and *learning*, by defining the hidden truth in a story, which is a *Type*].

"All these things happened unto them for types." Paul explains that the record of these events is given to us in the Bible for a special purpose:

To teach us certain lessons. These events not only actually happened, but they happened to teach us spiritual lessons also. Therefore, by this scripture we can see, in part, that there are lasting values for each person who applies himself to the study of Types.

4. The Gospel of John refers constantly to OT types: Lamb of God, Jacob's Ladder, The Tabernacle, The Temple, The Brazen Serpent, Jacob's Well, Manna, The Smitten Rock, The Light of the World, The Good Shepherd, The Corn of Wheat, The Laver, The True Vine.

Warning: *The study of **Types** is very helpful, but it demands **mental restraint and a controlled imagination.*** We must not, nor can we safely, refer to every portion, incident, person, etc., as a possible means for a type. We cannot spiritualize everything, and thus lose the lasting value by taking away the literal aspect of the story or scripture, etc.

TWO RULES TO FOLLOW:

1. *We should study all the OT types* ***in the light of the NT Teaching***.
2. And we should make our study of types *practical and helpful **for our daily living.***

APPENDIX II

Significance of Numbers in Scripture

In Daniel 8:13 "a certain saint" is asked a question about *numbers:* "How long?" The Hebrew name of the one who was questioned is *Palmoni*, which means "the numberer of secrets" or "the wonderful numberer." The Word of God holds numbers and their secrets in a very important place which is presided over by this *Wonderful Numberer*. Not only are events numbered, but even the *words* themselves. "Every word of God is in its right place."

1. Unity (Deuteronomy 6:4; John 17:11). Beginning (Begin with God; "In the Beginning, God"). God is First (One, the *first* number). Independence (Excludes difference; *There is no other*). Supremacy.

2. Fellowship, Testimony, Union (One and one), Choice Agreement, Dependence (Affirms difference; *There is another*).

3. Resurrection; Trinity; Manifestation (three parts of Tabernacle; Man a triune being; on third day Christ rose; Altar is three cubits high, etc.); Solidity (cubed, third dimension, etc.); Reality; Realization; Actuality; Fullness (all the fullness of the Godhead in Christ).

4. Earth; (Universal–Eden's four streams–Genesis 2:10; "Four Winds" that blow on the earth–Ezekiel 37:9; "Four Corners" limit the earth–see Isaiah 11:12; "Four-footed beasts tread the earth;" "Four beast governments" are to rule the earth;" "Wars, earthquakes, famines and pestilences" destroy the earth; four points of the compass, E.W.N.S.–1 Chronicles 9:24. Four Gospels Universality (Whosoever–Christ is the Universal One.)

5. God's Grace to Man in Man's Weakness. (Four and one–Whosoever and God; four fingers and one thumb, five digits on each hand; five toes on each foot; five natural senses; five spiritual senses; five commandments God-ward, five commandments man-ward; five ministry gifts to the Church, etc. five offerings brought Israel near to God, five wounds of Christ on the Cross reconciled man to God.)

6. Imperfection Man (On the sixth day man was created.) Man's work (six days man labors.) (666–three sixes–fullness of man's imperfection and work.)

7. Perfection Four and three–Agreement of earth and God's fullness. (In Revelation, all is perfected and we find 59 sevens. The perfection of the Word of God is found in a supernatural design of sevens in the Hebrew and Greek text that is never found in Apocryphal or other writings.) Rest, Dispensational Fullness.

8. New Creation New Birth Resurrection New Beginning New Life ("'Enough and more than Enough'–Christ's name in the Greek has the value of 888!" –Cheyne.)

9. Triple Manifestation (3x3–God's Number–Trinity–cubed. Nine manifestations of the fruit of the Spirit and nine gifts of the Spirit.

10. Testimony God-ward Completeness–nothing wanting, Union with God's grace (2x5).

11. Government under man, short of twelve. Man and God's grace in his weakness (6 and 5).

12. Divine Administration in Government God's Elect (12 stones in Breastplate, 12 loaves on Table, 12 tribes of Israel, 12 apostles, 12 gates of the City, 12x10 in upper room on Day of Pentecost, etc.).

13. Rebellion; (Genesis 14:4; Esther 3:12; Jeremiah 25:3).

20. 2x10.

24. Divine Worship, Kingly–Messianic Rule (12 and 12).

40. Probation–Complete testing Christ was tempted 40 days and 40 nights in the wilderness. He went into the city and appeared to many for 40 days after His resurrection. The Israelites were challenged by Goliath for 40 days. Moses had three periods of testing of 40 years each in his lifetime. It rained upon the earth for 40 days in the time of Noah. Trial.

50. Liberty Jubilee Pentecost 100 (10x10, 2x50, 5x20).

NOTE: We come to understand that the numbers in Scripture are significant and symbolic by a collation of the passages in which certain numbers occur and then by comparing the places.

APPENDIX III
God's Word and Women Preachers

(During the time I was an Instructor at Seattle Bible College [1960, 1961, 1966-1987], some of the students questioned me concerning the subject I am now writing for you. It was during the study of the Tabernacle and particularly concerning the Laver that I composed this article which I gave to each student in my classes.)

The Laver

In the Tabernacle of God in the wilderness there was a *Laver* located before the "Door" of the Sanctuary building. God had given instructions concerning the building of it as well as its location. The Laver was to be made of copper (brass) and this was a donation of the Jewish *women* who had received these prized copper looking glasses from the Egyptian women before they left the land of bondage. We read of their offering:

> *"And he made the laver of brass, and the foot of it of brass,* **of the lookingglasses** [looking-brasses] *of the* **women assembling,** *which* **assembled** *at the door of the tabernacle of the congregation"* (Exodus 38:8).

In Typology the Laver represents the **word of God.** The lookingglasses were made of highly polished brass (copper) into which the women would look to see a reflection of themselves. The Word of God is like a mirror which reflects what we look like and it tells of a remedy whereby we can be cleansed. These lookingglasses were donated by the Jewish women for the building of the Laver. The words "assembling" and "assembled" means that it was *by troops as an army* that these women met at the Door of the Tabernacle of the Congregation.

In this connection, **Psalm 68:11** tells the same: *"The Lord gave the word: great was the company of those that published it."* The word, "company," is in the feminine gender. The words of action (i.e., "published") telling what this feminine "company" is doing, is also in the feminine gender, since this is the proper Hebrew grammar. The word *"company"* implies that it is an army that assembles by troops. These words: "assembling" and "assembled" in Exodus 38:8 along with the word "company" in Psalm 68:11, indicate then that it is a **feminine army** that assembles before the Door of the Tabernacle at the Laver (God's Word)! The Hebrew text of Psalm 68:11 uses, instead of "company," the word *tseba-ah* to indicate that it is a "feminine army" which proclaims God's Word (the laver). So we can paraphrase Psalm 68:11 thus: *"The Lord gives the command; The **women** who proclaim the good tidings are a great host."*

Another portion of Scripture concerning *women preachers:*

"O Zion, that bringest good tidings, get thee up into the high mountain; O Jerusalem, that bringest good tidings, lift up thy voice with strength; lift it up, be not afraid; say unto the cities of Judah, Behold your God" (Isaiah 40:9)!

The words "Zion" and "Jerusalem" cannot be properly rendered rhetorically as the subjects of the verbs: *"O **thou** that tellest good tidings to Zion, get thee up into the high mountain; O **thou** that tellest good tidings to Jerusalem, lift up thy voice with strength; lift it up, be not afraid; say unto the cities of Judah, Behold your God!"*

Psalm 68:11 and Isaiah 40:9, in the Hebrew text, employ one and the same word in the same verbal form in each instance for the word signifying "to publish the tidings." In Psalm 68 it is said that *the women* publish, or preach, the good tidings; in the words of the prophet Isaiah, it is *woman* who is addressed and expressly commanded to preach the good tidings to Zion, to Jerusalem, and to the cities of Judah. Both words are participial in form and of the feminine gender. We will not enter in detail the words which indicate that the *woman* was to *preach* but you can consult a Hebrew student to help you to understand that Isaiah 40:9 is correctly translated as:

*"O **woman**, that publishest good tidings to Zion, get thee up into the high mountain; O **woman** that publishest good tidings to Jerusalem, lift up thy voice with strength; lift it up, be not afraid; say unto the cities of Judah, Behold your God!"*

We find here an explicit command that *woman* shall go forth into places of prominence ("get thee up into the high mountain"), and proclaim with a loud voice ("lift up thy voice with strength") to *entire cities* (not just a few women somewhere). Then beginning in verse 10 the message the women were to preach is given. This is their "sermon" they are to give without fear. It is concerning the Advent of Messiah, i.e., "Behold your God"!

It might surprise you to learn that there were **women priests** in the Old Testament account! They ministered in the services of the Temple. Women came at stated intervals, *as did the Levites and men priests* (see 1 Samuel 2:22)! The women served at the Tabernacle Door like the Levites did to render various kinds of services to the Lord. In 1 Samuel 2:22 it is stated that *women* **assembled by troops**. This is the same word used of the women *assembling by troops* to donate their copper lookingglasses for the building of the Laver. They were a feminine army which published the Word of God!

The Jewish Apostle Paul commended the *women* who were his fellowlaborers *in the gospel* as in the following Scripture:

"And I entreat thee also, true yokefellow, help those **women** *which* **laboured** *with me* **in the gospel**, *with Clement also, and with other my* **fellowlabourers**, *whose names are in the book of life"* (Philippians 4:3).

Notice that Paul called the women who helped him: *"fellow-labourers in the Gospel." "In the gospel,"* not doing housework, not serving at luncheons, not cooking meals, not preparing banquets for conferences, but *in the Gospel*, the same as he was doing! When we envisage a fellowlaborer, we see someone participating in the same activity together! This means that these women were preaching even as Paul was preaching–ministering even as Paul was ministering–*in the gospel*!

Not only in this instance does Paul call these women (and a man, Clement) his fellowlaborers in the gospel, but in other portions he names some *men* his *fellowlaborers:* (see Philemon 1:24). *"Philemon ... Marcus, Aristarchus, Demas, Lucas, my* **fellowlabourers**.*"* Also in 2 Thessalonians 3:2, *"And sent* **Timotheus**, *our brother, and* **minister** *of God, and our* **fellowlabourer** *IN THE GOSPEL OF CHRIST ..."*.

Romans 16 strikingly brings out the ministry of **women**! The list includes *Junia, Phebe, Priscilla, Mary, Tryphena, Tryphosa, Persis, Rufus' mother* and *Julia*. They laboured *in the Lord*, "laboured *much* in the Lord," facing dangers cheerfully and were entrusted with the office of *deacon* ("diakonos") as was *Phebe*. Phebe, *a woman*, carried the mighty fundamental Epistle to the *Romans*, more important than the law of Moses, to the center of the Gentile world!

Junia was identified by Paul as an *apostle* (Romans 16:7) and a kinsman of his. But many translators and scholars, unwilling to admit there could have been a *female apostle*, have since the 13th Century, masculinized her name to Junias or simply left it as Junia but considered that this name was that of a man.

Let us examine Romans 16:1. Paul commended *"Phebe, our sister, which is a servant of the church which is at Cenchrea."* The word translated "servant" in this verse, is *diakonos* which means "deacon," "deaconess," or *minister*. Vine, in his "Expository Dictionary of New Testament Words," observes of *diakonos*: "The word designates without distinction *any minister of the gospel*." The Newberry Bible defines "bishops," as well as "deacons" (Philippians 1:1) as "overseers" and "ministers."

Phebe is commended and called a "servant," but the Greek word here translated "servant" occurs 20 times in Paul's Epistles, and 16 times is translated "minister," three times as "deacon," and only *once* as "servant" when it applies to a *woman!* And she was *not* a *deaconess* in our modern understanding of the term, as *this office did not come into existence until the Third Century*! Furthermore, the word "deacon" applies to either *male* or *female*.

Let us study Romans 16:2. Phebe was plainly made a *prostatis* which means *"one who is placed over, to preside or rule."* (The word "prostatis" is taken from a derivative of *"proistemi,"* "to stand before," i.e. [in rank], "to preside" or [by implication] "to practice," "maintain," "be over," "to rule".) The Church Father, Origen, in commenting on Phebe, speaks of the ministry of women in high terms. He wrote:

> "Phebe was the *minister* of the Church at Cenchrea, seaport of Corinth, and *received her appointment from Paul*, who gave her a letter of introduction to the church at Rome, and advised them to stand by her! The Greek word 'prostatis,' here translated 'succourer,' *does not at all express her place and usefulness*. It does not do her justice. It means 'one who stands in front, a front-rank woman, a front-rank protectress, a chief, a *ruler*, a leader, a guardian.' Phebe was a *chief* in her sphere. The translators certainly did not wish to give woman her divinely appointed place, therefore they translated the word *'diakonos'* as 'servant' and the word *'prostatis'* as 'succourer.'"

In Romans 16:3, Paul called *Priscilla* his "fellow-worker in Christ." Priscilla, with her husband, *expounded the Word to a learned man and mighty in the Scriptures.* Priscilla and Aquila are called "helpers" by the translators, but they were really *fellowlabourers ("sunerguous,"* in Greek) with Paul. And Priscilla is named *first,* as being in the lead!

Some years after Pentecost we find in the Record that Philip, the evangelist, had *four* **daughters** *who did* **prophesy** (Acts 21:9). Those who prophesied *spoke forth for God*; they preached to both men and women; they ministered comfort, edification and consolation to others. The ministry of these four women who prophesied, or "told forth," was recognized in the Church as *normal* and *proper*!

There are those who say there were no women among the 12 disciples–that the Lord Jesus chose only **men**. *Neither were there* **Gentiles**! This does not mean that *Gentiles* cannot be ministers of the Word because Jesus did not choose Gentiles to be His 12 disciples! Jesus knew no double standard. His first appearance after His resurrection was to a **woman** making her the first herald of the very cornerstone truth of our Faith!

In the Upper Room, on the day of Pentecost, *women* were present. These women, as well as men, received the infilling of the Holy Spirit. Peter declared of this that it was the fulfillment of Joel's prophecy:

> *"And it shall come to pass in the last days, saith God, I will pour out of my Spirit upon all flesh: and your sons and your* **daughters shall prophesy***, and your young men shall see visions, and your old men shall dream dreams: And on my servants and on my* **handmaidens** *I will pour out in those days of my Spirit; and* **they shall prophesy***"* (Acts 2:17-18).

Women in the Church Service

1 Corinthians 11:5 says *"women ...* **prophesieth***"* (to *prophesy* is "to speak forth for God"). 1 Corinthians 14:28 tells that "the *man* is to keep silent (in the church)." 1 Corinthians 14:34 says *"Let your* **women** *keep* **silence** *... it is not permitted unto them to* **speak;** *... as* **also** *saith the law. ... it is a shame for* **women** *to* **speak** *in the church."* The words "to speak" is the Greek word, *laleo* meaning "to talk out" which indicates a

woman requesting publicly an answer to some *personal inquiry*. It does not have to do with *preaching*. "Let her ask at home," etc., tells that the "speaking out" was a personal question.

Did Paul say it was *the Law of God* that prohibited women speaking in the church? One could search the Hebrew Scriptures (OT) through and find no place where women are commanded by God not to speak in the assembly! It is a Jewish *tradition* which said, "It is a shame for a woman to let her voice be heard among men." *This is from the Talmud*. When Paul said "as also saith the *law*" he did not refer to *God's* law, but referred to the *Mishnah* (the "oral law" of the Jews). On the contrary, the Old Testament gives authority to several outstanding women to prophesy and to act as *leaders* in Israel: *Deborah* was a *Judge, Warrior, Seer (Prophetess), a Companion in battle, a Poet and Sacred Singer!* She was the daughter of lowly parents and the wife of *Lapidoth*, an ordinary man (Judges 4:4, 9-10, 14-15). She led both *men* and *women* who were **under her authority**! She declared: *"The LORD made me to have dominion over the mighty"* (Judges 5:13).

Huldah spoke: *"Thus saith the Lord,"* to the **priests** in the reign of Josiah. Strange, these priests and statesmen did not go to Jeremiah, her contemporary, for advice and counsel (2 Kings 22:14, 20)!

Women were *Nazarites* (Numbers 6:2), an office equal in importance to that of ***priests*** and ***prophets***. The Priest was man's representative with God; the Prophet was God's representative with man. Women were also *prophets* (as stated previously), so we find in the Old Testament that not only *men* but *women* as well were ***priests*** and ***prophets***!

We must not forget **Miriam**, the sister of Moses and Aaron, who was named by God together with her brothers as a **leader of God's people** (see Micah 6:4)! She was a ***prophetess***, and a singer-composer also. She prophesied in song and preached to both men and women. And she is **preaching TODAY** through ministers who repeat her prophetic words in Exodus 15:20-21!

Anna was a prophetess who **preached** Jesus!

> *"And there was one Anna, a **prophetess**, ... And she coming in that instant gave thanks likewise unto the Lord, and **spake of him to all them** that looked for redemption in Jerusalem"* (Luke 2:36, 38).

Notice that she preached to *all* who looked for redemption in Jerusalem which means both **men** and **women.**

*"But I suffer not a woman to teach, nor to usurp authority over **the** man, but to be in silence"* (1 Timothy 2:12).

This verse of Scripture has been much misunderstood because of incorrect translation. It seems to infer that a woman should not teach nor preach, also should not take authority over a man. The phrase, "usurp authority" is taken from the Greek and means "to dominate." "Over **the** man" (not just *any* man). The context shows THE man is her husband (see verse 15). In other words, "a woman should not dominate her husband"!

I quote from the William's translation in order to clarify this much misunderstood verse:

"I do not permit a married woman to practice teaching or domineering over her husband; she must keep quiet."

Paul says in 1 Corinthians 14 (in substance), that women shall not interrupt the assembly with their *speaking out*, and if they would learn anything, let them ask their husbands at home. *This refers to women in the **audience**, and not to women in the pulpit!* In Chapter 11 of this same letter, the privilege of women praying and preaching (prophesying) is recognized, honored, and regulated. And through it all, God will have *men* as well as **women** preserve order in His holy Assembly!

Let us look at another commandment concerning the position of officers in the Church:

*"A **bishop** then must be blameless, **the husband of one wife**, vigilant, sober, of good behaviour, given to hospitality, apt to teach"* (1 Timothy 3:2).

The **bishop** or **overseer** must possess the same qualifications and virtues as the **deacon** (see 1 Timothy 3:8, 12 and Philippians 1:1). **Bishops** is the Greek *episcopoas* (Acts 20:28) and is synonymous with **presbyters** (*presbuterous*) in Acts 20:17. The literal meaning of **bishop** in Greek is **overseer**.

1 Timothy 3:12 says: *"Let the **deacons** be the husbands of one wife, ruling their children and their own houses well."* Does this mean that only *men* can be **deacons** since he is to be the *husband* of one wife? Remember, the word *diakonos* is *minister* and the same qualifications for the *bishop* or *overseer* of the

church is the same for ALL God's *ministers* whether they be *male* or *female*! If a woman, then, is a *deacon* (*diakonos*), and *Phebe was*, she must be the wife of one husband! She must train and discipline her own children well. The husband, if a *deacon*, must also rule his household well.

It is recorded that not only women were officers and pastors of churches in public, but also that women presided over churches which met in their homes.[82] Too, women were involved in the first decision made by the early church (Acts 1:14-26).

When God called "witnesses" to Him, He did not specify whether these witnesses were to be either male or female. When He made believers as "*sons* of God" they were not all *men*. When God poured out the Gift of the Holy Spirit on His waiting *disciples* in the Upper Room, *there were **women** present* (Acts 1:14) *who also received the promise of the* Father! God promised to pour out of His Spirit upon *all* flesh, not only upon the *sons*, but also upon the *daughters* and **they shall prophesy** (see the promise in Joel 2:28 which is quoted in Acts 2:17)!

To sum it all let us find some of the ***women preachers*** in the Bible. Miriam (Exodus 15:20); Deborah (Judges 4:4); Huldah (2 Kings 22:14); Nodiah (Nehemiah 16:4); Mahershalalhashbaz's mother was a prophetess (Isaiah 8:3); Anna (Luke 2:36); Philip's four daughters (Acts 21:9); Phebe, Priscilla, Mary, Junia, Tryphena and Tryphosa (Romans 16) to name a few!

Supplement to the Preceding Article

In my files is a collection of many news items which include women in the ministry. These are interesting articles concerning women as military chaplains, pastors of large denominational churches, missionaries in various foreign fields, chaplains to the elderly and to women prisoners, priests and bishops of the Episcopal church, cantors of synagogues, etc. Catherine Booth was cofounder (with her husband William Booth) of the Salvation Army; Maria Woodworth Etter was used of God in signs and wonders who contributed substantially to the Pentecostal movement; Aimee Semple McPherson was the Founder of the Foursquare Gospel Church and L.I.F.E. Bible Institute which

---

[82]Acts 12:12, house of *Mary*; 16:13-15, 40 (house of *Lydia*); Romans 16:3-5 (house of *Priscilla* [and Aquila]); 1 Corinthians 1:11 (the Church is called "The house of *Cloe*"); 2 John (to the "elect *lady*").

sent out many preachers and missionaries around the world; Corrie ten Boom was used of God to save hundreds of Jews in "The Hiding Place" during the Holocaust. She was a world traveler, author and renowned *preacher* of the Gospel, etc. etc.

Christian Life Magazine, January, *1954 issue*, reported *The Ladies in the Pulpit* as follows:

> "An unofficial census shows that there are now 2,869 women pastors in the country (USA), and a total of 5,791 women have been officially ordained or licensed to preach. The same survey shows that 77 religious bodies or denominations now ordain women for the ministry. The number, it was stated, is on the increase. [I do not have the present statistics on this but it is much more than it was in 1954!]
>
> "Two of these women recently ordained have clergymen husbands. The first woman minister ever ordained in the Evangelical and Reformed Church's Northern Illinois synod was consecrated by her spouse, the Reverend Robert H. Klepper, at a service in Prospect Heights Community Church. The church called Mrs. Klepper, 37, as pastor a year ago. The other is Mrs. Mabel Lewis Sahakian, of Dedham, Mass., who was ordained in the Congregational Christian Church, while her husband, the Reverend D. William Sahakian, looked on!"

Some of these articles tell about *women* **Rabbis**! I will just quote some excerpts from one of them. It was headed by the title: *A Great Woman Rabbi* (written by Rabbi Pinhas H. Peli):

> "[I described] *Nehama Leibowitz* as the most outstanding living Israeli 'Rabbi.' This was long before there were actual women rabbis anywhere, and people were wondering: A woman rabbi? In Israel? And an Orthodox woman at that? ... we seem to have forgotten the original meaning of the word Rabbi in Jewish tradition. Rabbi really means a *Teacher* [of Tora], and this being so, *Nehama Leibowitz* is certainly one of the greatest rabbis of our generation. ... The main 'secret' of Nehama Leibowitz's art of teaching is the ancient pedagogical Socratic device of formulating the right questions. ... The art of the master teacher [which Nehama Leibowitz was] ... does not 'impose' his own knowledge and wisdom, but draws those out of his students."[83]

---

[83]*The Jerusalem Post*, week ending January 3, 1987. Rabbi Peli is Professor of Jewish thought and literature, *Ben-Gurion University of the Negev.*

APPENDIX IV
Treasures in the Snow

"Hast thou entered into the treasures of the snow?" (Job 38:22).

The Quiet Message of the New-Fallen Snow

By Timothy Wieferich

New-fallen snow speaks of a fresh start. The old is covered; the gray dullness of the path, the barren brown of the fields are forgotten as the world takes on a cloak of white. One feels he should walk with soft step lest he mar the blanket of beauty.

A gentle snowfall at New Year comes at a particularly appropriate time. It reminds us that God has given us a new opportunity. The old now is gone; the new year lies ahead, untouched, waiting for a path to be formed.

Look closely at the snow and learn all the beautiful variety of God's workings. A lasting debt of gratitude for our knowledge of this portion of His handiwork goes to a pioneer explorer of the treasures of the snow. His name was Wilson Bentley, and he was born in a tiny Vermont town called Jericho to a family of farmers back in 1865.

When Wilson was 10 years old, he asked his father for a camera outfit. The cost was $100, a big amount for the Bentleys; but as they saw the seriousness of their son in his request, they sacrificed to buy it.

At that young age, Wilson became deeply interested in the crystal structure of the snowflake. While other boys were making snowballs, he examined individual flakes under a magnifying glass, and he found no two alike. By means of the magnifying system attached to his camera, he was able to photograph the fragile ice crystals.

Wilson Bentley, using that same camera outfit, quietly spent his entire life on that farm. But before his death he had photographed some **400,000** snowflakes. Some days he photographed dozens. A record was 100 on one day.

Though Mr. Bentley spent more than a third of a century in photomicrography, he never was paid a dime for his work. It was just a hobby. However, his careful research opened up to all mankind the wonders of the snow. In those thousands of magnified snow pictures he never found two flakes alike.

Mr. Bentley discovered a snow crystal does not form itself all at once, but gradually grows around a tiny center or nucleus such as a microscopic speck of dust high in the air. It grows slowly but with perfect symmetry on all sides.

Almost invariably a hexagonal or *six-pointed* symmetry characterizes the crystals. E.J. Pace asked Bentley if he had any theory to account for this phenomenon. He replied: "No one knows but God, but here is my theory. As you know, snow crystals are formed from water vapor at temperatures below freezing, and water is composed of ***three*** molecules, two of hydrogen combined with one of oxygen. Each molecule is charged with both positive and negative electricity, the tendency of which is to polarize at opposite sides. The number ***three***, you see, enters the business at the start."

Mr. Bentley's remark about "***three*** at the start of the business" set Pace to thinking. "May not it be," he decided, "that the ***triune*** God, who fashions all the loveliness of creation, has signed His '***threeness***' in these fragile stars of ice crystals as an artist signs his name to his masterpiece?"

Mr. Pace examined the Hebrew word for *snow* and interestingly found it to be made up of units of ***three***. He said, "Hebrews ... used the letters of their alphabet as numbers. Only the casual glance of a Hebrew at the word *sheleg* (Hebrew for *snow*) would be needed to see that it reads ***333*** as well as *snow*. The Hebrew for the first letter answering to our 'sh' is ***300***, the second consonant 'l' is ***30***, and the final one is our 'g' or ***3***. Add them up, and we have ***333***." [Also, the Hebrew word for *snow*, *sheleg*, itself is composed of *3* letters, ג ל ש !]

Mr. Pace said, "Try to imagine how many millions of billions of snow crystals can fall upon an acre of ground in an hour's time and imagine, if you can, the staggering fact that each crystal bears an individuality all its own, a design and a pattern without a duplicate in this or any other storm! Such knowledge is too wonderful for me; it is high, I cannot attain unto it (Psalm 139:6)."

How beautifully God's care is shown in each snowflake! With billions of stars to consider, and with millions of His children on earth to receive care, our Father yet takes such pains with a tiny snowflake!

This new year as the snow falls, remember the Creator who has "signed His name to each crystal masterpiece." And remembering, move forward in the unbroken path, confident that He will be with you. The experiences He has chosen for the new year will vary like crystals of snow, but every one of them will be stamped with His faithfulness and adorned with His mercies.

The Lord who is concerned with each snowflake is concerned about those made in His image, His children, His own.

–Printed in *The Pentecostal Evangel*

APPENDIX V
The Tabernacle as Fulfilled in John's Gospel

Chapters 1 and 2 (THE GATE–The Incarnation)

Christ came into the world by way of the Incarnation. *"The Word was made flesh and dwelt [**tabernacled**] among us"* (1:14).

Chapter 3 (THE BRAZEN ALTAR–The Cross)

Presented in this chapter is man's need of the New Birth (3:3), making it necessary that Christ go to the *Cross* (3:14-16).

Chapter 4 (THE LAVER–The Word of God and His Holy Spirit)

The Word of God was given to the woman at the well, and that was the first recorded experience of the New Birth. The Laver speaks of regeneration (see Titus 3:5 where the Greek is "laver of regeneration"). The Laver itself is symbolic of the **Word of God**; the Water symbolizes the **Holy Spirit**. *We are born* (again) *of the Word of God by the regenerating work of* **the Holy Spirit**.

Chapter 5 (THE DOOR Before the Lord–The Way of Life and Healing)

After regeneration at the Laver, we approach the Tabernacle Building itself where we see the entrance curtain hanging from five pillars (Exodus 26:37). The five porches of the sheep gate suggest this (5:2). Here "before the Lord" (the Door) we find healing for soul and body (5:6-9, 24).

Chapter 6 (THE TABLE OF SHEWBREAD–The Bread of Life)

We enter through the Door into the Holy Place and in this Room we see the Showbread which portrays Christ, the Bread of Life. He offers Himself as "The True Bread" (6:32) and we feed on Him.

Chapter 7 (THE LAVER–Ability for Witnessing)

After regeneration and then feeding on the Bread, we come back to the Laver for the water of the Spirit in witnessing (7:37-39). We have been regenerated by the Spirit–now we are empowered by the Spirit.

Chapters 8 and 9 (THE CANDLESTICK–Light for Each Witness)

Now we see the Candlestick more fully, as Jesus declares, "I am the light of the world" (8:12; 9:5). We receive light from Him, and by the enablement of the Holy Spirit (*Oil* in the Candlestick) we become "witnessing lights" as well.

Chapter 10 (THE VEIL–The Way to God is Opened)

The Veil was torn in order for us to enter the Holy of Holies (Hebrews 10:19,20). The Good Shepherd was the Door (Veil) of the Sheep (10:7) and was "rent" for them (10:11; cf. 10:27-28).

Chapter 11 (THE HOLY OF HOLIES–The Presence of God)

In this Room we see the Glory of Him who is ever Living. He is the "Resurrection and the Life" (11:25; cf. 11:40).

Chapter 12 (BRAZEN ALTAR–The Believer's Cross)

After our entrance through the Veil into the Holy of Holies, we return to the Cross to learn of its deeper meaning. We met Christ here at the Cross–in Salvation, but now we meet Him here to share the Cross with Him (12:24-26; cf. 12:32-33; also see Galatians 2:20; 6:14).

Chapter 13 (THE LAVER–Empowerment for Daily Walk)

We come to the Laver now for cleansing in our daily walk (13:10). The Water tells of the Holy Spirit who enables us to live clean lives and to love as Christ loved (13:34, 35). The Laver is symbolic of the Word; the Water symbolizes the Holy Spirit (see John 15:3; Ephesians 5:26). *We are able to live and love as Christ lived and loved only as we receive* **the enablement of the Holy Spirit** !

Chapter 14 (THE HOLY PLACE–Fellowship with the Holy Trinity)

We enter the Father's House (14:1). In the Holy Place we have fellowship with the Father, Son, and the Holy Spirit, represented in the three articles of furniture located there (14:16, 23).

Chapter 15 (THE CANDLESTICK–Christians in Christ)

We learn that we, the Branches, are to abide in Christ, the Vine. We are a vital part of Him; He is a vital part of us. It is *one* Candlestick (15:5).

Chapter 16 (ALTAR OF INCENSE–Prayer in His Name)

We approach the Father in the Name of the Lord Jesus Christ by the Holy Spirit. The Altar represents Christ; the Incense represents the Holy Spirit (16:23-24; Hebrews 4:15-16).

Chapter 17 (THE ASCENDING INCENSE–Our High Priest's Prayer)

We see Christ praying, interceding for us to bring us into the Holy of Holies (see especially 17:24-26).

Chapters 18-21 (THE HOLY OF HOLIES–Entrance Gained)

Christ's death and resurrection brings us into the Holy of Holies (incense *beaten small*–His death; the fragrance and smoke of incense rises and fills the Tabernacle–His resurrection). We see in this room the *Holy Ark of the Covenant*. God's Presence is with us here. In these chapters, Christ's instructions for service and the promise of His presence ties in with *the Promise of the Father*.[84]

---

[84]See The Gospel of John, Chapter 14:15-21 and Chapter 15:26-27.

APPENDIX VI

The Tabernacle in the Revelation

The Book of Revelation is built on the imagery of the Tabernacle. Here we see its ultimate fulfillment for John heard a great voice out of Heaven saying: *"Behold, **the tabernacle of God** is with men, and **he** will dwell with them, and they shall be **his** people, and God himself shall be with them, and be their God"* (Revelation 21:3).

Ark of Covenant and Mercy Seat (Throne)	3:21; 4:2, 3; 11:19
Breastplate Stones	4:3; 21:11, 18-20
Cherubim ("Living Creatures," cf. Ezekiel 1:5, 10)	4:6, 7
Colors of Tabernacle (Rainbow)	4:3
Copper (brass)	1:15
Crowns of Gold	4:4; 14:14; 19:12
Glory of God (Cherubim)	4:5; 11:19; 15:8; 21:23
Gold	21:18, 21
Golden Altar (4 Horns)	5:8; 6:9; 8:3, 4; 9:13
Lamb–(27 times in Revelation– Sacrifice Altar)	5:6; 7:17
Lampstand	1:12; 2:1; 4:5
Laver (Sea of Glass)	4:6; 15:2
Linen Garments	3:4, 5; 6:11; 7:9, 13; 15:6; 19:8, 14
Linen Girdle (golden girdle)	1:13; 15:6
Mitre/Crown (w/Name of Lord)	14:1; 22:4
Pillar of Cloud	7; 14:14
Pillars	3: 12
Priesthood	4:1-5; 9-10; 5:10-11
Shewbread (Hidden Manna)	2:17
Song of Moses	15:3
Stones with Names (Thummim)	2:17; 3:12
Tabernacle of Testimony (etc.)	15:5
Table (Fellowship)	3:20
Tribes of Israel	7:4-8; 21:12
Trumpets	8:2

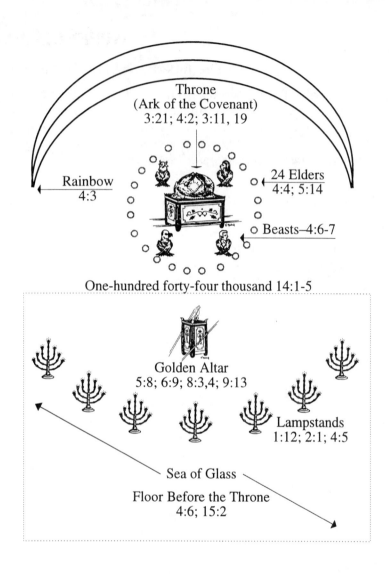

Tabernacle in the Book of Revelation

APPENDIX VII

The Open Place in the North

One of the most inspiring and thrilling of recent disclosures of astronomers is, there is a great empty space in the north in the nebula of the constellation of Orion, a heavenly cavern so gigantic that the mind of man cannot comprehend it and so brilliantly beautiful that words cannot adequately describe it.

The revelations were made possible by gigantic lenses, plus long exposures of photographic plates which in turn can be further magnified. This increases the vision of man so tremendously that he is able to peer into the depths of interstellar space and glimpse the vastness of infinity itself. What has been found correlates the words of Job: "He stretcheth out the north over the empty place" (Job 26:7).

All astronomers agree there is a huge opening in Orion which is perhaps more than 16,740,000,000,000 miles in diameter. The diameter around the earth's orbit is 186,000,000 miles, which in itself is incomprehensible to man; yet the opening into this heavenly cavern of Orion is 90,000 times as wide. In other words, there could be 30,000 solar systems like ours with a sun in the middle of each across the entrance of the opening in the north, and still have room to spare.

But surpassing the immensity of its size is its exquisite beauty and the luminous colors that are unlike any upon earth. Prof. Learkin of Matthew Lowe Observatory[85] gives us the following description:

> "These photographs reveal the opening and interior of the cavern so stupendous that our entire solar system would be lost therein. I have watched it since the days of youth in many telescopes of many powers, but never dreamed that the central region is the mouth of a colossal cave. Pen of writer and brush of artist alike are lifeless and inert in any attempt to describe this interior; For the depth of the Orion nebula appear like torn and twisted objects and river masses of shining glass, irregular pillars, columns of stalactites in glittering splendor and stalagmites from the mighty floor. The appearance is like that of light shining and glowing behind the clear walls of ivory and pearl, studded with millions of diamonds like shining stars."

---

[85] As a student at Southern California College, I visited this Observatory with the graduating class–what wonders we saw that day, wonders of God's creation!

"There must be some reason why all this grandeur is lavished on this one spot in the heavens. The colors are a hue peculiar to the Orion and studded around the opening so that they appear as a pavement of starry sand. No wonder the astronomers (many of them not religious) relate they seem to feel as if they were in some Almighty 'Presence' while scanning this part of the heavens and become speechless before this great outburst of grandeur extending for trillions of miles through space."

Here we think of the prophecy of Daniel 12:4, "But thou, O Daniel, shut up the words, and seal the book, even to the time of the end; many shall run to and fro, and knowledge shall be increased."

I wonder why, in Isaiah 14:12-16, at the time of Lucifer's fall, in v. 13, he states, "I will sit also upon the mount of the congregation, in the sides of the NORTH ... I will ascend above the heights of the clouds; I will be like the most high."

The NORTH has a great significance in God's Word. Could it be possible that Revelation 21 might have some connection here? We are sure that many changes of great magnitude are in the making for God's people, but the 'how' and the 'when' we cannot say; but all these things do encourage our HOPE and our spiritual ambition while we continue to serve.

Without doubt, Paul spoke more truth in his statement (1 Corinthians 2:9) than we realize; for "Eye hath not seen, nor ear heard, neither have entered into the heart of man, the things which God hath prepared for them that love Him"–beyond all power of comprehension!

THEREFORE, the Hope We Have: "Looking for that blessed hope, and the glorious appearing of the great God and our Saviour Jesus Christ; who gave Himself for us, that He might redeem us from ALL iniquity, and purify unto Himself a peculiar people, zealous of good works."

How true it is today that so many of God's dear children simply live and worship for a "blessing," not realizing the great depth and far-reaching meaning of LIFE in its fullness, with a 'God-given' plan for EACH OF US, and that part we may have in the great hereafter.

–Tract, *Evangelistic Crusade,* Apache Junction, Arizona

APPENDIX VIII
200 Questions and Answers

Explanation: I prepared this set of questions with their answers as a help to my students while teaching on these subjects (Typology and Tabernacle Study) at Seattle Bible College.

TYPOLOGY

In order to understand the Tabernacle Study more clearly one must have some knowledge of Typology (the science of Types). It is hoped that the following questions and answers will help you to interpret Typology correctly.

1. Give reasons why Typology is a neglected subject among Christians.
ANS. It is misunderstood. Some stretched the truths and distorted the Word of God by this study. They let their imaginations run wild and made types of everything in the Bible. Types were made into doctrines.

2. As concerning the doctrines found in the Bible, how can types be used?
ANS. To EXPLAIN a doctrine but never to MAKE a doctrine.

3. What is a type in the Bible?
ANS. A type is a person, thing, or event in the Bible which God has designed to be a sign, a shadow, pattern or picture of some person, thing, or event of the future. Strictly speaking, a type is a model or form which exemplifies or contrasts characteristics of the real thing.

4. What is an antitype?
ANS. It "lies alongside the type" as being similar. "Anti" means "against" as "alongside." The anti-type is the fulfillment of the type.

5. How do we establish a type?
ANS. The fulfillment must correspond. The correspondence of type with the antitype proves the design.

6. What is an archetype?
ANS. The original of the type.

The Tabernacle - Exodus 25:1-9

(Read these Scripture verses.)

7. Why is the "Tabernacle" the Chief Type in the Bible?

ANS. Because it is the most complete story of redemption.

8. What did God want the Children of Israel to see in the Tabernacle?

ANS. The attributes, life, death, and ministry of their **Messiah**. It is also a picture of those who are His followers, the Church.

9. What was God's desire in commanding the Israelites to build Him a Sanctuary?

ANS. That He might dwell "within" (among) them (see Exodus 25:8).

10. What was God's method of teaching in the Tabernacle?

ANS. By symbol, type and object lessons.

11. What does the New Testament call the type and symbolism of the Old Testament?

ANS. "Example"–"ensample"–1 Corinthians 10:11

"Shadow"–"copy"–Hebrews 8:5; 10:1

"Figure"–"parable"–Hebrews 9:9

"Patterns"–"copies"–Hebrews 9:23-24

"Shadow of things to come"– Colossians 2:17

12. How many main parts were there in the Tabernacle? Name them and what they represent.

ANS. Three. 1) The Holy of Holies represents the Spirit of God, the Father, and the spirit of man. 2) The Holy Place represents God, the Son, and the soul of man. 3) The Court which is a type of the body of man, and God, the Holy Spirit (who dwells within).

13. What do we learn in the order of the offering in that GOLD is the first metal, BLUE, the first color, LINEN the first material, OIL, the first ingredient?

ANS. Gold, blue, and linen represent God. God is FIRST. He begins from Himself.

14. What does the shittim (acacia) wood represent?

ANS. The humanity of Messiah Jesus.

15. How were the Children of Israel able to carry out God's instructions to build the Tabernacle? Give the Anti-types.

ANS. God gave them helpers: Bezaleel and *Aholiab* who "represented" the Holy Spirit and the Gifts of the Spirit (see Exodus 31:1-7).

16. How are we able to carry out God's instructions today?

ANS. He gives us the "Baptism of the Holy Ghost" and bestows upon us the Gifts of the Spirit.

The Workers - Exodus 25:2, 35:21, 36:5

(Read these Scripture verses.)

17. What characterized the giving on the part of the offerers toward the work of the Sanctuary?

ANS. Generosity and cheerfulness.

18. What did God demand on the part of those who were "wise-hearted"?

ANS. That they bring a CHOICE offering willingly. They observed this. They had to be stopped from giving; they brought too much!

The Materials - Exodus 25:3-7

(Read these Scripture verses.)

19. Where were the materials for the Tabernacle obtained?

ANS. The Children of Israel "spoiled" ("emptied") the Egyptians which God instructed them to do. They took what the Egyptians gave them in payment for their service while they were in slavery (see Exodus 12:35-35).

20. How many metals were employed in the construction of the Tabernacle? Name them.

ANS. Three. Gold, silver, and brass (copper).

21. How many colors were used? Name them.

ANS. Three. Blue, purple, scarlet.

22. How many materials or woven fabrics in the Tabernacle? Name them.

ANS. Two. Fine twined linen and goat's hair (woven into a canvas).

23. How many skins? Name them.

ANS. Two. Rams' skins dyed red and badgers' skin. (Some translators used the words, dolphin, seal, or porpoise instead of "badger.")

24. If we would estimate the cost of the Tabernacle today, what would it be?

ANS. Over $1 million. Some say close to $2 million.

The Holy of Holies and the Ark of the Covenant - Exodus 25:10-16

(Read these Scripture verses.; see placing of the furniture in Exodus 26:34-35 and in Exodus 40.)

25. What does the Holy of Holies represent?

ANS. 1. God, the Father. 2. God's Throne. 3. God's actual presence.

26. What does the Ark of the Covenant teach us in that it was the first article of furniture to be built and placed in the Holy of Holies?

ANS. That God begins from Himself. God is first. He proceeds from Heaven to Earth.

27. Of what materials was the Ark of the Covenant made and what do these materials represent?

ANS. Wood and gold. Wood–The humanity, Gold–the Divinity of Messiah Jesus.

28. What does the incorruptibility of the wood teach us?

ANS. The incorruptible humanity of Jesus, Son of God. He arose on the third day before corruption could work into His flesh (Psalm 16:10; Acts 13:35, 37).

29. What does the COMBINATION of gold and wood tell us?

ANS. The Incarnation. Jesus is the God-Man. He is the Son of God (gold), the Son of Man (wood).

30. What does the OVERLAYING OF THE GOLD on the wood tell us?

ANS. As the gold beautified the wood, so the Divinity of Messiah Jesus glorifies His humanity.

31. How many rings were to be cast for the Ark and what does this number signify?

ANS. Four, the Universal number. (4 corners of the earth, 4 winds, 4 main directions, 4 elements: earth, water, fire, gas).

32. What do the staves through the rings represent?

ANS. The wilderness journey of the God-Man.

33. What kind of flooring was in the Tabernacle? What does this teach us?

ANS. There was no prepared flooring. The Tabernacle was set on the sand or soil of the wilderness. God came all the way down to earth and walked upon the sandy floor of this desert world–tabernacled (lived) among us (see Numbers 5:17 about the floor).

34. Upon what did the Ark stand? What lesson do we learn by this?

ANS. The Ark was placed on the ground while stationary. Jesus, the Messiah, Who is the Ark, God's Presence and Throne, stood upon the "desert sands" of this earth.

35. What three objects were placed inside the Ark of the Covenant?

ANS. Hebrews 9:4 tells: the tablets of the law, the golden pot that held manna, and Aaron's rod that budded.

36. What do these 3 objects in the Ark symbolize?

ANS. 1. Tablets of the Law–Jesus, the Way. He is the fulfillment of the Law of God. He was the Law of God in the flesh; 2. The Golden Pot that held Manna–Jesus, the Truth. He is Deity (Golden Pot) and yet is human as the Manna that came down out of heaven. He is the Living Word; 3. Aaron's Rod that budded: = Jesus, the Life. As the almond stick was dead but budded, blossomed and brought forth the almond, so is Messiah Jesus. He was dead but He arose. He budded, blossomed, and was the Firstfruits of them that slept!

37. What does the crown of gold around the Ark represent?

ANS. Jesus, the KING, has *authority*. He *finished* the work.

38. Of what kind of pure gold was the Mercy Seat made?
ANS. Beaten

39. Of what does this kind of pure gold prophesy?
ANS. It prophesies of the sufferings of Messiah.

40. What does the absence of wood or alloy in the Mercy Seat teach us?
ANS. (Wood represents humanity.) Mercy was fashioned by GOD. Man did not have anything to do with it. It is PURE *GOLD* all the way through.

41. What reason could there be for God not directing a CHAIR to be built for the Tabernacle? What does the "sitting down" imply?
ANS. "Sitting down" implied a FINISHED WORK and the priests' work was never finished (see Hebrews 10:11-12). Only ONE priest sat down because HIS work was finished. Messiah is our High Priest Who sat down on God's Throne after He purged our sins (see Hebrews 1:3).

42. What is another word for "Mercy Seat" from the Hebrew text? What is the English word in the New Testament?
ANS. *Kapporeth* or "covering over"–"Propitiation" (see Romans 3:25, John 2:2, 1 John 4:10).

43. What was the three-fold purpose of the Mercy Seat?
ANS. 1. A place for God's Dwelling between the cherubim; 2. To "cover up" the articles of judgment inside the Ark so as to save the people from the wrath of God for their sin; 3. To hold the blood of atonement, the only PROPITIATION for sin.

44. Locate and explain the first appearance of the cherubim in the Bible and what was their chief service?
ANS. In the Garden of Eden God put cherubim and a flaming sword to keep the entrance to the Tree of Life. They were Guardians of God's Holiness and Executors of His Righteousness and Will.

45. Where were the cherubim located on the Mercy Seat?
ANS. On each end (in the length) and on top.

46. In what direction were the faces of these cherubim to be?

ANS. They faced each other but did not look at each other. Their faces were to be "toward the Mercy Seat."

47. Why were the cherubim's faces in this particular direction? And why were their wings stretched on high over the Ark?

ANS. They were not to look on one another nor on the gold, but upon the BLOOD of the sacrifice sprinkled on the Mercy Seat. They were Guardians of God's Holiness–their wings, protecting the blood of sacrifice which was man's only way of entrance to His holiness.

The Shewbread Table - Exodus 25:23-30

(Read these Scripture verses.)

48. What do the four feet of the Table on the ground represent?

ANS. The earthly walk of Him Who is the Universal Man, Messiah Jesus.

49. What surrounded the Table? the Bread? Explain the symbolisms.

ANS. A crown surrounded the Table and another crown surrounded the Bread. These were of pure gold. *Yeshua* is the KING of the Jews, His earthly people. He is the KING of Kings to His heavenly people. He is the CROWNING FEATURE of all our fellowship and He is able to keep us from falling from that fellowship.

50. What was the Bread on this Table called? (Give literal translation from the Hebrew.) What does this name tell us?

ANS. *Lehem ha-Panim* "Bread of Faces" ("a face that turns every way" which implies "Presence"). It is also called "Presence Bread," for the "faces" or "Presence of God" is continually with His people. And the faces of the redeemed people of the Lord are continually in the presence of God.

51. How many loaves or cakes of Bread were there and in what order were they to be placed upon the Table?
ANS. 12 loaves. They were six ON a *row* ("stack"). Each loaf was on top of another, 6 in one stack and 6 in another stack (see Leviticus 24:5-6).
52. Whom did the loaves of Bread represent in the time of Moses and whom do they represent today?
ANS. (First of all they represent Messiah, the Bread of Life.) Then they represent the 12 Tribes of Israel redeemed out of Egypt. Today these loaves represent the children of God redeemed from sin.
53. Who was to partake of this Bread? How many days was it to be set before the Lord before it was replaced with new loaves? Explain the typical teaching in that these loaves were first offered to God, then to the priests.
ANS. The priests partook of the Bread after it was before the Lord 6 days. On the seventh day after eating them, they were replaced with new loaves. Christ offered Himself first to God, then to His people. We, who are priests of God, must first offer ourselves to God, then to the people!
54. Explain the typical teaching in the fact that the Table was on the NORTH SIDE, the place of judgment.
ANS. When we come to the Lord's Table (Communion) we examine ourselves or JUDGE ourselves before we partake of His fellowship and service.

The Golden Lampstand - Exodus 25:31-40

(Read these Scripture verses.)

55. What does the Golden Lampstand (as a unit) symbolize?
ANS. Jesus, the true Light (also those who are in Him who are lights).
56. What does the absence of alloy or wood in the Lampstand imply?
ANS. Gold is all the way through. GOD is the Creator of Light. MAN did not advise God in creating light; it is *Divine* throughout.
57. What does the beaten gold represent?
ANS. The sufferings of Messiah Jesus.

58. Why were not any measurements given for the Lampstand? Give symbolism.

ANS. Light cannot be measured. It is limitless. Messiah, the Light, cannot be measured in His love and mercy. His grace is limitless.

59. Give symbolic meaning of the design of the ALMOND in the branches of the Lampstand.

ANS. The almond tree is the first tree to bud, blossom, and bring forth the almond after the death of winter, telling us of Messiah who is the Resurrection and the Life. It is because of His Resurrection that the branches, which the redeemed ones are, can have life and bear fruit.

60. Whom does the Central Shaft represent, the Central Branch, the Design of the Almond in bud, blossom, and fruit?

ANS. Central Shaft–God, the Father, Central Branch–God, the Son; Design of the Almond–the work of God, the Holy Spirit.

61. What do the seven branches hold on top of each one?

ANS. A lamp with oil in it.

62. What does the oil symbolize?

ANS. The Holy Spirit.

63. When and how was the Lampstand lighted?

ANS. *"Aaron and his sons shall order it from evening to morning"* (Exodus 27:21). Oil was put into the lamps, a wick in the oil, and the wick was lighted with a coal of fire from off the altar of sacrifice.

64. What do the snuffdishes, tongs, etc. represent?

ANS. They are "helps" for the lighting and trimming of the lamps and all made of pure gold. They are symbols of the Holy Spirit and His work.

The Coverings - Exodus 26:1-14

(Read these Scripture verses.)

65. How were the Boards of the Tabernacle completed, or, of what was the ceiling and roof of the Tabernacle building made?

ANS. Coverings of two curtains and two animal skins.

66. Why did God give directions for the ceiling and roof before the framework and foundation of the building?

ANS. The Boards of the framework represent the Church. The Coverings (ceiling and roof) represent Messiah. Messiah is FIRST. The ceiling and roof is nearer to heaven–the Boards, nearer to earth. The Lord begins with Himself, proceeds from Heaven to Earth.

67. Of what material was the inside or First Covering made? What is its spiritual application?

ANS. Fine-twined linen. Righteousness.

68. Give the Hebrew name for the First Covering and what is the English translation?

ANS. *Mishkan*, "dwelling." It is called "The Tabernacle."

69. This *First Covering* completed the Boards. Make typical comparisons.

ANS. The first Covering is Messiah and His righteousness. The Boards (the Church) is made COMPLETE in Him and receives His righteousness.

70. Explain "cunning work" and give symbolic meaning.

ANS. "Cunning work" was a weaving through and through the material so that the design could be seen on both sides. The "cunning work" symbolizes the ministry of the Holy Spirit.

71. What were the four faces of the cherubim in Ezekiel's vision and give typical meaning of each one (see Ezekiel 1:5, 70, "living creatures" are the cherubim).

ANS. **OX**, the patient, enduring servant of man. Jesus, the Saviour. He is as the Ox pulling us out of sin. The OX also was the Sacrifice on the Altar of Burnt Offering which also speaks of Jesus, the Supreme Sacrifice on the Altar of the Cross.

LION, the King of beasts, having dominion and power on earth. Jesus, the Great Physician. He is the LION of the Tribe of Judah and has dominion and power on earth. He came to destroy the works of the devil.

EAGLE, the King of the birds, who soars high into the heavens. Jesus, the mighty Baptizer. He baptizes us with the Holy Ghost and causes us to rise with eagle's wings into the heavens with Him. The eagle is the deadly enemy of the serpent! Jesus has power and dominion in heaven and earth. He promised us to have the power to tread upon serpents and over all the power of the enemy!

MAN, the King of men. Jesus, our soon-coming King. The government shall be upon His shoulders. He shall rule over men and reign forever.

72. How many panels comprised the Mishkan covering and what does this number represent?

ANS. Ten–completeness, nothing wanting.

73. What joined the two sets of five panels to make it one Tabernacle? Make symbolic comparisons.

ANS. 50 loops of blue and taches or clasps of gold. The number 50–Pentecost. Blue–Glory of heaven. Gold–Deity.

74. Where was this "joining" of the Mishkan Covering to be located relative to the inside of the building?

ANS. The loops of blue and the gold taches were to be *above the Veil.* (The Veil represented Messiah's "flesh," His humanity.)

75. How was the Mishkan or Tabernacle Covering kept from flying in the wind?

ANS. It was held to the ground by cords and copper pins.

76. What was the Second Covering (over the Linen Covering) called? (Give Hebrew word and English translation.)

ANS. *Ohel*–"Tent"

77. Of what material was the Second Covering (*Ohel*) made and who made this Covering?

ANS. Goat's hair spun into a canvas by the women who were "wise hearted;" *"whose heart stirred them up in wisdom"* (see Exodus 35:25-26).

78. What does the material of the Ohel represent?

ANS. Made of Goats' Hair: The goat represents sin. Messiah is the Anti-type of this Covering. He came in the likeness of "sinful flesh," however sinless, but was made the sin offering (as was the kid of the goat) on the Cross of Calvary. He was as the sinner tenting in goat's hair. He knew no sin but became sin for us that we might become the righteousness of God in Him (see 2 Corinthians 5:21).

79. (a) How many panels comprised the Ohel Covering? (b) What joined the 2 sets of panels of the Ohel?

ANS. (a) Eleven. (b) Fifty loops (unknown of what they were made), and 50 copper taches or clasps.

80. Where was the "joining" of the two sets of panels of the Ohel Covering to be located relative to the inside of the Tabernacle building?

ANS. Above the VEIL. (The Veil represents Messiah's "flesh," His humanity.)

81. What was to be done with the "extra" curtain panel of the Ohel Covering? Why?

ANS. It was to be doubled and shown a little on the entrance of the Building. This was always to remind the Children of Israel of their sin–that they needed a Sin-Offering, and that their coming Messiah would be that Sin-Offering.

82. What does the copper taches of the Ohel (Tent) symbolize?

ANS. God's judgment for sin. Messiah received God's judgment for our sin. (The copper taches were over the Veil which was a symbol of His humanity.)

83. What does the 50 loops of the Mishkan Covering typify? of the Ohel Covering?

ANS. 50 of the Mishkan–*Pentecost*. Because Messiah rose from the dead, God is free to pour out His gifts upon His people. 50 of the Ohel–*Jubilee* (slaves set free). Because Messiah died, man is free to receive God's Gifts.

84. What was the "color" of the Tent or Ohel Covering? Why?

ANS. Black, for this is the symbol of sin in keeping with the goat which represents sin. (The Egyptians owned black-haired goats which the Israelites obtained when they left Egypt.)

85. What is the material of the covering over the Ohel Covering?

ANS. Rams' skin.

86. Of what is the ram a type?

ANS. Consecration of the priesthood and substitution.

87. Explain the antitype of the rams' skin.

ANS. Messiah consecrated Himself to the service of God to the place of substitution. He delighted to do the will of God and humbled Himself even to the death of the cross.

88. What was the measurement of the rams' skin covering? Explain.

ANS. God gave no directions for the measurements of this Covering. Messiah's consecration to the will of God and His substitutionary death cannot be measured.

89. What color was the rams' skin Covering? Give symbolic meaning.

ANS. It was to be dyed RED. Man was to dye it this color. It is the color of blood, of sacrifice, of suffering, of death. Man's sins made the rams' skins that blood-red color! Man's sins made it necessary for Messiah to consecrate Himself to His substitutionary death on Calvary.

90. Why is the skin of the outer Covering of the Tabernacle not known?

ANS. Because it tells us of Messiah who is the Unknown Man.

91. What is this skin according to some translators?

ANS. Seal, porpoise, dolphin, goat, leather, or badger. In the Septuagint it is "a skin dyed blue." Jewish translators left it untranslated, using the Hebrew word, *tachash* in place of the skin.

92. What was the appearance of this skin of the outer covering of the Tabernacle? Give antitype. What was its purpose? Make comparisons with Messiah.

ANS. Unattractive. Messiah was unattractive in the sense that He was as other men and the Jews expected their Messiah to come in pomp and glory. Isaiah describes Him as having *"no form or comeliness and when we shall see him, there is no beauty that we should desire him."* As the outer skin protected the under skin, curtains, and contents of the Tabernacle from the storms and the hot, scorching sun, so Messiah, the Servant, the Saviour, protects us from the storms of life and the hot, scorching sun of God's wrath upon us for our sin.

93. What Coverings could the Children of Israel see on the Tabernacle building?

ANS. The outer skin and a little of the goats' hair covering hanging down on the entrance. This brings to mind: *"There is no beauty in him that we should desire him"* (Isaiah 53:2). They did not see the beautiful Mishkan covering, neither the rams' skin dyed red!

94. What Coverings could the priests see?

ANS. The Mishkan Covering, the doubled Covering Curtain of the Ohel, and the outer skin.

The Boards - Exodus 26:15-30

(Read these Scripture verses.)

95. Of what were the Boards of the Tabernacle made?

ANS. Acacia wood overlaid with gold.

96. What is the Antitype of the Boards?

ANS. The redeemed people of God, the Church.

97. What is the Antitype of the Corner Boards?

ANS. Messiah, the Chief Cornerston*e. "The Stone which the builders refused has become the HEAD STONE of the CORNER"* (Psalm 118:22).

98. Give *seven* similarities of the Boards with their Antitype (the Church).

ANS. 1) **Acacia tree chopped down.** The individual to be in the Church is first brought down.

2) **Wood transferred to a new place in the desert.** Individual (to be in the Church) transferred to a new position in the world, that of standing on redemption ground, in Messiah Jesus.

3) **Wood overlaid with gold.** Individual given power to become a son of God, a partaker of His Divinity.

4) **Board standing in silver sockets.** Individual standing on redemption ground. In the world but not a part of the world.

5) **Boards facing the sun-rising.** Church to face Jesus, the Sun.

6) **Many Boards, one Building.** Many members, one body.

7) **Boards facing the Tribe of Judah.** Church to continually show forth the Praises ("Judah" means "Praise") of God.

99. What was a part of the Boards, made of the same materials, which grasped and stood in the silver sockets?

ANS. Two tenons (*yadoth*), "hands" on the bottom of each board.

100. Where was the silver obtained for the foundation of the Boards? Give symbolisms.

ANS. (See Exodus 30:11-16.) Each Israelite, 20 years and over, must pay a half-shekel for the work of the Sanctuary. It was a silver piece, about 32 or 35 cents in present day coinage before inflation. The poor were not to give less and the rich were not to give more. All had the same atonement price. It was a memorial of the blood of the lamb which delivered them from death and bondage. This silver foundation, upon which the Boards stood, kept them from falling and also kept them from sinking into the sands of the desert. Those who would be a part of the Church of the living God must have the "half-shekel," the redemption price. The Church stands upon this foundation in the desert of this world. Believers are in the world but are not a part of the world. They are kept from sinking down into the sands of sin because of the "silver" foundation beneath them!

101. What kept the Boards from tipping from side to side?

ANS. 5 bars (rods) placed alongside the Boards north, south, and west. (5 bars or rods on each side, 15 bars in all.)

102. What do the 5 bars represent? Explain.

ANS. The FIVE ministry gifts which God has given to the Church (typified in the Boards). These gifts are: Apostles, Prophets, Evangelists, Pastors and Teachers. They are given to keep the Church from tossing to and fro in the "desert" world with every wind of doctrine (see Ephesians 4:11-16).

The Veil and the Door - Exodus 26:31-33
(Read these Scripture verses.)

103. Where was the Veil located?

ANS. It "divided" the Holy of Holies from the Holy Place. In other words, it was located between these two rooms.

104. Of what colors was the Veil made and of what kind of sewing?

ANS. Blue, Purple, and Scarlet. The sewing was that of cunning work which was the same as in the Mishkan Covering.

105. What were the differences of the Veil from the Door?

ANS. The Veil was made of "cunning work" whereas the Door was made of "needlework." The Veil had the cherubim in it whereas the Door did not. The Veil hung upon four pillars. The Door hung upon five pillars.

106. What is the Veil in relation to the Christian walk?

ANS. The Veil is more beautiful through and through than the Door. The Cherubim are guardians of God's Holiness. The Veil tells of a more beautiful walk in the Lord. It is the Way of Holiness.

107. What did the beautiful Veil do for the priests?

ANS. It hid the glory of God and shut them out from His holy presence.

108. What did the Veil represent?

ANS. Messiah's "flesh" or humanity.

109. What is the typical meaning of the rending or tearing of the Veil?

ANS. The death of Messiah.

110. What did the rending or tearing of the Veil do for the believer?

ANS. It made a new and a Living Way into the presence of God.

111. Describe the material and colors of the Door and the kind of sewing in it.

ANS. The Door of the Tabernacle building (that is, the Entrance) was made of fine-twined linen, of blue, purple and scarlet with needlework.

112. Explain: "wrought (made) with needlework" and apply this in symbolisms.

ANS. Needlework is sewing or embroidery only on one side of the material. The beauties of the colors and design were not clearly seen on the outside. One would have to come inside before beholding them. So it is with any individual who desires to see Messiah in His beauty. He must come inside.

113. Upon what did the Door hang and what could this represent?

ANS. The Door hung on five pillars made of acacia wood overlaid with gold. It could represent the five redemptive names of Messiah as He hung upon the Cross, which Names are: "Wonderful, Counsellor, Mighty God, Everlasting Father, Prince of Peace" as in Isaiah 9:6.

114. In what did these five pillars stand? Give symbolisms.

ANS. Brass (copper) sockets. Copper symbolizes the judgment of God for sin. He who is the Wonderful, the Counsellor, the Mighty God, the Everlasting Father, the Prince of Peace (the five pillars) is standing in the copper sockets. This means that the Messiah has been judged for our sin and it is past!

115. Where was the Door of the Tabernacle located? Give significance.

ANS. At the entrance to the Building at the East side facing the Gate and the Tribe of Judah. Again we see Messiah Who is the Door. He came from Judah's Tribe. Judah means "Praise." Messiah is the Door of Praise to God.

The Altar of Sacrifice - Exodus 27:1-8

(Read these Scripture verses.)

116. Of what materials was the Altar of Sacrifice made and what is the significance of each?

ANS. Acacia wood–humanity; copper (brass)–God's judgment for sin.

117. Of what measurement was this altar? Give symbolic meanings.

ANS. 5 cubits square and 3 cubits high. 5—God's grace to man in man's weakness is found here. 3—The Trinity at work in this grace (also, it was on the *third* day Messiah arose!) This altar speaks of death but also tells of LIFE out of DEATH.

118. What do the measurements of this Altar make it distinct from all the other articles of furniture of the Tabernacle?

ANS. It was the largest of all the furniture.

119. Of what is the Altar of Sacrifice a symbol? Give a similar outstanding symbol made of the same materials as this Altar to which Messiah referred in a prophecy of His own death.

ANS. The Cross of Calvary. The symbol in the Old Testament is the Serpent in the Wilderness (see John 3:14).

120. What does the copper (brass) on the wood tell us?

ANS. God's judgment for sin (copper) was laid on Messiah's humanity (wood). The Scriptures say that He bore our sins in His own body on the tree (see 1 Peter 2:24).

121. How many copper instruments were there for service at the Altar and what does this represent?

ANS. Five (the number of God's grace). These five copper instruments then represent God's grace measuring out sin's penalty by the "help" of the Holy Spirit.

122. Why was the Altar to be "hollow with boards"?

ANS. So that the Israelites could fill this "hollow" with earth or stones for this was the only kind of altar God commanded of them for sacrifices (see Exodus 20:24-26). It was upon the EARTH that the Cross (the Sacrificial Altar) was erected.

123. What do the four horns on the Altar of Copper represent?

ANS. The strength and power of the Son of God.

124. On what side of the Altar were the sacrifices slain and why?

ANS. On the North Side. God directed it to be the place of judgment.

125. Name the Five Great Offerings.

ANS. The Burnt Offering, The Meat (Meal) Offering, The Peace Offering, The Sin Offering, and The Trespass Offering.

126. Describe the Grate and Network of Copper.

ANS. The Grate came up to the middle location on the Altar surrounding it. Upon this grate the priests ministered, for it was a ledge under the "compass" ("rim") or "top margin" (on the outside; also see Exodus 27:4-5; 38:4).

127. Compare and give typical significance of the measurement for the Grate in its height with that of the Mercy Seat.

ANS. The copper speaks of God's judgment for sin and, coming up to the middle of the Altar would make it one-and-a-half cubits which was the height of the Mercy Seat. God is a God of love and mercy, but He is also a God of judgment and wrath. Sin must be punished. The height of the Mercy Seat and the Grate being the same tells us that God is "equal" in His Mercy and Judgment. He "punished" His Son for us so that He then could offer His mercy!

128. Draw from memory a diagram which shows the cross formation in the Tabernacle furniture. (Place and name the furniture in their positions on your diagram.)

ANS. See illustration on page 122.

The Court Fence - Exodus 27:9-14; 17-19

(Read these Scripture verses.)

Tabernacle, Dwelling Place of God
Camp of Israel, Dwelling Place of Man
Fence occupied the position between them as a Mediator. (A Mediator is one who takes an official and accepted position between two parties. He is a *Go-Between*.)

129. Of what material was the Court Fence curtain made and of what is this material a symbol?

ANS. Fine twined linen–righteousness. Linen comes from flax; flax comes from the earth. Linen tells of Messiah's righteous humanity.

130. What is the Bible word for "curtain" here as it pertains to the Court Fence?

ANS. "A hanging."

131. What is the measurement (in length) of the Court curtain, excluding the Gate? (Give significance of this measurement.)

ANS. 280 cubits 280 days of gestation for human birth. Messiah was born into the HUMAN family. He is the Son of man and as MAN was *righteous*. The curtains of the Court Fence symbolize His righteous HUMANITY.

132. Explain the similarity of measurement for the Mishkan Covering and the Court Fence curtain and give application.

ANS. The Mishkan Covering was composed of 10 curtains (panels) of 28 cubits length in each. If these were placed end to end lengthwise it would equal 280 cubits, the same measurement of the Court Fence curtain (excluding the Gate)! The Mishkan Covering was inside, representing Heaven; the Fence Curtain was on the outside, representing Earth. Messiah is the same in His righteousness in Heaven as He was when He walked upon the earth; He is both righteous inwardly and outwardly. He is Human and Divine forever!

133. What held up the Fence curtain and who does this represent?

ANS. The Pillars held up the Fence. The Pillars represent the Church and the Church displays the righteousness of Messiah.

134. Of what material were the Court Pillars and give spiritual application.

ANS. It is unknown as of what the pillars were made. The Church is unknown to the world even as Messiah is unknown.

135. What is the number of the pillars and give applications.

ANS. 60; 6 is the number representing MAN and 10 is the number representing completeness, nothing wanting. The 60 pillars represent man who is complete. Only is man complete as he is united to Messiah Jesus. Thus the 60 pillars speak of the Church of the Living God.

136. In what do these pillars stand and give applications.

ANS. The pillars stand in copper, a symbol of God's judgment for sin. The copper is not around them or upon them, but is beneath them. The Church has already been judged for sin–in Jesus. It is PAST!

137. What is above on the pillars? Give applications.

ANS. On the pillars were silver capitols or chapters (Exodus 38:17). Silver is a symbol of redemption through the blood of the Lamb. The pillars are adorned with the silver. The Church shows forth the beauties of redemption which is in Messiah Jesus.

138. What joins the Pillars to each other? Give significance.

ANS. Silver fillets. They were to be filleted (united). Silver is a symbol of redemption. The silver fillets signify Redemption through the blood of the Lamb and this unites all the Church together.

139. Of what did this Fence remind the Israelites who were encamped around it?

ANS. That God is righteous and demands righteousness of man in order that he might enter His holy presence.

140. What 4 things could this Fence be to the Children of Israel?

ANS. 1) A barrier. It shut man out; 2) A protection. It closed God in; 3) A line of demarcation. It marked the Way of Holiness from the Way of Worldliness; 4) It provided a means for approach to God (in the Fence was a Gate). Only through Messiah's righteousness can a man come to God and God has provided Him for the world.

141. Explain pins and cords of the Court Fence.

ANS. **Pins of copper**–"A Nail in a sure place" (Isaiah 22:23). Messiah is called "The Nail" and the "Anchor" of our soul. We died with Him. Nail (the tent pin) was hammered into earth and we were buried with Him (Nail deep in the earth), but Hallelujah, the top of the Nail was **above** the earth. *We rise with Him* to walk in newness of life and shall rise with Him in the First Resurrection!

Cords–Drawing and holding power. Messiah draws us with cords of love. Holds us steady from winds, etc.

142. What measurement did God require of the entire Court? What is the significance of this measurement number?

ANS. *Fifty by fifty everywhere* (Exodus 27:18-Hebrew rendering). This made a perfect rectangle composed of two 50 by 50 squares. *Fifty* is the number representing *Pentecost* and *Jubilee*. The first "square" has as its center the Cross (Altar of Sacrifice) where sin is atoned for. The "square" beyond had as its center the Presence of God Within (the Ark of the Covenant) which represents the Baptism of the Holy Ghost. The first square is for the sinner–50 for Jubilee, when the slaves are set free. The second square is for the saint–50 for Pentecost, when God empowers the freed slave by His Spirit!

The Gate, the Door and the Veil - Exodus 27:16; 26:36; 26:31-33

(Read these Scripture verses.)

143. Where was the Gate located and what does this tell us?

ANS. In the East, where was the Tribe of Judah and where the sun rises. Messiah is the Gate. He came from the Tribe of Judah, and is the Sun Who rises with healing in His wings."

144. Of what material and colors was the Gate? Give symbolic applications.

ANS. Fine-twined linen = righteousness of Messiah. Blue, heaven - He came from heaven, the Son of God. Scarlet (red), earth; He came from earth, the Son of man. Purple (blue and red combined), the blending color = heaven and earth = the God-Man.

145. Explain "wrought with needlework" of which this Gate was made, and make applications.

ANS. (Same for the Door; see #112.) Needlework is sewing or embroidery on one side of the material. The beauties of the colors were not seen clearly on the outside. So it is with any individual as he stands outside of salvation. He cannot see the "colors." However, as he steps inside, coming through the Gate which is Messiah, he can see the beauties and the loveliness of the Saviour.

146. How many Pillars were to hold up the Gate curtain? Give significance.

ANS. Four. Four represents the Universe with its 4 corners, 4 winds, 4 main directions, 4 elements, etc. The Gate represents the UNIVERSAL ONE, the Messiah of Israel, the Saviour of the world.

147. Give the measurements for the Gate and give its symbolic meanings.

ANS. 20 cubits by 5 cubits which when multiplied (20x5) equals 100. The Gate is 100% the way into salvation through the Supreme Sacrifice on the Altar of the Cross.

148. Give the measurements for the Door and give typical meaning.

ANS. 10 cubits by 10 cubits which when multiplied (10x10) equals 100. The Door is 100% the way into fellowship, service, nourishment and satisfaction. (The Door is the Entrance into the Holy Place.)

149. Give the measurements for the Veil and give typical meaning.

ANS. 10 cubits by 10 cubits which when multiplied (10x10) equals 100. The Veil is 100% the way into the Holiness, glory, power, and presence of God. (The Veil was the entrance of the Holy of Holies.)

150. Explain the differences as pertaining to the measurements of the Door and the Gate. Give applications.

ANS. The Gate (Entrance into the Court of Salvation) was wider and lower than the Door. More come into the Way of Salvation–it is easy of access. The Door is higher and narrower. There is a higher and narrower way in the Christian realm. There are fewer who come this way. It is the Door of Fellowship with God and Service to God. The Gate is for the sinner. The Door is for the saint.

151. What is the Veil in relation to the Christian walk?

ANS. The Veil is more beautiful through and through than the Gate and the Door. The Cherubim (embroidered on the Veil) are Guardians of God's Holiness. The Veil tells of a more beautiful walk in the Lord. It is the Way of Holiness.

152. How did Israel's representative priests enter the Gate? and what spiritual truth do we see here?

ANS. Through the side. Christ is the Gate. We enter His wonderful salvation through His riven side!

The Tabernacle Priesthood

(Read Exodus 28 & 29.)

153. List Company "**C**" (We C Jesus).

ANS. **C** hosen–"Take Aaron thy brother and his sons with him" (Exodus 28:1).

C alled "from among the children of Israel" (Exodus 28:1).

C ommit–"that he may minister unto Me in the priest's office" (Exodus 28:1).

C leansed (by the water in the Laver (Exodus 30:17-21).

C lothed (in holy garments–Exodus 28:2).

C onsecrated (by the blood application, Exodus 29: 19-20).

C hristed ("anointed" with the anointing oil (Exodus 29:21).

C onformed (see Leviticus, "The Priest's Handbook").

C ommissioned (Duties assigned: Numbers 1:49-54.)

154. Who were to make the clothing for the priests?

ANS. Those who were wisehearted filled with the spirit of wisdom (Exodus 28:3).

155. With what part of the garments does God begin in His instructions and with what part does He end? What is the typical meaning?

ANS. He begins with the Breastplate, typical of God's wisdom, glory and power, and ends with the fine-twined linen symbolical of the righteous humanity of Messiah. God begins from Himself–from heaven and comes to display His righteousness upon earth.

156. Name each part of the Garments for Glory and Beauty of the High Priest.

ANS. 1. The Breastplate with Urim and Thummim (The Breastplate of Decision or Judgment); 2. The Shoulder Stones of Onyx; 3. The Ephod with The "Curious" Girdle (or "embroidered" belt) of the Ephod; 4. The Blue Robe (The Robe of Blue, also called "Robe of the Ephod") with the Bells and the Pomegranates on its hem; 5. The Broidered Coat (The Linen Coat) and Linen Girdle or Belt of "needlework;" 6. The Mitre or Linen Bonnet; 7. The Linen Breeches (Pants); 8. The Holy Crown (Gold plate on the Linen Bonnet.)

157. What do these *8* parts of the Glory Garments represent?

ANS. *8* is the symbolical number for *resurrection*, a new beginning, new life, the first of a new week, eternity–therefore telling us of "Messiah who is the Resurrection, the First of a New Life, of a new beginning, and the Father of Eternity" as in Isaiah 9:6.

158. (God gave no directions for a seam of the Robe of Blue–no beginning–no ending). What does the *seamlessness* of the blue Robe teach? What truth do we learn in that the binding around the neck was to be that it could not be torn?

ANS. Messiah has the power of an ENDLESS LIFE. No man took His life from Him. He laid it down of Himself.

159. What is the typical meaning of the bells and pomegranates on the hem of the blue Robe?

ANS. Golden Bell has a tongue in it–Divine Testimony–the Power of God; Pomegranate (This was only the form of the actual pomegranate which had many seeds inside)–Fruitfulness; Messiah's Testimony was clear and pure because He bore fruit. There is a clear, ringing Divine testimony given forth when backed up by the Divine fruit of a life. It is by "fruits" we are known.

160. In what book and chapters of the Bible written by Paul do we find "bells" and "pomegranates" intimated?

ANS. 1 Corinthians 12–bell (power of God–Divine Testimony); 1 Corinthians 13–pomegranate (fruit of Divine Love); 1 Corinthians 14–bell (power of God–Divine Testimony).

The bells do not clang up against each other and cause discord because of the softness of the pomegranate (pad) between them. All the gifts of the Spirit are to be motivated by Divine Love or they are as nothing in the sight of God.

161. What do the girdles (belts), which girded the linen coat and ephod, represent?

ANS. Service.

162. Of what significance to Israel was the 12 stones of the Breastplate upon the HEART of the High Priest? Of what significance were the two stones, with six names each engraved upon them, on the shoulder pads of the High Priest?

ANS. The High Priest carried them (Israel) in his heart of LOVE and bore them up in strength upon his shoulders.

163. What is the typical meaning of the blood application to the **ear, thumb**, and **toe**?

ANS. Ear–consecrated to HEAR the Word of the Lord; Thumb–consecrated to WORK or serve the Lord; Toe–consecrated to WALK in the ways of the Lord.

164. What do we learn in that the oil is applied after the blood?

ANS. The blood is typical of the life laid down for our sin–salvation. Oil is a symbol of the Holy Spirit. First the blood, then the oil. First we are saved, then we are baptized with and anointed of the Holy Spirit.

165. Name the three families of Levites and their position around the Tabernacle Fence in front of the tribes of Israel.

ANS. Sons of Gershon (the Gershonites)–West; Sons of Merari (the Merarites)–North; Sons of Kohath (the Kohathites)–South

166. Give the Camp location of Moses, Aaron and his sons who were of the priestly family of Kohath.

ANS. East of the Gate of the Court Fence.

167. Name the 12 tribes of Israel and their Camp location. (Be able to draw diagram with names of Levites and Israelites in their correct positions.)

ANS. East–Judah, Isaachar, Zebulun; South–Reuben, Simeon, Gad; West–Ephraim, Manasseh, Benjamin; North–Dan, Asher, Naphtali

168. What supernatural phenomena occurred after the Tabernacle was completed and anointed? Give significance.

ANS. (See Exodus 40:34.) A cloud covered it and the glory of the Lord filled it. God was not only WITH them, but dwelt IN them. So it is with each believer. It is God's desire to be WITH us (We are the Tabernacles of God) and also to make His abode WITHIN us.

The Altar of Incense - Exodus 30:1-10

(Read these Scripture verses.)

169. Why is the Altar of Incense (or Golden Altar) commanded to be built AFTER the Altar of Sacrifice?

ANS. The Golden Altar is for the SAINT, the Copper Altar for the SINNER. An individual must meet God at the Copper Altar before he can meet God at the Golden Altar.

170. For what purpose was this Second Altar and what does this action represent?

ANS. To burn incense upon. This represents prayer and praise.

171. Give at least three titles of Messiah that are represented in the Golden altar.

ANS. Intercessor, Mediator, High Priest.

172. What was commanded not to be offered on the Golden Altar and why?

ANS. Strange incense–only the prepared incense God had ordered was to be offered here. Burnt sacrifice, meat (meal) offering or drink offering also was forbidden for this had already been offered. Messiah died ONCE and for all.

173. Who was to do service at this Golden Altar and when?

ANS. Aaron–morning and evening.

174. Of what materials was this Altar made and what do they represent?

ANS. Gold–Divinity. Wood–Humanity.

175. What difference from the other articles of furniture that are measured do we notice concerning the measurement of this Golden Altar and what does this tell us?

ANS. It is the *highest* measured article of furniture and since this Altar represents prayer, it tells us that PRAYER is the highest form of activity of the Christian.

176. How was the incense caused to ascend? Give significance.

ANS. It was lighted by a coal of fire from off the Copper Altar. This teaches that all prayer fired with the Holy Ghost ascends to God on the basis of the Sacrifice of Calvary. Sin must first be dealt with before the cloud of incense can rise to God.

177. What two features were located on the top of the Golden Altar? Give symbolisms.

ANS. A crown of gold and four horns of acacia wood overlaid with gold. The Crown–authority and kingship of the Great Intercessor. The horns–power and strength of the great High Priest. Four (horns)–universality of the Mediator.

178. What held the staves with which this Altar was to be carried? Give representations.

ANS. Two rings. TWO is the number for union and agreement. Represents Messiah in union and agreement with the Holy Spirit in His work of intercession and prayer. As concerning prayer which this Altar represents, this verse of Scripture comes to mind: *"If any TWO ... agree as touching one thing* [in prayer] *... it shall be done ..."* There is to be union of the believer and the Holy Spirit in prayer. We know not how to pray as we ought, but the Spirit knows the mind and will of God and helps us to get our answer through.

RINGS–Eternal Love. Messiah's High Priestly work was carried on by rings of God's Love. Our prayers and intercession should also be propelled by Divine Love.

179. Where was the Golden Altar located and what does this teach?

ANS. Just before the Veil which separated the Holy Place from the Holy of Holies. Messiah is the Mediator. We come into the Holiest (to God) by Him. Prayer is the activity which brings us into God's Presence.

180. What was the ritual involving the Golden Altar on the Day of Atonement as concerning the blood?

ANS. The blood of atonement was to be put upon its horns.

181. What great truth does this ritual emphasize?

ANS. It is only on the basis of the blood atonement that anyone can come to God.

The Atonement Money - Exodus 30:11-16

(Read these Scripture verses.)

182. What is the significance of the required atonement money or ransom price mentioned here immediately after God gave commandment concerning the blood application on the horns of the Golden Altar?

ANS. Each one must have the "ransom price," the atonement through the blood of God's Lamb, before approaching Him in the Holy Place of prayer.

183. Who was to have this ransom for his soul? Give applications.

ANS. Everyone who was numbered with the Israelites. Everyone who would be "numbered" or considered in the family of God must have a ransom for his soul. The Lord Jesus paid the ransom; we must accept it or we have no access to the Golden Altar or to the Mercy Seat.

184. How is physical healing associated and included in the atonement money or "half shekel of the sanctuary"?

ANS. God promised that no "plague" ("physical disease" in Hebrew) would come upon them if they had the "ransom for their soul."

185. Explain the equality of rich and poor who give "the ransom price." Make applications.

ANS. The rich were not to give more than a half-shekel (which, before inflation was about 32 or 35 cents) and the poor were not to give less. All had the same half-shekel to give. This teaches that God is not a respecter of persons (Acts 10:34). All are equal in His sight and all must come God's way through the same atonement purchased by Messiah with His own precious blood.

The Laver Exodus 30:17-21

(Read these Scripture verses.)

186. Of what material was the Laver made and of what is this a type or symbol?

ANS. Copper. God's judgment for sin.

187. Where was the Laver located?

ANS. Between the Door of the Tabernacle Building and the Copper Altar in the Court.

188. Who was to use this Laver, when was it to be used, and for what purpose?

ANS. The priests were to use this Laver for their washing (cleansing) before and after the handling of the sacrifice and before entering the Holy Place. They were to wash at the Laver daily.

189. What was the penalty for failure to wash daily and what does this represent?

ANS. Death. Separation from the presence of God.

190. Where was the copper obtained for the making of the Laver?

ANS. The highly polished copper looking-glasses of the women who obtained them from the Egyptian women and who donated them willingly for the Sanctuary (see Exodus 38:8).

191. Of what was the Laver a symbol? the water? Apply the activity of the priests in connection with the Laver.

ANS. The lookingglasses–**The Word of God.** The water–**the Holy Spirit.** The priests would come to the Laver, see a reflection of themselves in the water, wash their hands and feet with the water–thereby cleansing themselves from defilement. So the Christian looks into the mirror of God's Word, judges himself there, washes himself with the remedy provided therein, and so is he cleansed from defilement contacted in his daily walk.

192. What does God's Word tell us if we judge ourselves?

ANS. That we will not be judged.

193. What also was reflected in the Laver because of their position in the Court? Give applications.

ANS. The Door of the Tabernacle and the Copper Altar. The Door represents Messiah. The Altar of Copper is a symbol of the Cross. The Word of God reflects Messiah and Him Crucified.

194. What was the measure of the Laver? What does this tell us?

ANS. No measurements given. The Word of God is immeasurable!

195. What does the location of the Laver teach?

ANS. We must be cleansed before we can enter beyond the Door into the Holy Place with God and before we can offer any service to Him.

196. Give references and write out portion in the New Testament where the term "laver" is used (from the Greek) for a spiritual washing or cleansing.

ANS. Ephesians 5:26–*"by the washing* [laver] *of water by the word."* Titus 3:5–*"saved us, through the washing* [laver] *of regeneration and renewing of the Holy Spirit."*

197. The Laver was located before the Door into the Holy Place of the Tabernacle (where was the Table of Shewbread). What does this teach?

ANS. Children should wash their hands before they eat. We are to be cleansed before we can come to God's Table and feast with Him (1 Corinthians 11:28-31).

198. What do we learn by God's commandment for the priests to wash *thereat*?

ANS. They did not wash *inside* the Laver but at the side of it. Washing IN the water which was in the Laver would pollute it for the other priests. The Word of God and the Holy Spirit cannot be polluted by man's opinions and ideas. We wash THEREAT. (The Hebrew is "out of" or "from.")

199. What is symbolized by the hands and feet of the priests which were to be cleansed?

ANS. *Hands*–their work or service was to be pure before the Lord. *Feet*–Their walk and their standing or conduct was also to be clean.

200. Compare by a verse of Scripture God's requirements symbolized in the Copper Altar and the Copper Laver.

ANS. *Copper Altar–*"Without the **shedding of blood** there can be no remission [for sin]."
Copper Laver–"Without **holiness** no man shall see the Lord."

The Copper Laver and Copper Altar of Solomon's Temple
(as imagined by the artist).

BIBLIOGRAPHY

Baxter, J. Sidlow. *Explore the Book.* Grand Rapids, Michigan, Zondervan, c1960.

Brown, Arthur I. *God and You. Wonders of the Human Body.* Findlay, Ohio, Fundamental Truth Publishers, n.d.

Bullinger, E.W. *Number in Scripture.* London, The Lamp Press Ltd., 6th edition, 1952.

Burney, C.F. *Outlines of OT Theology.* New York, Edwin S. Gorham, Church Missions House 2nd edition, 1904.

Callaway, T.W. *Christ in the OT.* New York, Loizeaux Brothers, c1950.

Chambers, Laurence T. *Tabernacle Studies.* Grand Rapids, Michigan, Zondervan Publishing House, c1958.

Cohen, A. (ed.). *The Soncino Chumash.* London, The Soncino Press, 1956.

Dake, Finis Jennings. *Dake's Annotated Reference Bible.* Atlanta, Georgia, Dake Bible Sales, c1963.

Davis, John D. *The Westminster Dictionary of the Bible.* Philadelphia, The Westminster Press, c1944.

DeHaan, M.R. *The Tabernacle, The House of Blood.* Grand Rapids, Michigan, Zondervan Publishing House, c1955.

DeHass, Jacob (ed.). *The Encyclopedia of Jewish Knowledge.* New York, Behrman's Jewish Book House, 1946.

Dolman, D.H. *Simple Talks on the Tabernacle.* Grand Rapids, Michigan, Zondervan Publishing House, c1941.

Edersheim, Alfred. *The Life and Times of Jesus the Messiah, Vol. I & II.* New York, Longmans, Green and Company, 1904.

Enelow, H.G. *A Jewish View of Jesus.* New York, Bloch Publishing Company, 1931.

Fairbairn, Patrick. *The Typology of Scripture, Vol. I &II.* Grand Rapids, Michigan, Zondervan Publishing. House, n.d.

Fuller, Charles E. *The Tabernacle in the Wilderness.* Westwood, New Jersey, Fleming H. Revell Company, c1940.

Grant F.W. *Atonement in Type, Prophecy and Accomplishment.* New York, Loizeaux Brothers, 8th printing, 1956.

Gray, James M. *Christ in the Sacrificial Offerings.* Chicago, The Bible Institute Colportage Association, c1924.

Habershon, Ada R. *The Study of Types.* Grand Rapids, Michigan, Kregel Publications, 1957.

Hains, Edmont. *The Tabernacle.* Grand Rapids, Michigan, Zondervan Publishing House, c1950.

Haldeman, I.M. *The Tabernacle Priesthood and Offerings.* Chicago, Fleming H. Revell Company, c 1925.

Hanke, Howard A. *The Tabernacle in the Wilderness.* Grand Rapids, Michigan, William B. Eerdmans Publishing Company, 1953.

Harrison, Norman B. *The Gospel of John.* A Study Book, Minneapolis, Minnesota, The Harrison Service, c1938.

Heslop, W.G. *Lessons from Leviticus.* Grand Rapids, Michigan, Baker Book House, 2nd edition, 1945.

Hottel, W.S. *Typical Truth in the Tabernacle.* Cleveland, Ohio, Union Gospel Press, 1943.

Hengstenberg, E.W. *Christology of the Old Testament.* American reprint edition, Grand Rapids, Michigan, Kregel Publications, c1970.

Klinck, Arthur. *Home Life in Bible Times.* St. Louis, Missouri, Concordia Publishing House, 1947.

Lev, Mark. *Lectures on Messianic Prophecy.* Philadelphia, c by Mark Lev, 1917.

Little, David. *The Tabernacle in the Wilderness.* New York, Loizeaux Brothers, 1942.

Mackie, George. *Bible Manners and Customs.* New York, Fleming H. Revell Company, n.d.

McCord, Iris Ikeler. *The Tabernacle, Its God-Appointed Structure and Service.* Chicago, Moody Press, c 1927.

McGee, J. Vernon. *The Tabernacle, God's Portrait of Christ.* Wheaton, Illinois, Van Kampen Press, n.d.

Miller, H.S. *The Gospel in the Hebrew Tabernacle, Priesthood and Offerings.* New York, The Word-Bearer Press, c1939.

Moorehead, W.G. *The Tabernacle.* Grand Rapids, Michigan, Kregel Publications, 1957.

Needham, George C. *Shadow and Substance.* Springfield, Missouri, Gospel Publishing House, reprinted 1958.

Newberry, Thomas. *Solomon's Temple and Its Teaching*. Fincastle, Virginia, Scripture Truth Book Co., n.d.

Orr, James (General Editor). *International Standard Bible Encyclopaedia*. Grand Rapids, Michigan, Wm. B. Eerdmans Publishing Co., c1939.

Partridge, William Peyton. *The Tabernacle and Other Bible Object Lessons*. London, The London Bible and Book Saloon, n.d.

Pink, Arthur W. *Gleanings in Genesis, Vol. I & II*. Chicago, Illinois, Moody Press, c1922.

Pollock, A.J. *The Tabernacle's Typical Teaching*. London, The Central Bible Truth Depot, n.d.

Pont, Charles E. *Tabernacle Alphabet*. New York, Loizeaux Brothers, c1946.

Potter, Charles T. *Christ and Christian Experience in the Tabernacle*. Cincinnati, Ohio, God's Revivalist, c1903.

Ridout, S. *Lectures on the Tabernacle*. New York, Loizeaux Brothers, 6th printing, 1952.

Sale-Harrison, L. Palestine, *God's Monument of Prophecy*. Wheaton, Illinois; Van Kampen Press.

Seiss, Joseph A. *The Gospel in Leviticus*. Grand Rapids, Michigan, Zondervan Publishing House, n.d.

Sheldrake, Leonard. *Tabernacle Types and Shadows*. Grand Rapids, Michigan, Gospel Folio Press, n.d.,

Simpson, A.B. *Christ in the Tabernacle*. Harrisburg, Pennsylvania, Christian Publications, Inc., n.d.

Slemming, Charles W. *These Are the Garments*. Grand Rapids, Michigan, Zondervan Publishing House, n.d.

____. *Made According to the Pattern*. Wheaton, Illinois, Van Kampen Press, 1951.

Soltau, Henry W. *The Tabernacle, The Priesthood and the Offerings*. Fincastle, Virginia, Scripture Truth Book Company, 1965.

Spink, James F. *Types and Shadows of Christ in the Tabernacle*. New York, Loizeaux Brothers, 1946.

Spurgeon, C.H. *Treasure of the Old Testament*. London, Marshall, Morgan and Scott, Ltd., n.d.

Street, Harold B. *The Believer-Priest in the Tabernacle Furniture*. Chicago, Moody Press, c1946.

Strong, James. *The Tabernacle of Israel.* Grand Rapids, Michigan, Baker Book House, 1952.

Talbot, Louis T. *Christ in the Tabernacle.* Wheaton, Illinois, Van Kampen Press, c1942.

Terry, Milton S. *Biblical Hermeneutics.* Grand Rapids, Michigan, Zondervan Publishing House, 1967.

Vine, W.E. *An Expository Dictionary of the New Testament Words.* Westwood, New Jersey, Fleming H. Revell Company, 17th impression, 1966.

Whiston, A.M. (trans.). *The Life and Works of Flavius Josephus. Antiquities of the Jews.* Philadelphia, The John C. Winston Company, n.d.

White, Frank H. *Christ in the Tabernacle.* London, S.W. Partridge & Company, 1910.

Wight, Fred Hartley. *Devotional Studies of Old Testament Types.* Chicago, Moody Press, c1956.

Wright, Walter C. *The Sacrificial System of the Old Testament.* Cleveland, Ohio, Union Gospel Press, c1942.

General Index

A

Aaron's Rod, 245
acacia nilotica, 81
agate, 161
agony, 114, 151
Ahisamach, 17
ahmahd, 78
Aholiab, 16, 17
Aholiah, 243
alloy, 246, 248
almond, 245, 249
almond-cakes, 28
amethyst, 161
Anchor, 261
antelope, 73
anti-type, 241
antitype, 241
Apocryphal, 221
apparel, 33
Arab, 69
arak, 24
archetype, 241
architect, 3
Ark of God, 27
army, 191, 222, 224
aromatic gums, 207
astronomers, 239, 240
atom, 15
ayphod, 156

B

Babylonian, 20
badger, 244, 253
barah, 91
barley bread, 28
barrier, 101, 128, 131, 181
bas-relief, 57
basin, 193
bastions, 86
beasts, 250
Bedouin, 69, 70, 140
beneficial, 93
Benjamin, 159, 169, 267
Benoni, 159
beriah, 91
Betselel, 16
betszer, 11
Bezaleel, 243
black-balling, 165
blanket, 231
blasphemy, 112
bleaching, 63
borrowed, 9
brass pin, 3
broken heart, 151
brown, 11, 70, 107, 231
buttress, 86

C

Cabinet, 1
Caiphas, 152
cakes, 248
calamus, 201
calf, 10
calyx, 51, 52
calyxes, 51
camera, 231
camp, 4, 17, 109, 128, 204
canvas, 69, 72
capporeth, 22
capsule, 22
carbon, 59
carnality, 59
cassia, 201
cavern, 20, 239
centurion, 63
Ceylon, 200
chalcedony, 161
challah, 45
chapiters, 136, 261
char, 59, 143
charcoal, 161
chashav, 64
cheating, 9
cheerfully, 8, 9, 10, 224
cherubs, 31, 35, 66
chiselers, 112
chiton, 33
cinnamon, 200, 201
clasp, 68
coals, 109, 182, 183, 208
coinage, 187
collation, 221
comeliness, 253
Comforter, 14, 26
commerce, 80
Communion, 248
completeness, 251, 260
consecrate, 9
cord, 3, 140
cords, 251, 261
corps, 66
counterfeit, 45
coupled, 68, 85
crab, 207
crest, 79
crystal, 231, 232, 233
cubitum, 20
curds, 28

D

Decision, 265
defense, 11
defilement, 23, 70, 154, 196
dermis, 81
desecration, 23
diadem, 41
diakonos, 224, 225, 228, 229
diameter, 81, 239
disc, 153
Divine Enabler, 25, 52, 90
dolphin, 244, 253
dominion, 250, 251
dove, 5
dross, 22
dye, 253

E

eagle, 250
earrings, 10
earthquake, 96
East Indies, 207
Easter Day, 119
edifice, 15
Egyptians, 243, 252
El, 16
elliptically, 69
embroidery, 257, 262
Emmaus, 3
empowered, 26, 43, 44, 55, 60, 156, 206, 235
endearment, 172
Ephod, 265
ephod, 12, 64, 156, 166, 266
epidermis, 82
episcopoas, 228

executant, 23
explorer, 231

F

female apostle, 225
fill the hand, 9
fillets, 261
five porches, 234
flag, 108
foreign, 143, 183, 188
fumigation, 181

G

galbanum spice, 207
Garden of Eden, 13, 114, 119
genetic, 171
Gershonites, 169, 171, 172
gestation, 130
gibbet, 75, 119
Go-Between, 7, 22, 40
goblets, 43
golden calf, 10
Golden Censer, 181, 182, 190
Golden Scissors, 143
goral, 166
grate, 259
gray, 11
green, 11, 28
green corn, 28
guard, 23, 154
Guardians, 246, 247, 263
gum arabic, 80

H

habergeon, 150
half-a-log, 142

hallowed, 8, 211
halved, 137
hanging, 254, 260
Hanukkah, 142
hapto, 155
heave offering, 8, 109, 116
heave-shoulder, 8
Heavenly Blueprint, 16
hem, 265
Herod's Temple, 27, 36, 58, 135
hexagonal, 232
hieron, 13
hin, 202
Hiram, 17
hobby, 232
Holiness, 246, 247, 256, 261, 263
Holy Shade Cloud, 17
house of clay, 15
house of hair, 69
Huldah, 227
Hur, 16, 17
hydrogen, 232

I

ice crystals, 231, 232
idolatry, 10
imaginations, 241
imbalance, 137
impotence, 146
impoverished, 9
Incarnate Word, 7, 168
incorruptible, 21, 78, 79, 80, 193
inflation, 187
instruments, 15, 44, 59, 100, 109, 126

interpenetrate, 64
interstellar, 239
intertwined, 65, 100, 156
iron, 11, 94, 161
Ishmael, 69

J

jasper, 161
Jehovah Jireh, 72
Jehovah Tsidkenu, 11
Jehovah-Nissi, 67
Jehovah-shammah, 24
Jericho, 231
Jeshurun, 172
Jordan, 5, 65, 168, 202, 204, 211
Jubilee, 50, 68, 71, 130, 221, 252, 262
Junia, 224, 225, 229

K

Kadesh, 80
kaphar, 22
Kapporeth, 29, 32, 33, 186
kapporeth, 29
karkob, 110
kashah, 49
Kedar, 69, 74
ketallage, 33
kethoneth
kid, 251
Kittel,, 153
knop, 50, 51, 52, 53
Kohath, 25, 169, 173
Kohathite, 109
Kohathites, 169, 172
Korah, 28, 108
kritikos, 193

L

Lamb's wife, 11
Lapidoth, 227
laver of regeneration, 193, 234
lavished, 9
Lazarus, 28
ledge, 110
Lenten season, 119
Levites, 266, 267
lilies, 51
logeion, 162
longitudinal, 108
looking glasses, 191, 192, 198, 222
loutron, 193
lubricant, 141
Lucifer's, 240
luou, 193
lymph, 151

M

magnanimous, 24
magnifying glass, 231
Mahershalalhashbaz, 229
mallet, 140
mantlerock, 96
marred, 118, 135
masculinized, 225
Master-Builder, 16
mechanical arts, 15
Mediator, 259, 267, 268, 269
mediator, 7, 128, 131, 143, 181
menorah, 48, 60
Merarites, 169, 172
metaphorically, 2
meticulous, 15
metonymy, 165

microscopic, 232
Mikdash, 13
Mikshah, 49
mikshah, 56
mirror, 271
Mishkan, 250, 251, 252, 254, 256, 260
Mishna, 45, 181
Mitre, 265
mitre, 64, 148, 153
mixed multitude, 7
mizbeach, 105
mizbeah, 117
Moab, 80
molecules, 232
mor, 199
morbid, 114
Mordecai, 64
mortises, 88
Mosaic, 33, 57
myrrh, 199, 200

N

nachash, 108
naos, 13
Naphtali, 162
nathan, 164
Nazirites, 227
Nebuchadnezzar, 27, 58
nebula, 239
nechosheth, 106
needlework, 256, 257, 262, 265
Nehushtan, 108
New Jerusalem, 11, 160, 161, 167
nucleus, 232

O

obnoxious, 197

Observatory
  Mt. Lowe, 239
odem, 162
Ohel, 69, 70, 72, 101, 251, 252, 254
oil and frankincense, 6
oiled bread, 5
omdiim, 78, 98
Omnipotence, 146
onycha, 207
onyx, 12, 19, 157, 159
Orient, 171
Orion, 239, 240
ornamental work, 17
Ouches, 161
oxygen, 232

P

Palmoni, 220
parable, 242
parallelogram, 88
participial, 223
pattern, 241
pavement, 240
pedagogical, 230
Pentecost, 251, 252, 262
percolating, 157
pericardium, 151
permeate, 15, 21
perpetual, 142, 182
Pharisee, 185
phenomena, 267
phenomenon, 232
photomicrography, 232
Physician, 250
Physiology, 130
Pidyon Haben, 188

plague, 269
poetry, 172
polarize, 232
pomegranate, 51, 152, 153, 154, 176
pomegranates, 265
porpoise, 244, 253
pouch, 164
preeminence, 12
presbuterous, 228
priesthood, 252
prism, 50, 153
prize, 9
proistemi, 225
property, 188
Propitiary, 186
propitiation, 29, 30, 31, 33, 107, 186
prostatis, 225
Publican, 185
purged, 246
pyre, 119

Q

qeresh, 81, 82

R

Rabbinical, 29, 91
Rabbinists, 1
rail, 23, 41
ram, 12, 72, 73, 77, 168, 252
ransom, 269, 270
raqam, 64
ravel, 67
reconciliation, 33
rectangle, 130, 137
red meat, 28
regeneration, 26, 193, 234, 235
reinforcement, 110

Reuben, 267
revelry, 44
reward, 9
ribbons, 67
Righteous Branch, 53
rim, 259
rings, 245, 268
robbing, 9
Rock Hounds, 157
rom, 8
Rome, 57
rupture, 151

S

sac, 151
sack, 63
Sacred Chest, 21
sacred lots, 167
sacrilege, 112
sandstorms, 21
science, 241
seal, 244
seismographic, 96
selvedge, 67, 68, 71
seneh, 78
sepals, 51, 52, 54
seraph, 108
serpent, 251
servitude, 9
shaal, 9
shadow, 1, 16, 216, 217, 219, 241
shaken, 62, 135
sheep gate, 234
Shekinah, 21, 23, 35, 62, 75, 134, 204, 210
shesh, 63
shittah, 78, 93
shittim, 242
shoham, 157

shotet, 78
shulhan, 38
sieve, 110
silex, 161
silver hook, 3
similitudes, 1
skeleton, 81
slaves, 15, 68, 71, 83, 189
snowfall, 231
snowflake, 231, 233
snuffdishes, 249
snuffers, 59
Socratic, 230
sojourn, 27, 43
solar, 239
splendid, 17
spoiled, 9
stake, 108, 140
stalactites, 239
stalagmites, 239
stamens, 51, 52, 207
stauros, 108
stem, 51, 199
storax tree, 207
strained honey, 28
stripped, 9
sunerguous, 226
supernatural, 267
sweat, 147, 175
sweet milk, 28
symbolisms, 257

T

tachash, 74, 253
Talmudists, 1
tam, 85, 86
tamam, 165
tamiym, 165
tavek, 13, 19
teleological, 58
telescopes, 239
tenons, 255
tent of flesh, 14
tent of my father, 17
terebinth, 199
terumah, 8
textile, 17
thereat, 272
thigh, 50
threshold, 193
thumiaterion, 181
tokens, 154, 155
tongs, 249
towel, 157
transportation, 24
trillions, 240
troops, 191, 222, 224
Tryphena, 224, 229
Tryphosa, 229
tsalal, 17
tsel, 16
tumbling, 157
tweezers, 59
twinned, 86
twisted, 63
Typology, 241
tzitzit, 67

U

unction, 203
Uri, 17

V

venom, 107, 108

Vermont, 231
virgin, 3, 5

W

wafers, 28
wall gems, 160, 167
wick, 249
wicks, 59, 143, 144
Wilson Bentley, 231
wine, 43, 44, 46, 47, 94, 143
wings, 247, 250, 262
winter, 249
womb, 5
women priests, 224
Wonderful Numberer, 220
world-conscious, 2
woven fabrics, 11

Y

yadoth, 82, 85, 255
yathed, 140
Yom Kippur, 153, 187

Z

Zered, 80
zinc, 106